RIVERMAN

RIVERMAN

An American Odyssey

Ben McGrath

ALFRED A. KNOPF
New York
2022

THIS IS A BORZOI BOOK
PUBLISHED BY ALFRED A. KNOPF

Copyright © 2022 by Ben McGrath

Library of Congress Cataloging-in-Publication Data
Names: McGrath, Ben, author.
Title: Riverman : an American odyssey / Ben McGrath.
Description: First edition. | New York : Alfred A. Knopf, [2022]
Identifiers: LCCN 2021021709 | ISBN 9780451494009 (hardcover) |
ISBN 9781101973615 (paperback) | ISBN 9780451494016 (ebook)
Subjects: LCSH: Conant, Richard Perry. | Canoes and canoeing—
United States. | Adventure and adventurers—United States—
Biography. | Canoeing accidents—United States.
Classification: LCC GV782.42.C67 M34 2022 | DDC 797.122092 [B]—dc23
LC record available at https://lccn.loc.gov/2021021709

Photographic Credits
Conant in Trenton: James Halliday (top); Jonathan Gordon (bottom)
Conant in Upstate New York: Brad Rappleyea
All other images are from Dick Conant's personal collection.
Front-of-jacket images by Dick Conant
Jacket design by Jenny Carrow
Maps by Mapping Specialist Ltd.

Manufactured in the United States of America
First Edition

For Ian and Sam

When you get sold a lemon you make lemonade. Don't cry over spilt milk. Lap it up. Don't be a fuddy-duddy. Don't be a habbernow throwing a habdab. Don't be a crybaby bellyacher. DO something. Hold your head up high. Take a walk in the sun. Eat chocolate. Swim in the water and paddle down the river. That's the ticket. That's the way. That's the Tao. Persevere. Hah! And now, for something mildly amusing . . . my journey.

—DICK CONANT

RIVERMAN

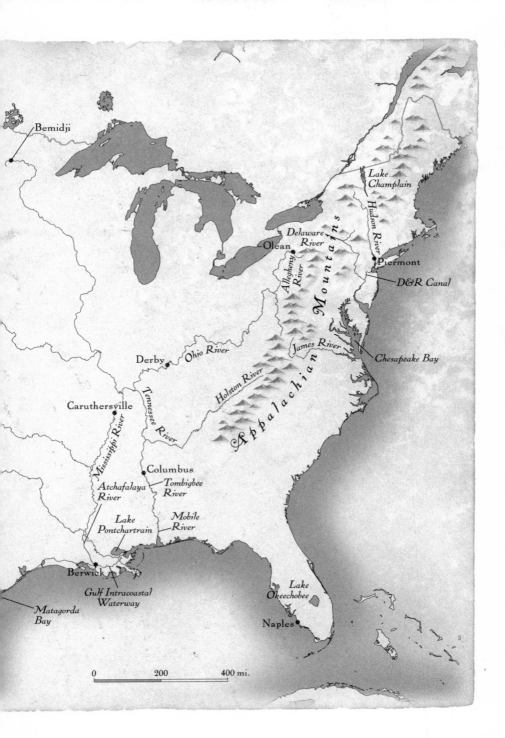

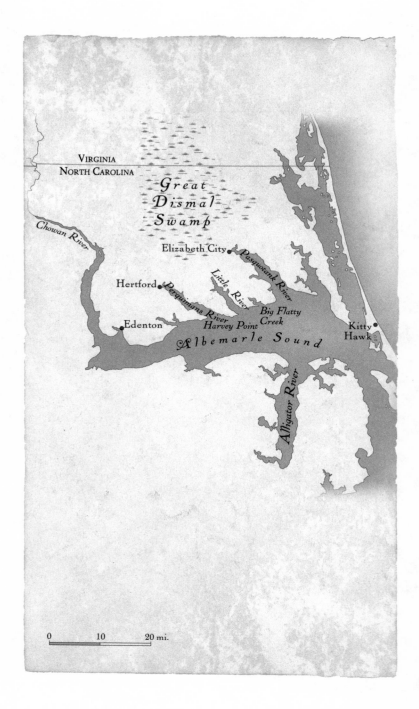

VIRGINIA
NORTH CAROLINA

*Great
Dismal
Swamp*

Chowan River

Elizabeth City

Hertford

Pasquotank River

Little River

Perquimans River

*Big Flatty
Creek*

Edenton

Harvey Point

Kitty
Hawk

Albemarle Sound

Alligator River

0   10   20 mi.

Prologue

A streak of red on the shore: whatever it was, it hadn't been there on Thursday, the last time Barry Lowry went fishing for stripers. It was Saturday morning now, the end of a stormy late-November week in 2014. Lowry, a North Carolina soybean farmer, and his six-year-old son, Brayden, had just reached planing speed when they noticed the unfamiliar object. Lowry idled his engine, raised a pair of binoculars—"Oh, crap!" he muttered—and then lowered them. Trying not to alarm Brayden, he reached for his CB and radioed Grover Sanders, a fellow farmer who'd been out hunting ducks since dawn. Sanders had thirty years on Lowry, and an untrimmed white beard that conveyed authority.

"Can you come down here for a second?" Lowry asked.

"Boy, *what* are you doing?" Sanders said. This wasn't the first time Lowry had sought his help on the water.

"I see something by the stumps that looks like a boat, and I'm not going over there by myself."

"Oh, Lord."

Sanders recommended, instead, that the Lowrys retreat and join him in his skiff for a group inspection.

The stumps were cypress knees that perforate the northern

shore of Albemarle Sound, giving the water the color of tea. Sanders had been out that way—just east of the mouth of Big Flatty Creek—the previous evening, at dusk, and saw nothing amiss. "So it come up during the night," he said.

Approaching slowly, they could see now that the red object was an overturned canoe. Sanders eyed the scene warily from a semicircular perimeter for fifteen minutes, while trying to steer clear of the stumps, a couple of which had snagged the errant boat. Ropes pulsed beneath it. They formed a kind of loose cage, trapping bags—or, as Sanders soon discovered, bags within bags within knotted bags, containing enough air that they amounted to a flotation device. Fearing what else might turn up when they righted the canoe, the two men ordered Brayden into the skiff's stern. Then Sanders unsheathed a knife and began to saw at the ropes.

Relief—there was no trace of a body—gave way to confusion. A paddle was secured lengthwise, along the canoe's starboard gunwale, so tight that it would seem not to have been in recent use. A spare? They scanned the nearby coast, fronting a thousand or more acres of swampy cypress and gum forest. Nothing. Behind them, to the south, lay a full horizon of sloshing, brackish water. Sanders called his friend Randy Cartwright, the Pasquotank County sheriff, on his cell phone. They dragged the canoe, which was made of plastic, up onto the skiff, over the bow, along with as many of the bags as they could fit, and headed inland, via a narrow canal, passing the rickety docks and large oyster middens of a shellfishing operation called Frog Island. A sheriff's deputy and two officers of the North Carolina Wildlife Resources Commission, John Beardsley and Chase Vaughan, met them there and began combing through the effects, looking for clues.

No one had been reported missing in Pasquotank or its neighboring counties. The sheer quantity of maps and other gear packed into the canoe suggested a long voyage. So did a collection of sodden newspapers from towns nowhere close. *The Poughkeepsie Journal. The Times of Trenton.* They were dealing with a worldly voyager, from the looks of things: here was an interview with the economist Paul Krugman, clipped and saved from *Princeton Magazine;* and there was an issue of *The New Yorker* from a dozen weeks back. One of the maps—a bicycle map, of Plattsburgh, New York—had some handwriting in the margins. The deputy studied it closely.

A businessman goes down to the river with a bottle of pills and liquor, intent on suicide. He gets nice and comfortable on a blanket when the landowner arrives carrying a shotgun. "What are you doing on my land?" "Suicide. Say, may I borrow your gun? It'd be quicker than pills." "Sure, here." So the businessman shot the farmer, thought twice about it, and kept the gun.

But there were no weapons in evidence. Recovered artifacts included seventeen toothbrushes, fourteen Chapsticks, six cigarette lighters, a sewing kit, a socket, a digital camera, three Louis L'Amour novels, a mud-caked Samsung flip phone, two thumb drives, eleven pens, a deck of playing cards, a marine radio, a four-foot extension cord, two CVS key fobs, *John Paul Jones: A Sailor's Biography.* A Dell laptop case contained no laptop. When the contents had been inventoried and hung out to dry in a storage shed, using the severed ropes as makeshift clotheslines, they occupied two full trailer bays. Packing it all into a fourteen-foot canoe came to seem like an engineering marvel, as remarkable in its way as the vessel's unheralded arrival in such remote country.

The phone, when it was finally charged and turned on, flashed a message indicating an account balance of $0.00. The last incoming call, from a number in Bozeman, Montana, was logged on September 20, 2011, more than three years earlier. The last outgoing call, to Livingston, Montana, was November 24, 2011.

Receipts and other assorted documents bore notes and inscriptions, written in blue and black ink:

"If you allow poverty to hold you back, it means you have neither imagination nor will."

"Idea—SciFi: USB port from human nervous system directly into Internet."

"I have been denied what our men are supposed to do. So I do what I want, which is to navigate."

"I'm not good @ everything. I'm good @ long-distance canoe."

Some of the receipts had been traced over with a ballpoint pen, as if to preserve the information from the fading effects of time and sunlight. Not just the essential numbers but "Expect More Pay Less" and "Your associate today is: Samantha."

. . .

Recreational boating accidents in North Carolina fall under the jurisdiction of the Wildlife Resources Commission, and Officer Beardsley, a thirty-year-old army veteran, assumed control of the investigation at Frog Island. He was immediately struck by the quality of the two sleeping bags they found. Beardsley had used similar equipment while camping for weeks in the mountainous region near Afghanistan's border with Pakistan. He remembered waking up comfortably with ice in his zipper. This canoeist, he felt, was amply prepared for winter.

Amid the papers arrayed in front of him on the dock, a handwritten phone number caught his attention. Not a local number; it appeared to be in New York. There was a name written above it. It was a start, at least—a shot in the dark.

1

Stone-Age Mentality

T he most wonderful day in the very full, topsy-turvy life of Richard Perry Conant occurred in his forty-ninth year, in the summer of 1999. An auspicious start: he awoke without feeling ill. He was camped in a grove on the east bank of the Yellowstone River, whose water he had drunk, untreated, in great quantities the night before. Was it Monday? He wasn't quite sure. Happily, he was losing track of time. A little more than a week had passed since he'd quit his job, as a janitor at the VA hospital in Boise, declaring himself fed up with the Clinton impeachment indulgence and maybe modernity itself. Before leaving, he'd stashed some frozen fish in the attic of the house he'd been renting, a stink bomb on delayed fuse. Then he'd driven to Yellowstone National Park, where he spied elk, goats, buffalo, and—on the Blacktail Plateau, amid lush meadows—a black bear. Finally, he'd gone to Walmart and bought a canoe, which he launched near the border of Montana and Wyoming. Destination: Gulf of Mexico.

Conant was now downstream of Yankee Jim Canyon, a narrow cleaving of the Absaroka and Gallatin ranges that chokes the river into an angry froth. He had capsized a couple of days earlier while struggling with a rapid known as Boateater, and been fortunate to lose only a machete and a hat in the process. The water was frigid, and he'd briefly reconsidered his options, among them adding outriggers for stability. But he no longer had access to a car, with which to resupply. As he stood on a bridge that morning, gazing nervously ahead, a truck driver stopped and asked, only half joking, if someone had drowned. Not so funny. Conant ate a quick breakfast (hot yams, more river water), and set about rearranging his gear, which included Pepto Bismol and a marble composition book in which he'd jotted a few reminders: "REMEDY FOR BUGS. KEEP SWATTING. How to get through rapids—hold on tight. CLOSE EYES." Forget the outriggers. He was under way, a lone canoeist amid scattered dories in a seven-knot current, at around 10 a.m.

The canyon walls receded and he shot out into the valley, flanked in the near distance by ten-thousand-foot peaks. Cottonwoods lining the banks yielded summer snow to the flukey breeze. On the water, swirling eddies materialized and vanished inexplicably, while rainbow trout breached in the periphery of his vision. Paradise Valley: a name well deserved. Conant had traveled much of the world, and set foot in all forty-eight contiguous states, and he deemed this the most picturesque river valley he had experienced up close.

Afternoon brought heavy weather and a slalom course, as the straightaways shortened and he coped ably with shoals and rapids. Somehow, in the course of sliding forty-five miles, he scraped just two rocks. And then, half an hour before sunset, he arrived, brimming with adrenaline, in Livingston, a town that seemed composed of equal parts galleries and saloons. Yuppies and cowboys. A man like Conant—an old art major with Falstaffian appetites—could imagine getting used to such a place.

But he was on a mission, of a sort. He had notions of spending Christmas in Mississippi (Natchez or Vicksburg), and of ring-ing in the millennium in New Orleans. He thought it best not to "tarry," as he liked to say, thinking of his deceased father, an army colonel with a performative sense of rectitude. He won a little money gambling at a hotel casino on the south end of town, and spent the extra cash on Bernard DeVoto's abridged *Journals of Lewis and Clark*, good companionship for a transcontinental river trip.

In a park near some ballfields, while Conant repacked his boat, a young brunette was walking her dog. They got to talking. Her name was Tracy. She seemed intrigued by his plans, maybe even impressed by his derring-do. Conant, who had been dressing more or less exclusively in bib overalls since Woodstock, had grown familiar in recent years with being regarded as a misfit rather than a rugged charmer: a janitor, after all, in spite of a graduate education. A gifted natural athlete, he now carried well over two hundred pounds on his six-foot-one frame. No matter his evocative blue eyes and wispy blond hair. He was highly perceptive, and sometimes sensitive to a fault. Yet here was someone, perhaps, who saw him the way he was still determined to see himself: intelligent, adventurous, charismatic, *ambitious*.

Tracy asked what he planned to do when he was finished with the journey. It was a natural question, and a heady one. What *should* a middle-aged man who has quit his job and stink-bombed his home hope for, after conquering more than three thousand miles on one of the earth's longest unbroken chains of river— Yellowstone to Missouri to Mississippi? He liked university towns and big skies. He liked hospitals: before becoming a janitor, he'd worked as a scrub, prepping for surgery. He said that he was thinking of settling nearby, in Bozeman, with an eye toward studying bacteriology. A little late to resume a medical career, but the vigorous long paddle into town had left him feeling youthful and optimistic. Reflecting on the exchange as he continued downriver, he recalled a bashful glimmer in the woman's eyes at the prospect of his returning. "I hope I see Tracy again," he wrote in his composition book.

. . .

After a week afloat, he found himself occasionally unsteady on his feet, the ground seeming to rise and fall beneath him, as though carried by waves. He learned to avoid the gunpowder-gray sand, which was deceptively yielding, and capable of sucking the shoes off his ankles, in favor of gravel bars, the rockier the better. The river shed two thousand feet in elevation in a couple hundred miles, and then, having left the mountains behind, began to slow. The temperature climbed above a hundred. The lush valley turned into prairie badlands, with red streaks and coal in the ochre bluffs. He saw paw prints larger than his own hands, and a bobcat the height of a German shepherd.

The vertigo subsided, but bugs were a persistent problem: black flies so adept at the hit-and-run that Conant found himself unable to distinguish between real bites and phantom bites—a kind of preemptive paranoia; gnats, which he inhaled by the cloudful; and mosquitos, never more annoying than when they dive-bombed the moisture of his eyeballs and got trapped in his defensive lids. While studying the ingredients lists in many of the itch-relief products available in drugstores, he noticed that ammonia kept recurring. So he scoured the cleaning supplies, and bought himself a pint of Parsons' Household, for a buck-fifty. After a localized experiment produced no skin rashes, he began buying the stuff in bulk and applying it as a comprehensive daily salve. On his hands and feet, and even his face, meanwhile, he used Bag Balm, a lanolin-based livestock disinfectant, to seal cracks and stave off chilblains. When he ran out of shoe grease for his boots, he tried the Bag Balm on them, as well, and found that it repelled moisture just as effectively, and for half the price.

The frames of his glasses were pitted with metal that began to rust after the capsizing at Yankee Jim Canyon, but he was regaining his night vision, a source of pride from his navy days as a ship's navigator. Approaching Sidney, near the North Dakota border, he saw five shooting stars, and later made his way back to the canoe from town by starlight, through fields of wheat and corn. The air was so clear, and free of dust, that he realized he had gone a couple of weeks without the urge to pick his nose. For reading and writing at camp, he built what he thought of as a Chinese lantern, standing a white plastic dishwashing basin on its side and placing a row of citronella gel candles behind it, shielded from wind. By the end of August, he had regressed to a "stone-age mentality," as he put it, fashioning acoustic chambers (for his radio) and cooking stoves out of sedimentary rocks, and burning the coal for fuel. He had also acquired a passenger: a mouse, which was nibbling holes in his dry bags in search of food.

Conant's merger with the Missouri was uneventful, but the addition of the Little Muddy River, outside Williston, produced a labyrinth of delta hedgerows and willow islands in which he got lost. While seeking a place to camp, amid electrical storms, he was chased by a steer. He found a cave with bones littered around the entrance and built himself a sleeping coffin out of driftwood, "a Lincoln Log kind of a deal."

After the labyrinth, the Missouri was less a river than a chain of elongated lakes, with scalloped shorelines, backed up behind massive dams. In the mornings, he was sometimes greeted by thousands of large-scaled carp at the surface, so plentiful that he had to be careful not to bat them with his paddle. For long stretches he could detect no current, but there were genuine sea swells and surfable breakers. He felt as if he were on the Atlantic. When paddling into headwinds, he learned to time his strokes to coincide with the arrival of cresting waves by his side, thereby shortening his reach by several inches. With following seas, he tried to absorb wave thrusts on his starboard aft quarter and then grab the crests with his paddle as they passed by.

October brought screeching ravens, the smell of fresh wild mint, and, one morning, a thick fog that yielded to slanting sleet that blasted his corneas. A couple of days later, observing great cumulus formations drifting west in a continuous stream over the Lower Brule Sioux Reservation, in South Dakota, he suddenly realized that the eastern half of the sky was entirely blue. Then he saw wisps of moisture rising from the middle of the river: a cloud fountain.

He enjoyed vivid dreams: porpoises jumping the turnstiles of a flooded subway station. He learned to stow primo driftwood in his cooler, so that he'd have dry kindling even when it rained. He discovered a nice thing about traveling south at a dammed river's pace through the fall: the elongation of peak foliage, soon to be stretching into a third month.

The trip's rough midpoint, both by distance and thematically, was Sioux City, Iowa, where the shipping channel begins—or ends, if you're a tugboat captain traveling upstream from New Orleans. Conant celebrated the conclusion of the wilder half of his journey by checking his blood pressure at a supermarket kiosk. It had plunged from 200/100 to 120/77. No better medicine. A few days later, near Decatur, Nebraska, he was awakened for the first time by the sound of a tug pushing a barge. "I scrutinized the resulting wave action," he wrote. "It did not swamp my boat as I feared it might. These waves were navigable. Safety will require constant vigilance." Ahead lay Omaha, Kansas City, St. Louis, Memphis: a buoyant highway.

2

Things That Are Real

I met Dick Conant fifteen years later, on Labor Day morning in 2014. My two-year-old son, Ian, and I were down at the west bank of the Hudson River, in Piermont, New York, a small village twenty miles north of midtown Manhattan, when a neighbor of ours appeared and gestured at a filthy vessel lashed to an iron loop in his seawall. It was a plastic red canoe, packed as if for the apocalypse with army-surplus duffels and tarps and trash bags. The neighbor, named Scott, said that the boat's owner was in the midst of paddling "from Canada to Florida" and was presently enjoying a pit stop inside his house.

We didn't know Scott especially well at that point. My wife, Leah, and Ian and I had relocated to Piermont the previous year from a waterfront neighborhood in Brooklyn, where a hurricane had deposited a fish in our basement, like a Mafia warning. From one flood zone to another, I joked of the move, though our new house was at least perched on a hillside, whereas Scott's was nearly flush against the seawall. I admired it mostly from the comfortable remove of a second-story window in my home office, through which I could see Scott emerge, often still dressed in a bathrobe, to . . . train seagulls? That's what it looked like, at any rate. He had them eating out of his hand. I'd been told that he sold linoleum flooring for a living and gave out the most desirable candy on Halloween. In our passing interactions, he exuded a kind of laconic charisma, frequently ending conversations with the phrase "Happy day." Leah called him Lebowski.

It was his fifty-sixth birthday, we learned, and there were several guests seated around a long table in his living room. The man at the head of the table, facing down a kingly spread of caviar and donuts and drinking a vodka cocktail, seemed a stranger not just to Piermont but to the twenty-first century. He wore denim overalls, a faded baseball cap, and muddy brown boots, and had a patchy, rust-colored beard. A summer spent on the water had given him the complexion of a boiled lobster, to go with the build of a manatee. He offered a handshake stronger than any I can recall and spoke his full name proudly, with equal emphasis on every syllable: *Dick-Coe-Nant.* I asked if it was true that he was headed for Florida. He nodded and specified, "Naples." Not twenty minutes earlier, I gathered, he had floated into view of the wall of picture windows before us, through which the flexing water, in the glare of morning sunlight, appeared like molten lead.

Conant was sixty-three, and gave only retirement as an explanation for his slo-mo southern migration. (He joked that he was a snowbird, laughing with great heaves of his gut.) But he spoke in a mellifluous high timbre that was almost childlike. Thinking out loud, I mentioned that Naples was not on the Atlantic but the Gulf Coast. It must have come off sounding skeptical. (*You do realize you're traveling by canoe, don't you? Can you* get *there from here?*) Conant was accustomed to being doubted, and to remaining gracious rather than defensive. He stifled a smirk, cocked his head back, and shook an index finger as if to say, "Don't get me started." The short version is that there is a canal extending east and west from Lake Okeechobee, connecting the two sides. The longer version was implied—as he looked to be navigating a map in his mind, lost in a blur of logistics for several seconds—but left unsaid for the sake of polite company. (I later came to understand that he was debating an explanation of the Intracoastal Waterway, a chain of estuaries, rivers, bays, and man-made canals that enables safer shipping along the Eastern Seaboard and over to Mexico.)

One of the other guests slipped upstairs and returned bearing a framed newspaper clipping from 1977, the year I was born. It described the bicycle journey of our host, Scott Rosenberg, then eighteen years old, and a friend, from Rockland County, New York, to Cocoa Beach, Florida, while subsisting on a couple hundred bucks and the kindness of strangers. Were such characters magnetized to one another? They'd met the previous day, I soon learned, at a beach five or six miles north of us, where Scott had arrived by kayak and Conant by canoe, from opposite directions. Scott had made a mental note to keep an eye trained out his window thereafter, realizing that he could have a surprising source of entertainment to beckon ashore for his birthday guests. He said that he viewed his hospitality to the southbound paddler as a form of "paying it forward," from one adventurous spirit to another.

My son, barely verbal, was not then capable of appreciating the novelty at hand, so we soon bid the traveler good luck and returned to the slippery rocks and sea glass on the river's shore, while my mind, alight with childhood memories of *Treasure Island* and *Where the Wild Things Are,* started composing a bedtime story for future use, about the sudden arrival of a bearded giant from a distant land, with a grip that could kill and a belly laugh as disarming as St. Nick's.

That evening, after Ian had gone to sleep, I sent an email to a friend in Manhattan. "So we're down at the water this morning," it began. "And our neighbor Scott, the guy whose house is right there on the other side of the stone wall, waved me over and invited me in . . . where he was feeding breakfast to a man who looked like Santa Claus crossed with a lobster, in overalls." The note went on to mention the coincidence of Scott's own bicycle journey. The subject line was "river town," implying archly that such whimsy was par for the course. If only I'd known how true that would prove to be.

·   ·   ·

Moving "upriver," as I liked to say, I had consoled myself with the notion that I wasn't settling into a normative middle age so much as reconnecting with my youthful escapism, at the dawn of parenthood. (Rivers, Thoreau wrote, "are the constant lure, when they flow by our doors, to distant enterprise and adventure.") The Hudson at Piermont is two and a half miles wide—the Tappan Zee, a Dutch word for sea. On foggy mornings, and during snowstorms, the distant eastern shore vanishes, and it's possible, if you have a yearning cast of mind, to imagine that you've been marooned—not simply in a bedroom community, but on the edge of something vast and ultimately unknowable, keeping time less according to commuter bus schedules than to the magical permanence of tides. At the closing meeting for our house, one of the sellers—a professional riverboat captain—mentioned that the Hudson, though regarded by millions primarily as a transit obstacle, was, in fact, "as wild as the Serengeti." It was exactly what I wanted to hear. Not for me Kerouac's dreamscape of the open road, which had forever seemed proscribed, the dominion of crossing guards and police cruisers, whereas setting oneself afloat felt otherworldly and limitless.

By any reasonable definition, Piermont is now a prosperous suburb of New York City. Yet, like many river towns, the most ancient of human settlements, it is the sort of place that regards as newcomers all whose surnames can't be found on street signs, while retaining a feeling of being left behind, not simply by the descending current but by the march of history. The name is an amalgam of two defining geographic features: "pier," for the mile-long spur, jutting out toward the channel, that was built for Erie-bound freight trains that stopped arriving in 1861; and "mont," for the minor mountain—a glorified hill, really—that tumbles down to the river. At the summit are the graffitied remains of a nuclear missile base, a relic of the Cold War now obscured by forest. And at the base, across the street from Scott's house, sits a boulder bearing a plaque that identifies the anchorage out yonder as the site of a seventeen-gun salute, in 1783, from Sir Guy Carleton to George Washington: Britain's first formal recognition of American sovereignty. When my family arrived, the crumbling Dutch Sandstone looming above the boulder was owned by an octogenarian who wore a tricorne.

I've mentioned the hurricane, and the fish in the Brooklyn basement. Discovering it—still moist, and cold—was actually a momentary thrill, in that it seemed to lend some primal grandeur to our bourgeois misery. We'd been renting a place a couple of blocks from the docking station for the *Queen Mary 2,* the world's last great ocean liner, which had felt to me like a link to a past when people who wanted to travel great distances to exotic places took to what Ishmael, in the incantatory opening of *Moby Dick,* called "the watery part of the world." Here, in an overwhelming surge, that world had come right to my (useless) door. I remember, in the storm's aftermath, commiserating with an artist friend in the neighborhood about our respective experiences and watching his eyes excite at my mention of the fish, which seemed to complement his attempt to paddle a raft through his studio when the harbor breached. He talked about staging an exhibit—nature reclaiming the Bloombergian city!—like the opening scene of an environmental thriller, and asked me to send him a picture. I never did. Nor did I tell him why: because I'd already concluded that the fish, which was toothless and small enough to hold in one's palm, had traveled no farther than from the koi pond next door.

In my day job as a journalist, I've seen more than enough stunts, and had Dick Conant's peculiar voyage come to my attention by way of a press release, touting yet another attempt at some kind of arbitrary "record" in a postmodern world lacking authentic frontiers, I might have dismissed or ignored it, as emblematic of the koi pond, not the Serengeti. But I googled him that night, after emailing my friend, and was further intrigued by the scant digital traces that he seemed to have left. There was a short article from the *Bozeman Daily Chronicle,* in 2002, about a "weather watcher" for Montana State University, headlined "Richard Conant keeps an eye on Mother Nature." It revealed little other than that its subject was "one man in a 107-year lineage of official Bozeman weather readers," and that he observed the mercury "with a physician's care"; the accompanying photograph showed a large man with his back turned to the camera. The denim overalls, however, looked familiar.

And there was a thread on a Texas kayak fishermen's forum, beginning with a post from New Year's Day, 2008. "I thought your membership would be interested in the adventures of Dick Conant," it read. "Mr. Conant is paddling a dark green heavily loaded 16' canoe along our stretch of the intercoastal waterway. He left Buffalo New York in early July, paddling alone down the rivers from New York to the Mississippi and then to the GIWW"— the Gulf Intracoastal Waterway. A few people responded to say that they, too, had met him ("He told me had a real tough time in Matagorda Bay"), while others wished they had ("What a journey! Epic proportions"). And that was about it.

Leah was then eight months pregnant with our second son. Neither of us had been sleeping well for weeks, and late that night, acting on a flight impulse and inspired by our unusual visitor, I gave up trying and slipped out of the house to launch a kayak—also red, also plastic—that I'd bought from a sketchy man on Craigslist.

The ambient illumination from streetlights revealed that Conant's canoe was no longer tied to Scott's seawall. I pushed off from shore, alone with my regret over the missed opportunity to gather at least a few more vivid details of his adventures, for the bedtime story, if nothing else: strike one. To my right, or south, were a couple of marinas mostly full of motorboats, and, beyond them, at the foot of the long pier, a small public beach where Lycra-clad rowers launch sculls. On either side of the pier, the water is shallow and often calm, more lagoon than river. I pointed east, parallel to the pier, and glided out, round the end, turning south and into the pull of the current and the outgoing tide just as a pink glow was beginning to emanate from the treetops in Westchester. Ahead and to my right, now, was what Dutch settlers called the Slote, meaning ditch, referring to the marshy inlet that represents the first navigable break in the Palisades cliffs. A wall of green stalks with a hint of autumnal gold frosting the top: my own private wilderness.

Shortnose sturgeon—spiny bottom-feeders, contemporaries of the dinosaurs—shot out of the water like torpedoes, and then belly-flopped. Scientists still aren't sure why they jump. They have—around here, at least—no natural predators from which to escape. Yet after seventy million years they still haven't bothered to learn a graceful reentry. One theory holds that the flights and flops are a form of communication: percussive splashdowns as barbaric yawps, a way of marking territory. I prefer to think of it more as a prehistoric cannonball: the age-old wisdom of child's play. The pink sky turned orange, then yellow, neon shading into pastel, and I finally turned around when I reached a string of small white floats tended by a local character known as Crabman.

On the north side of the pier, behind tufts of marsh grass, I now noticed a red boat not unlike my own. I don't know if it was my disappointment at the shattered illusion of aloneness or the fact that I was focused more immediately on fighting the current to make it home before breakfast, but somehow it didn't dawn on me until after I was back on solid ground and ascending the hill that the other red boat must have been Conant's.

Strike two.

. . .

After breakfast, I caught a bus to Times Square (going *underneath* the river, through the Lincoln Tunnel), to the offices of *The New Yorker,* where I worked. The absence of a window near my desk contributed to a feeling of claustrophobia, and I found myself staring at a printout I'd made of the Texas fishermen's forum. Abruptly, I decided to commute back home, thinking that I might embark on a fool's errand of trying to find Conant again. This time, instead of taking the tunnel, I rode a bus over the George Washington Bridge, so that I could train my eyes on the water below, looking—in vain—for riparian Santa. It was hard to guess how far south Conant might already have traveled, but I resigned myself to the idea that if I didn't catch him before he slipped under the bridge, I wasn't going to be able to. He'd be lost—ostensibly forever—in an urban mess of ferries and barges and bulkheads.

Fortunately, the western shoreline between the bridge and Piermont is almost entirely wooded parkland, and accessible to the public. When I got home, I grabbed a pair of binoculars, and drove south, first, to a marina in Alpine, New Jersey, just across the state line. I asked some men who were smoking in the parking lot if they had seen a hillbilly in a canoe. "You mean the guy going to Florida?" one asked. Apparently Conant had long since come and gone, on an unfulfilled quest for ice. "I think it was around ten this morning," the man said.

It was now after two. Not promising. But maybe Conant, unlike me, had stopped for lunch. (Was he frying up white perch or tommy cod from the river?) I drove south another five miles, to a boat basin near the bridge, in the town of Englewood Cliffs. Inside an office on the dock, I found a female clerk and repeated my hillbilly-in-a-canoe line. She shot back a blank stare. I tried elaborating on the nature and scope of Conant's journey, such as I (barely) understood it, and she finally cut me off: "Some people have too much time on their hands."

I was actually in a bit of a hurry—on the hook for daycare pickup duty in less than two hours. Yet I felt reasonably sure that I had Conant's position pegged to somewhere between the two marinas, so I began hiking quickly upriver, along a rocky trail. Raising the binoculars after a couple of minutes, I spotted something colorful just beyond the nearest jetty, a few hundred yards ahead. It turned out to be a deflated mylar balloon.

I had the printout of the fishermen's forum in my bag with me, along with a notebook, a trail map, and a digital recorder. Looking at the printout again, as I dithered, I was beset by a feeling of inadequacy. Conant had evidently made it all the way to Texas once before, from considerably north of where I now stood, sweating uncomfortably in ninety-degree heat. If nothing else, he wasn't the kind of person who gives up on a crazy idea.

So I trudged on, and, after a mile, looking through the binoculars again, I spied the flash of a yellow paddle blade. There he was, bobbing in the ebb tide, riding so low that he appeared almost to be sitting on water.

"I'm due for a good break," Conant said, after noticing my exuberant arm waving and carefully backing his canoe in to a sandy beach beneath the Palisades, near some jet-skiers who had come over from the Bronx side to swim. "It don't look like much, but these damn swells are coming from the southeast. They're not hitting me in my face, but they're reducing my progress tremendously." He arranged several sticks of driftwood in a kind of ladder formation—a makeshift dry dock on which to slide the boat above the high-water mark. Yesterday's overalls were draped over a green tarp in the bow, air-drying after a laundry dunking earlier in the morning. He was wearing navy swimming trunks, and, underneath a black life vest, a salt- and sweat-stained T-shirt that read "New Orleans French Quarter." It looked like it might have been light blue once, before the sun bleached its pigmentation. His bare feet were slightly gnarled, and enormous.

Conant wrapped a long yellow rope around the aluminum shaft of his paddle a few times and then stowed it carefully, seemingly out of habit. The rope was knotted just beneath the paddle's T-shaped handle. Its other end ran through a loop on a white rubber bumper as well as through the handle of an empty detergent bottle, which appeared to be serving as a buoy. Another cluster of knots tethered the buoy, the bumper, and ultimately the paddle to a cable lock on a bracket built across the canoe's stern. This guy meant business.

"Do you have something to drink, like a soda pop?" he asked. I mistook it for a request, and stammered a little, while apologizing for arriving empty-handed. "Would you *like* one?" he said. I declined, not wanting to waste his supplies. "It's no waste— believe me," he said, his voice dissolving into warm laughter. "I'm going to get a glass of water myself." He lifted the green tarp and revealed a large Coleman cooler amidships. Then he unscrewed the cap of an empty Gatorade bottle and dipped it into the melted ice in the cooler. After he'd replaced the cap and given the bottle a few vigorous shakes, the water inside looked only semitranslucent. He pointed in the cooler to a Mt. Olive jar stuffed with kosher franks, and said, "I take hot dogs and I put 'em in pickle juice. If I run out of ice, the brine will keep them from going bad." Raising a bag of produce, he added, "I got peaches—you want one?"

Conant grabbed a folded brown tarp from behind his seat in the stern and spread it on some nearby grass, unnervingly close to a patch of poison ivy, warning that he was going to seek "as close to a prone position as possible." He urged me to take a tarp as well, cautioning against deer ticks. I then showed him my printout, with various Texans remarking on his prior travels from Buffalo. He seemed amused—evidently not a self-googler—though he felt compelled to correct it. "That's pretty close," he said. "Actually, *near* Buffalo. Place called Olean"—Oh-lee-ann. "On the headwaters of the Allegheny River. I took the Allegheny down to Pittsburgh, where it joins the Monongahela and forms the Ohio. I took the Ohio down to the Mississippi, as far as the mouth of the old Red River, which has a lock in it now—it's what they call a flood-control management area. And the Atchafalaya—I got on the Atchafalaya, went through the lock, goes up ten to twelve feet. Took the Atchafalaya down to Morgan City, and there's a town on the left side of the river whose name I forgot. I got on the Gulf Intracoastal there, in Louisiana. I took the Intracoastal all the way down to South Texas."

I had scarcely finished connecting the squiggly lines on the imperfect map in my mind before he began describing another voyage ("if you can keep up with me") that made the previous one sound like a lap around a duck pond. It involved descending the full length of the Mississippi and then *ascending* several rivers (the Mobile, the Tombigbee, the Tennessee, the Holston) through the Southeast, before hitching a ride over the Appalachians, relaunching on the James River, in Virginia, and making his way down to Hampton Roads ("where the *Monitor* and the *Merrimack* had their battle in the Civil War") and eventually Portsmouth. There was a naval hospital there, where he sought a tune-up. The whole adventure lasted nearly fourteen months. Midway through his recounting, around the time he was extolling the virtues of a "goooood Baptist family" he'd met in Louisiana, he paused to notice a fresh welt on the arm that was propping up his head, and exclaimed, "Gosh, look at these bugs! I hope I didn't run into a bunch of fire ants. Sometimes I do that."

His digital watch, I noticed, was set to mountain standard time. "Yeah, I'm from Bozeman, Montana," he explained. "I met my girl near there. I met my girl in Livingston, which is across the mountain pass."

"I was an army brat," he went on, and said that, as a matter of fact, he had spent the greatest portion of his childhood just five miles west of Piermont, right near me. A Rockland County local, after all that. He even had a brother who still lived nearby. "I was going to call him, but I didn't," he said, and then his eyes—a piercing blue, accentuated in contrast with his scorched skin—drifted out over the water again.

.   .   .

By sheer luck, I'd flagged him down at what he deemed an enviable campsite, with a narrow grass strip abutting some stone ruins, and a view of northern Manhattan across the river. He began to settle in, especially after examining a New York State road atlas and concluding that he'd traveled nearly a dozen miles since dawn. "Golly, I did well this afternoon, despite that wind," he said. "I ain't going no further. That's a good day's work."

The atlas itself was a marvel, its pages covered in blue ink—tidy block letters, all caps—such that in places you could scarcely make out the underlying map details. It could have passed for the work of an outsider artist. "I started keeping a regular journal, but I found that I was so tired at the end of the day," he said. "So what I do is, I keep notes as I go, and that way I don't have to remember things at night." He had a computer buried deep in a dry bag so that he could type up "a prose account" of the journey when it was complete. "I've written three books," he said. "I'm just not *published*. Because, by the time I get done writing, I'm so tired of living in the city that I'm ready to go out on another trip!" His notes on the atlas included descriptions of wind and current and waterfowl, as well as of various social interactions, and other stray thoughts. Up by the Indian Point nuclear plant, he'd written "Drowning Mona," the title of a comedy, set nearby, in which a character played by Bette Midler mysteriously drives off a cliff to her death in the Hudson River.

At night, meanwhile, instead of journaling, he read novels, seeking an escape from his escapism. "Now I'm reading Clive Cussler, something about treasure," he said. "When I'm home in Montana, I don't read fiction. I read history and scientific works. Archaeology, physics, astronomy: things that are real. But my life there is, like, sedate. When I get out here, my days are filled with rational thought. It's constant intellectual and physical interaction with my environment: with the weather, with the river, with the rocks. So I'm totally immersed in reality during my daylight hours, and when I go to camp at night, I do something I don't do at home: I read these novels. I stop in little towns. At the local library, they have this thing they've been doing the past few years—in the front of the library, there's usually free books. I think they get donated? So I get the authors I like, and when I'm done with 'em, I either throw 'em away or burn 'em in a campfire." He must have noticed a faint twitch of disapproval on my face, because he quickly added, "What I *can't* do is take 'em with me after I'm done."

We both looked over at his canoe, with its tarped mounds, and Conant smiled. He seemed to suggest that he was *strategically*, not wantonly, overloaded. He had a half-dozen gallon-size jugs onboard, capable of carrying up to fifty pounds of water weight, and he stowed them around the bottom of the hull in varying arrangements, as ballast to counteract wave action, having learned from some towboat captains down south that they sometimes used more fuel pushing empty barges than full loads, because of the effort required to hold a steady course. When he was anticipating turbulence, he drank deeply without replenishing, to increase his canoe's buoyancy. He was doing that right now, in fact, because the harbor in the city was likely to present "confused seas—waves coming from one direction and another— and if I'm more buoyant I can rock and roll a lot better."

It was a delicate calculus—thirst insurance versus maneuverability—especially given that he had long since reached the brackish stage of the river, with salinity increasing by the mile, which ruled out boiling his means of conveyance as a last resort. He said he'd resorted to that option twice while upstate. But an urban environment such as he was now approaching seemed likely to promise ample spigots or grocery stores, he figured. "I don't expect to hit anyplace that's really remote until I get to central New Jersey."

I grew up in New Jersey. Not *central* New Jersey, but I've got a lifetime's experience with the fact that most people from elsewhere don't much care to parse the regions. It is, of course, the most densely populated state in the country. There is the New York City part of Jersey and the Philadelphia part of Jersey. And the Shore, but that's not what he meant; he said the salt concentration in ocean water activated skin allergies, and was best avoided. The idea that you could lose yourself in the middle—that an accomplished Montana outdoorsman, no less, could manage to conceive of sliding inland on inevitably polluted watercourses and anticipate a feeling of remoteness—was, to this product of *Sopranos* territory, enchanting. Was it even *possible* to traverse the state by boat? I'd never considered it. The ever-shrinking woods I used to try to disappear in as a boy, while hoping for absolution from travel soccer, abutted a condominium development called Rio Vista, which was a kind of quintessential Jersey joke: there was no view to speak of, and certainly no river.

Looking back at his atlas, and at a tide chart by his side, Conant shifted his focus to the more immediate challenges of an industrial environment: the city and the harbor ahead, where the biggest problem, aside from confused seas, was finding accessible and suitably private campsites. To the extent possible, he preferred not to trespass or to appear "slovenly," as he put it. "People get offended if you sleep out in the open," he said. "I can travel at night, if necessary—or, you know what I did once? On the Mississippi, I was coming up to a dam, and these signs that said, 'Do not go further.' So I pulled up to this arsenal. You know, 'Do not enter. U.S. government property.' I had no choice. I tied myself off to a tree and to a log that was horizontal, and I went to sleep right in the boat. And I actually got shuteye, too!"

Conant informed me that we were in a waxing moon cycle ("It's going to be bright tonight—take a look before you go to bed"), and he hoped for low cloud cover that would trap the skyscrapers' lights, further illuminating the river at night. "I looked at this on Google," he said, pointing on a map to the area around the Statue of Liberty. "And it looks like if I got there after dark . . ." He acknowledged that what he was envisioning might be illegal. "I shouldn't tell you my secrets," he said, and added that he was thinking of paddling over to Ellis Island. "I've never been."

. . .

I had to leave, in order not to be criminally late to pick up my son. Conant, sensing my unease, mentioned that he might stick around another day, in case I wanted to come visit again. "I don't want you chasing me around like you did today," he said. Because he had no schedule to maintain, he thought he might benefit from resting his muscles a little longer for the difficult stretch ahead. Also, he could use the time to drink more water, in preparation for rocking and rolling.

"Let me tell you one more story before you go," he said, as I made a rapid calculation of how many minutes I could save by driving seventy instead of the usual sixty on the parkway. "I see lots of wonderful birds on trips like this. When I first started seeing great blue herons, many years ago, I was just enthralled with 'em—such a graceful bird. They have this guttural squawk. I don't know if you've ever heard it? Very rarely have I seen them actually catch fish, because when I come by, they're wary of me. And they can just jump up and be airborne—that's how graceful they are. They're amazing, *amazing* animals.

"One day, I was paddling down the Mississippi River, doing what I call night passage. I had a full moon, was maybe a hundred or two hundred yards from shore. So I'm on the edge of the current, you know? I'm on the margin. I'm not doing four knots, but I'm moving. *Two* knots—that's enough. That's what I do on slack water anyhow. And I just thought, Well, I'll sit back." He gestured toward the rubber bumper tethered to the canoe's stern, which I now understood to be a pillow. "You see I have a little resting thing. So I'm looking at the moon and just relaxing. All of a sudden, out of nowhere, this *huge* male comes swooping in right next to my port gunwale. And he was just about to put his talons—he had these really long, skinny fingers—with both feet, he was just about ready to grab my gunwale. Which is bad news, man, because he could tip me. And I went *whooooaaaa*—like that, right?—and he goes—I'll do what he did—he goes *doink*." Conant turned his head sharply and exposed the whites of his eyes. "So he's looking at me, right? But he never did grab my gunwale. He just flapped his wings—he was hovering. He flapped his wings I think three or four times. I could feel the wind in my face. And his beak, it looked like a dagger, man! Eh heh heh heh. He's, like, *this* close to my face. And he's got these beady eyes. The moon was glinting off the surface of his eyeballs. We're looking at each other like this." He flashed a look of alarm, and then smiled.

"Then all of a sudden he goes *whooof:* couple flaps, and he was gone." Conant closed his eyes for a moment, scratching behind his ear. "I thought I'd leave you with that," he said, chuckling. "I don't play patty-cake with wild animals. Sorry! I wish I was like that guy from Alaska that was making friends with all the bears— and then the bears ate him?"

Before I left, he asked if he could keep the printout from the Texas fishermen's forum, and suggested that I write my name and number on the back, for future reference.

.   .   .

The next afternoon, I found Conant "dreaming," as he soon put it, amid a spread of cheese and condiments. "Do you need some-thing to drink?" he asked, after snapping to, and suggested once again that I grab a tarp from his boat to defend against ticks. "If you get thirsty, let me know," he reiterated. He mentioned that I was not his first visitor of the day. A man had come by to fish early in the morning, before work. "All's we did is talk about the river, his life, my life," Conant said. Then he relayed much of what he'd learned: the man's name, age, and hometown, as well as his work history (a truck driver turned dispatcher) and the whereabouts of his parents. "You can write that down," he said.

He was eager to apologize for something he'd said the day before, and he hoped that I wasn't offended. I couldn't fathom what he was referring to. As I was leaving, he reminded me, he had said that he didn't care whether or not I managed to publish an article about his voyage. It was a harmless remark—sweet, even. As I understood it, he had meant to emphasize that he valued the companionship, and my interest in his adventures, more than any esteem publicity might bring him. ("I *love* telling about my trips," he'd said.) He was trying to absolve me of any obligation to labor further on his behalf.

Apparently, though, he'd been worrying about it ever since. For one thing, he now explained, it wasn't true. He recognized having one's work published as a form of professional success, and he wished to contribute to mine. ("This is your life's work!") And then there was the matter of his own manuscripts—two of which, he now said, he was carrying with him on flash drives. "I was going to give you one, but I thought Nah, that's going over the edge," he said. "But you know what I can do is, if we develop a certain email rapport, so to speak, I'll send you a snippet, I guess. Maybe twenty to thirty pages? Something particularly neat that you might like." He still imagined that he might get around to trying to find a wider audience for his writing, and he wondered if validation from *The New Yorker* might help. He had mentioned me that morning to the trucker fisherman, who told him that the magazine was a big deal, read by mayors and governors. "He said it's for the upper crust!" Conant added, and then snorted, pantomiming disavowal. "I'm kind of poor."

. . .

My interest this day was more transactional. Though I had enjoyed hearing his stories maybe as much as he had enjoyed sharing them, I now had some basic logistical questions, with the article in mind. Typically, a member of *The New Yorker*'s fact-checking department would follow up with the subject of a piece like this one before we went to press, to verify details and proper context, but it had occurred to me that that might be a challenge here. "When the time comes," I began, "is there a way that we can get in touch with you?"

"No," he said, and chuckled, as though the idea were indeed laughable. "I got a cell phone, but I rarely charge it," he went on. "You know, on my other trips, I didn't have one at all—until, like, I think the last half of my last trip, I got one." Whatever the case, he wasn't interested in using it for our convenience. I admit that I was more impressed than annoyed, and a little envious of his self-possession.

So I was left with my digital recorder and the hope that I might get him on the record addressing anything I thought the editors might conceivably want to know. Like, for instance: "When you go on a trip like this, you're gone for a long time. Do you give up your apartment for the time being? Or your house?"

He laughed again, more nervously this time, and paused. "That's kind of sensitive," he said. He paused some more, mumbled about how he supposed it would "get out anyhow," then took a deep breath and said, "Well, one of the reasons I go on these trips is because I don't *have* an apartment. I'm homeless. *People* call it homeless. I don't." I'd planned to ask next about how he financed his travel, but he kept going and answered without my prompting. "I was discriminated against in both housing *and* employment," he continued. "I was having a rough time.

And I managed without going to jail or getting thrown into a mental hospital. Now I'm old enough where I can collect Social Security—and going on a trip like this? It's cheap. Even though I make very little on Social Security, on a trip like this I can actually save big dollars." He laughed again. "Like I said, this is *much* too sensitive. But! It's the truth."

A day without transit, lacking the charge that comes from physical exertion or the distraction of constantly engaging with a dynamic environment, had left him faintly melancholic compared with the previous day's exuberance. He spoke candidly about his "checkered career," including stints on the railroad and in the navy, and described the medications he was on, and the reasons (uric acid, high blood pressure, a "missing" enzyme), and said that the VA clinics he frequented would give him only a two-week supply, which served as an incentive to keep moving. ("There's one or two in each state that I'm going to, so I should be okay.")

The lone stabilizing force in his life, as he now talked about it, seemed to be the "unusual" woman he'd met in Livingston the year before he settled across the mountain pass in Bozeman. Her name was Tracy—"and I don't want to give you her last name," he said. "We're not legally affianced or nothing." He described their relationship as "very strange but constant," and acknowledged that it was difficult to explain, in light of his itinerant ways. "She comes from a wealthy family out of Seattle," he said, hastening to add, "I didn't know she was wealthy when I met her." He sounded a little defensive, perhaps anxious about the judgments others might make about his intentions or his worthiness. "I very close to proposed to her within five minutes," he said. "And then I was on my way down the river."

At some point, after I'd lost control of the interrogation and submitted once more to the undammed stream of his consciousness, I noticed that he was sipping soy sauce straight from the bottle and pouring himself capfuls of Tabasco, and remarked on it. He seemed briefly embarrassed, as if caught engaging in a private ritual. "It's something I get into when I'm under way," he explained. "All's it does is it just flavors my mouth. I'm energizing the flavor buds."

Referring to my neighbor, he asked, "Did Scott tell you about Tracy following me around the country?" Then he launched a torrent of a monologue that began with a smoked sausage he'd bought at a grocery store in Minnesota, in 2009, near the beginning of the dizzying downstream-upstream voyage that he'd described the day before. "I pickled it like I pickle my other stuff, but unfortunately it had a bug," he explained. "Many microbes will not live in that acetic acid and salt and garlic, but this particular bacteria *thrived* in the pickle juice. Anyhow, as I was getting down towards, oh, mid- and southern Missouri, I ate some of that, and I got sick as a dog."

His sickness coincided with his arrival at a teardrop-shaped island in the Mississippi called Jones Towhead, downriver and around the bend from Chester, Illinois, the commemorative home of Popeye the Sailor. He set up camp in a glade on the northern end, under a light canopy of eighty-foot trees. "At the same time, within the nearest surrounding—I think it was seventeen—counties, in Missouri and Illinois, they had this deluge, just a magnificent rainfall, about five inches of rain that lasted over about two days," he went on. "And I had dysentery. Not only do you have to evacuate all the time, but I lost my energy completely. And as the river was rising, I had to move my tent and my gear. So I would move my gear, you know, up five feet in elevation, but maybe thirty-five or forty yards back, because you got a grade going up the towhead.

"So I'd go to sleep, and wake up in the morning, and the water would be lapping at my feet, and I'd have to get up and move my tent again. But the dysentery was so bad that I could only move like twenty feet at a time, and I'd collapse. When I say collapse, I mean totally on my face in the mud. Can't get up. Had to wait another twenty minutes to get enough—I think it's ATP?—into my muscles to where I could move again." (ATP, or adenosine triphosphate, is a molecule that transports energy within cells.) "It was the most devastating thing. And so that's what I'd do: I'd get up, move my gear, fall down, wait for it to pass, get up, move my gear. Make about four or five trips, then collapse in my tent again. Drink water, try to stay hydrated, go back to sleep. Wake up, the water would be at my feet again. It was just—the water *kept rising.*"

He stuck twigs upright in the mud to chart the river's rate of encroachment, which he estimated at six or more inches in elevation an hour. "So this went on for about two more days. The river level rose about twenty feet. Finally, I got to the top of the towhead, and I thought, Oh my god, *when's this river gonna stop?* There was only maybe eighteen inches of elevation left. Only the very top of the towhead was still above water." He looked up and his heart sank: there was driftwood suspended in branches above his head, evidence that it could get much worse. The river, meanwhile, was delivering not just tree limbs but washing machines and the sides of barns swiftly past him.

Then the rate slowed to an inch an hour, and finally his twigs were remaining high and dry.

"The Mississippi is just—I call it the Behemoth," he said. "I was lucky that it stopped. Anyhow, I had to stay on that island for about ten days to recuperate. I ran out of water, so I collected rainwater off the roof of my tent, and I boiled some river water." Boiling the Mississippi was a cumbersome project, involving stages of centrifugal sloshing and straining, to reduce sediment "and heavy metals and other noxious chemicals that cling to the mud." During his convalescence, he watched the ground beneath the canopy blossom into a fragrant carpet of daisies, and he observed the resumption of barge traffic, as the trash flushed out. He felt like Odysseus when he was enticed by the Sirens: "The water is calling me but I should not go." He forced himself to wait until his appetite had returned, and he tested his strength by hauling ever-larger logs—two and then three hundred pounds apiece—to his bonfire.

"I was scared," he said. "I had made it through a tremendous challenge, but I just had more respect for the river than I had ever had before. And by the time I got to—oh, what's the name of that town? General Grant had his headquarters there before he went to Columbus . . ." He meant Cape Girardeau, Missouri, the birthplace of Rush Limbaugh. "I forget the name of it. But I got acquainted with the townspeople, and almost—well, I got acquainted with a young woman, but I didn't fall in love, let's just put it that way. I was *tempted* to. I was so glad to be around a woman. And I think it was the fear of dying that I had gotten on that towhead that made me enjoy this person's presence. It made me feel alive again."

It was at this point that what had sounded to me like a survival narrative turned out to be a meditation on the redemptive power of constancy and faith. With his ego and self-confidence restored, he said, he got back on the river—"Told her, 'I really got to go, I'm not coming back'"—and, not long after, during a stopover in the Missouri bootheel ("the result of gerrymandering back in the eighteen hundreds"), he received a surprise visit, not for the first time, from Tracy, who was camouflaged in a wig. He was quickly attracted but didn't recognize her at first. He found himself telling her, "I got a sweetheart back home, and I know if I stick around here much longer I'm going to do or say something that I'll regret." He had a wistful smile as he recounted the episode and trailed off without mentioning what happened next, then allowed that he was anticipating another similar rendezvous as he headed south toward Naples.

"I tell this to some people and they say, 'Well, she's stalking you,'" he continued. "Well, that's fine with me! First of all, I have nothing to worry about. I don't cheat on her. She might get some false stories, but anytime she's ever checked on me, she's always found me to be fair and square. Plus, the other thing is she's looking to see if I'm healthy and alive. I appreciate that. I really do. Nobody else does that."

He mentioned that during his most recent VA check-in—"It's north of Beacon, I'm trying to remember the name . . . Castle Point!, which is really in the town of—it's got an old-timey name? Wappinger"—one of the nurses had suggested including Tracy as an emergency contact in their database. "They asked me, if I had a disaster, would I want her to find out about it." He declined. "I didn't tell 'em why," he said. "Because she'd know ahead of time. She'd know before anybody else."

"Unless I'm delusional," he added. "But I don't think I am."

A group of teenage boys on dirt bikes had arrived at the beach near Conant's campsite, and one of them began idly tugging at a set of wheels, for portaging, in the bow of the canoe, while maintaining eye contact with me from a distance of maybe thirty feet, as if to assert his fearlessness. If Conant saw the boy, he didn't let on. He was lying back again, his tongue energized with the residue of Tabasco and his cheeks flushed with longing. I'd hoped to wait until the teens moved on before taking my leave, but daycare pickup loomed. "I wish we could get better acquainted, but time is of the essence," Conant said, excusing me. "You're a family man."

I texted Scott when I got home, expressing my concern—about what, exactly? That the boys might have teased Conant? That he was relying on a guardian angel? It sounds so foolish in retrospect. Here was a bear of a man who had crisscrossed the country, alone, in a canoe, and evidently braved Montana winters sleeping outside, and I was trying to protect him from being harassed by suburban teenagers? Yet something about the phrase "she's looking to see if I'm healthy and alive" stuck with me. Along with the follow-up: "nobody else does that." There was a plaintiveness that started to feel like an omen, or a call to action.

Scott seemed untroubled by the flimsiness of my apprehension and responded to my text with the suggestion that we embark on a reconnaissance mission—another opportunity to spend time with a cool character, if nothing else. In addition to filling Conant's cooler with steak and vegetables, Scott told me, he had sent him off on Labor Day afternoon with a copy of his favorite book, *T. Jay's Log: The Last Voyage of the Frisco Felucca II*, which he stockpiled by scouring eBay and other online resellers and distributed with missionary zeal. It recounts, in journal form, a crossing of the Pacific Ocean on a converted lifeboat. I'll quote here from the flap copy:

"In the first few moments of the trip, the *Felucca*'s engine bursts into flame; they sail the entire rest of the way without an engine. Only a couple of days later, they lose their rudder not far from shore, and their beloved *Felucca* is towed by the United States Coast Guard—which promptly loses their boat at sea!"

Peril is part of the bargain, Scott seemed to be suggesting. And so, a few hours later, after my son had gone to sleep, we drove back down to Jersey, donned headlamps, and slipped into the woods, in violation of park rules forbidding visitors after dark.

. . .

If anything is likely to spook a solo traveler, it's got to be the unexpected sight of lights approaching from behind trees. Conant, jolted awake by our voices, was initially relieved to recognize a pair of familiar faces. Then he quickly grew suspicious, as I fumbled at explaining our rationale for the visit, mentioning the boy who'd looked as if he might have had sabotage or theft on his mind. "Wait a minute," he said, drawing out the first syllable, and I could see his eyes darting around me, as if trying to summon danger from the shadows. Maybe he *hadn't* noticed the kids, in which case I must have sounded like I was playing head games, describing a ghost. Or else he'd seen the boys come and go, without incident—after all, here he was, and there was the canoe, looking undisturbed—in which case I was the one raising the specter of threat retroactively.

The moment passed. Good nature prevailed. He warmed back up to his sociable self, and we three began exploring the nearby ruins together, speculating about their origins. Conant pegged them—correctly, it turned out—as a relic of the WPA era. An old bathhouse. Admiring the lights of northern Manhattan across the river, Scott recalled once circumnavigating the island in a kayak, timing his trip such that he rounded the Battery on a slack tide. I felt like an interloper at a secret meeting of the Explorers Club. Conant retrieved a digital camera from one of the bags in his canoe and asked if he could take our picture. He hugged us both. In spite of his girth, there was nothing soft about him. "These adventures are incredible," he said, repeating a sentiment that he'd voiced earlier in the day. "They really are. They're wonderful to have. They're dangerous, and full of excitement. However, at this point in my life, I've had enough of this excitement. I'd much rather be at home with a woman, and a family like you have, than out here on the water. But this is the alternative."

. . .

A police cruiser was waiting by Scott's car when we returned. Under my breath, I rehearsed what I might say if asked to explain our presence, fearing that in my misplaced concern about Conant I'd only managed to expose him to greater risk. A journalist always has an excuse; his subjects don't enjoy the same luxury. I've never been particularly good under pressure. I suppose that's one of the things I admired about Conant. He seemed so self-assured amid constant uncertainty. But, of course, as a perpetual visitor, he was at the whim of local authority.

An officer shone a flashlight in our eyes. He informed us that the park was closed. We said we were just leaving. He regarded us skeptically but didn't inquire any further—white privilege, perhaps. We managed to drive away without revealing that we'd left anyone behind at the riverfront.

. . .

Conant's casual mention of the possibility that he might be delusional, if only to dismiss it, gave me some pause as I reviewed my notes for the article. With the exception of the trucker fisherman who'd told him about *The New Yorker*'s moneyed readership, he hadn't provided last names for any of the people in his anecdotes. Some of those were pretty extraordinary. There was a NASA consultant, for instance ("he did programs for the Saturn rocket"), whom he credited with spontaneously chauffeuring him and his canoe over the Appalachians. From the details he provided, that seemed like a minimum of eighteen hours of round-trip generosity. The story, like all his others, was so incidentally specific—he'd mentioned the guy's missionary trip to Alaska, and attending Sunday school with him in Huntsville—that I didn't exactly doubt it, but what if he was omitting some essential context, like the fact that they were old friends from college, say, or the part where Conant stole his wallet? Even if I wasn't going to quote him at length, as I've done here, I was reluctant to assert his legitimacy, in the magazine, as an unheralded bard of American rivers without at least *some* corroboration.

My one shot, I realized, lay with a dive bar in the bootheel that he said he'd visited five years back, shortly after that near-death experience on a flooding towhead. "Place is called Woody's," he'd said. "And you can mention that, because it's well known in the Midwest, just a laid-back place where people are really happy and friendly and nobody is turned away."

Uh, sorry to bother you, but I'm calling from New York with an unusual question: Do you by any chance remember a large man in a canoe, dressed in overalls?

"I think about him often!"

The speaker was MaryBeth Johnson, who identified herself as a co-owner of the establishment and the daughter of the eponymous Woody. "What struck me is how he looked like a grandpa," she went on. "Like, what the heck is this old man doing by himself out on the river?" She mentioned that he "seemed very educated" and that they still had some annotated navigational charts that he'd left behind as souvenirs.

Duly reassured, I began to write: "Dick Conant likes to say that the Mississippi River, on which he has passed many months living out of a canoe, is a 'vibrant monster you just let out of its cage,' whereas the Hudson is merely 'an old uncle that has his moods.' . . ."

3

A Fine Line

Nearly three months later, on November 29, I was just sitting down to lunch with my wife and our toddler and newborn son when my phone buzzed. I didn't recognize the area code, and Leah flashed a look of disapproval when I answered anyway, on a whim.

"Ben McGrath?" a man said, and introduced himself as John Beardsley, a wildlife ranger in North Carolina. "I'm investigating a missing boater."

It took me only a couple of dumbfounded seconds to realize that he was calling about Conant. I explained that I was a journalist, and that I had written a short article (title: "Southbound") about the boater in question, describing his intention to reach Florida. I also mentioned that he had emailed me five or six weeks earlier, in late October. His note said:

Dear Ben, I just read your article and I am pleased. I am in Delaware City, DE, and am preparing for the next leg across Chesapeake Bay. I am healthy. My best to you, your wife and children and our friend Scott and all. I will write again when I can. My laptop went under with some waves but local libraries help, like this one. Good job. Your friend, Dick Conant.

So that explained the empty laptop case, at least.

Beardsley wasn't especially forthcoming about the circumstances under which the boat had been found. He mentioned duck hunters but didn't say that the canoe was upside down, for instance, and I, envisioning the filthy vessel stashed carefully on a mudflat, amid tall reeds, suggested that he check the nearest library, or perhaps a dive bar, where Conant might be establishing his Huck Finn bona fides by pantomiming frantic paddle strokes and recounting the time he almost got run over by a barge on the Mississippi, at night. Or was there a VA hospital in the area? I recalled Conant's impressive mental map of inland waterways, studded with clinics where he could renew his scrips. While my mind raced backward, re-sorting old memories, I took the opportunity to extemporize about Conant's many peculiarities and charms, and to theorize about his troubles.

"Do you think he might be dangerous?" Beardsley asked.

I didn't—or I hadn't, before the question had been put to me, in the disquieting context at hand: a sudden phone call from a stranger four hundred miles away, speaking about an investigation into a passing acquaintance who was traveling with my contact information.

Beardsley, polite but perhaps impatient, then reminded me about the northeaster a few days earlier that had made a hash of Thanksgiving travel up and down the coast, dumping several inches of snow outside my window. He asked for my help in alerting Conant's relatives to the developing situation.

I'd long wondered about them. Conant told me that he was one of nine siblings.

"Normally, I don't call them until I'm almost done, because that way they don't worry," he said. I'd been tempted, back in September, to find the brother who apparently lived near me and let him know that Dick was out on the river. Ultimately, though, I'd decided against even sending him a copy of the finished article, fearing it would come off as presumptuous. All families are complicated, let alone enormous ones. Who was I to intervene?

Reviewing my notes now, with some expanding guilt over my previous inaction, I saw that he had named his brother Joe, "down in Peachtree City, Georgia," as his closest kin. "He used to fly for Delta," he said. "His wife is one of those fussbudgets that everybody who has a birthday gets a card. So she's just kind of like the glue that keeps our disparate family together." I looked up the Conants in Peachtree City and sent Beardsley their phone number.

Meanwhile, a sinking feeling: as I continued reviewing my notes—spellbound anew by the ebbing and flowing of Conant's enthusiastic narration—I saw that he had identified North Carolina in particular as a problem spot on his itinerary. "I'll be far away from the Intracoastal Waterway," he'd said. "Now, it's settled land, but it's *sparsely* settled, and if I get to a place where I can't get ahold of people"—he raised the hypothetical scenario of a broken leg—"I usually have about three weeks of rations on board."

.   .   .

The absence of a life jacket among the wreckage was small cause for optimism, assuming it wasn't cause for utter despair. Albemarle Sound is vast, stretching more than fifty miles west from Kitty Hawk, on the Outer Banks, to the so-called Site X, where archaeologists lately have been digging for evidence of the lost colony of Roanoke—from the birthplace of flight, a triumph of

American exploration, to the cypress swamps at the heart of the New World's first missing-persons case. It's encircled, too, by rivers and creeks; Big Flatty, the smallest of those, is a mile across at the mouth, and worms its way inland some four miles north and west, flanked on either side by tilled fields and thick forest of cypress, tupelo, and pine. Facing south from the site of the canoe's discovery, it is ten miles across to more forest: a "mitigation bank" for the endangered red-cockaded woodpecker. If the waterways of central New Jersey can be considered remote, then the Albemarle might as well be the moon.

The sound's tides are not so much lunar as wind-driven: deeper (and saltier) when blowing from the east, and shallower (and fresher) when blowing from the west. The previous couple of days, since the storm, had brought stiff winds, primarily from the northwest. Shallowness, in general, is one of the sound's defining features. At its deepest, in the middle, the water might be twenty feet, but "with normal tides," as Grover Sanders, the farmer and duck hunter who hauled the canoe in, says, "there's nothing but four foot of water until you get a right good ways out there." You can almost walk.

The breadth of the fetch—the distance traveled by wind over open water—combined with the relative lack of depth makes it a deceptively dangerous body of water, as waves will bunch together in a squall, producing an aquatic rodeo. The same is true of Chesapeake Bay, to its north. An experienced boater in the region explains: "Any day of the week, if I'm in a decent boat, I would rather be fifty miles off the coast, dealing with thirty-foot seas, than in the Albemarle Sound or the Chesapeake, dealing with three-footers or four-footers." The first case is more like a roller coaster, frightening but manageable. "If you're out in the ocean and you're down in the trough, you see this mountain of water coming at you, like, 'Oh my god!' And you're going to ride up that, and when you get to the top you're going to see for miles. And then you go down in the trough again. You got these two mountains of water, one in front, and one behind you, but other than you being rather excited, not a whole lot's going on. When you're in the Albemarle or Chesapeake Bay, the first wave isn't off of you before the second wave hits you, and it's: *bam bam bam*. Those three-and-a-half- or four-footers are liable to drown your ass."

As far as Officer Beardsley and the others knew, their missing boater had survived the Chesapeake's chop intact. Another stroke of fortune: the nation's largest Coast Guard facility, Air Station Elizabeth City, sits on the western bank of the Pasquotank River, which spills into the sound just a few miles east of Big Flatty Creek. In the early afternoon, an hour or two after my phone conversation with Beardsley, the base dispatched a twenty-nine-foot boat to aid in the search, and diverted a Coast Guard Auxiliary plane to fly a grid pattern overhead. The boat had a crew of four, including a young petty officer nicknamed the Hawk, for his exceptional vision.

"Usually, I can spot anything and everything," the Hawk says. (His civilian name is Dan Langley.) "When we get these reports, sometimes it's super vague. 'New York to Florida,' that's all we heard. So why would he be going to Big Flatty? Where's he been sleeping?" They went up into the creek, looking for evidence of a campsite, if not a body itself, and then, finding nothing, headed southeast, into the wind and in the direction of the Alligator River, a dozen miles distant. The Alligator is part of the Intracoastal Waterway: a plausible route to Florida, used frequently by yachting retirees.

The water temperature was fifty-three degrees (brumating, or dormant, conditions for gators), slightly warmer than the air. Conant's weight would have worked in his favor, as fat storage delays the onset of hypothermia. But if the northeaster Beardsley mentioned had indeed been the cause of the separation of the snowbird and his canoe, Conant would have either been adrift for at least forty-eight hours or found his way to land.

The plane overhead saw only slop, increasing in turbulence as the day wore on. In late afternoon, peering through binoculars as the Coast Guard boat neared the mouth of the Alligator, the Hawk spied another overturned vessel, and was briefly excited at the thought that this could be a related discovery. It turned out to be a johnboat—or a portion of one, which looked to have been abandoned for many weeks, if not months.

"That sound's no play toy," Grover Sanders says.

· · ·

Officers Beardsley and Vaughan, from the Wildlife Resources Commission, returned to the cypress knees and began exploring the shoreline in wading boots. They found two more large green duffel bags in the water, stuffed with clothes. Behind the stumps was wet sandy ground, traversable with some difficulty. "But inland a little bit? I call it that nasty mud," Vaughan says. "You'll suck right up to your thigh."

"You'll go over your *head* in mud in there," Grover Sanders adds. "I'm serious. The old-timers, when I was a boy, told me they used to log in there. They built a tram road. Then they barged the logs up and down the river to the sawmill in Elizabeth City. And the old-timers told me they could take a twenty-foot pole in some spots and push it out of sight in them swamps—and I believe 'em. I mean there's no bottom to it."

The old tram road—now a footpath, used by hunters—arrives at the water's edge a few hundred yards east of where the canoe was discovered. It was deer and duck season, which meant that hounds, at least, might be rooting around in the nearer swamp woods on occasion.

Imagining that their missing boater might have trundled ashore, cold and wet, Beardsley and Vaughan looked for evidence of a fire. He'd have had access to a bounty of driftwood and light-wood knots, which, with the aid of a cigarette lighter, should have burned more easily than charcoal.

Vaughan also called the local paper, the *Daily Advance*, which ran a story on the front page of its Sunday edition the next morning ("Canoe found, search ongoing"), along with an 800 number for tips.

.   .   .

The first lead came from Mid-Atlantic Christian University, known locally as the Bible College, in Elizabeth City, approximately eighteen miles from the site of the canoe's recovery. A woman named Katherine Smith was reading the *Daily Advance* online, the weekend after Thanksgiving, and noticed the story about a rescue operation in progress. She alerted her husband, Dan, the enrollment director at the college. He called the sheriff.

It had been just after Veterans Day, on the twelfth or thirteenth, Dan Smith recalled. Another cold snap. He was out for a morning walk with his golden retriever, Baxter, when he noticed a sleeping bag on the dock where he keeps his sailboat. Baxter started to charge at the newcomer, and Smith had to call him off. "I don't need the guy getting startled with a hundred-pound golden licking his face, and then rolling into the water," Smith recalled thinking. He brought Baxter back inside and fed him breakfast, and when he returned to the dock, alone, fifteen minutes later, the sleeping bag and whoever had been using it were gone. Then Smith noticed an unfamiliar and well stuffed canoe tied to one of the slips, using the hitch knots of an experienced boater. "I just felt nudged," he said. "I pulled a bunch of acrylic and wool socks out of my drawer, and I had, like, fifty dollars in cash—put it in a shopping bag, double-bagged it, and just kind of tossed it into his boat."

The next night, a student at the college reported that she'd discovered a scary man sleeping under a gazebo near the river. Smith went out again and introduced himself. He had once offered an empty dorm room to a young man attempting to circumnavigate the United States in an open boat, and figured that he might do the same here, in light of the temperature, which had dipped below forty. The man explained that he was a navy vet, and that he had arrived in town via the Dismal Swamp Canal, which connects the Elizabeth River, in Virginia, with the Pasquotank. He was heading next for Albemarle Sound, en route to Florida. He told Smith, "If you don't mind, I'm perfectly comfortable, and if the weather does what I think it's going to do, I'll just be gone in the morning."

Relieved that he no longer needed to worry about "some wacko homeless guy being on campus," as he put it, Smith gave the man a business card, lest he change his mind about the dorm room or come to need any other help. They talked some more, about life on the water, and retirement: Smith and his wife, both in their fifties, were looking forward to the idea of spending a few years on their sailboat. "He said, 'Yeah, I just kind of crawl along the coastline,'" Smith explained. "Because he said something about how he could almost always find a dry place to sleep. He goes, 'A few times, I've had to sleep in the canoe, and you've never seen an art form unless you've done that.' I can't even imagine. But he said it can be done!"

"I was just enchanted," Smith went on. "The few minutes we talked, he was just very impressive—had such a calm demeanor, and was so unassuming. I remember walking into the house and telling Katherine, 'You wouldn't believe the guy who's out there.' Because you just never know who's going to wander in and out of your life. Sooner or later we're going to be some of those wanderers."

.   .   .

More people in Elizabeth City came forward. A regular customer at the Colonial Restaurant, a few blocks from the river, reported seeing a weathered-looking stranger—"looked like he made his living in the log woods"—eating breakfast there a couple of mornings, in the middle of the month. The owner of a bookshop on Water Street said she'd sold a lovesick Montana man a regional boating guide, and learned that he wished to reconnect with a brother in Georgia. And employees at the public library recalled helping a man they nicknamed Grizzly Adams photocopy maps. (They had to remind him to put his socks back on, because he was making himself overly at home.) But neither the boating guide nor Dan Smith's business card was among the items recovered outside Big Flatty Creek, and the timeline of these sightings was also puzzling, not to mention concerning. More than two weeks had passed since anyone could confidently place the visitor in town, and the boat hadn't made it all that far in the interim, raising the possibility that boat and boater had been separated, or parted ways, even before the recent northeaster.

I heard from John Beardsley, the wildlife officer, again on Monday morning, December 1, two days after the jarring phone call. In one of Conant's apparent interactions, Beardsley said, "he mentioned some intentions of going to Edenton," North Carolina's oldest permanent settlement, a well-preserved town named for a former governor and friend of Blackbeard the pirate. Edenton is some thirty miles west of Big Flatty Creek, along the sound's northern shore, near the mouth of the Chowan River. This suggested that the efforts of the Hawk and his Coast Guard colleagues, as they traversed the middle of the sound, south and north, that first afternoon, had perhaps been wasted. But Beardsley emphasized that "multiple aircraft" had been deployed, and added that he had made a few phone calls down to Edenton, where nobody seemed to remember being enchanted by a wanderer or spooked by a wacko homeless guy. He said that they were suspending the search "until we find more concrete evidence." The area in play was too vast to continue casting about aimlessly. He would continue to keep an eye out during his regular boat patrols, but it was "peak hunting time," as he later put it, and his efforts were needed elsewhere.

During our first conversation, Beardsley had asked that I not interfere with his "active investigation" by making direct contact with the Conant family. Now that the investigation had gone passive, I was stymied by the same caution that had prevented me from reaching out to them in the first place, before his disappearance. Where to begin? *You don't know me, but I met your brother on the Hudson River. He was amazing, but it seemed complicated.*

Then I received a note, online, from a man named Chris Kelly, an old friend of the Conants from Rockland County. He was acting on behalf of a couple of "Dicky's" brothers who still lived in the area and wanted to meet me.

. . .

I liked Rob and Roger Conant, the fourth- and seventh-born siblings, almost immediately, much as I had their brother. Dick, or Dicky, came fifth: the middle child. They shared his warm smile and his pretension-busting irreverence. Both were bald and solidly built. Neither was a giant. Rob had a gray brush above his upper lip, and was a social worker with the archdiocese. A bachelor. Roger had a darker goatee, neatly trimmed. He worked at Pfizer. He and his wife, Sharon, had been married since graduating from high school, in the early seventies, and were grandparents several times over. The two brothers seemed close, and touched that I had thought Dicky worthy of attention. But also a little surprised and curious about what others might have made of the story.

Nobody in the family had seen Dicky since 2008, when, in the aftermath of his canoe trip to Texas, he hopscotched up and down the East Coast, by bus, visiting many of his siblings as well as their elderly mother, whose funeral he then skipped a few years later. That was the way it had been for some time with Dicky. You could go years without hearing from him, they said, and then he'd turn up, beaming and full of outlandish tales.

To an outsider, I had to admit, their brother's elusiveness and unaccountability were large parts of his appeal, even as I now realized that they'd facilitated the predicament at hand. After the publication of my piece, I told them, I'd received a note from a German graduate student who was doing research at Columbia. "How and where is it possible to meet Dick Conant?" he asked. "Your article reminded me of Forrest Gump running across the country, and that story strikes me as very American." The student had imagined well-wishers cheering Conant on from the banks, not quite knowing why, or even launching boats of their own to paddle in his wake for a mile or two, seeking spillover enlightenment. "It seems to me that Americans love to have this 'free-yourself-from-all-societal-expectations' option in the back of their minds and idolize people who take such liberties." Eerily prescient, perhaps, he also cited *Into the Wild,* whose protagonist, Christopher McCandless, pursued pure freedom to his ultimate demise, starving alone in an abandoned Alaskan school bus.

My initial reaction, upon reading the note, was to blanch at the prospect of a parade of onlookers. Conant seemed to relish his privacy. Or maybe it was I who relished Conant's privacy. In spite of the fact that I'd written about him, with his blessing, I'd felt a twinge of possessiveness—like an anthropologist studying one of the last uncontacted civilizations—at the thought that my bedtime story could become a public spectacle. The magic in such travels lay in chance encounters; appointments and heralded arrivals would only break the spell.

Forrest Gump, in my recollection, was a guileless dope, whose life kept improbably intersecting with history and celebrity, whereas one of the things I appreciated about Conant was his hard-earned wisdom, and his honesty about the costs associated with freedom. He wasn't an evangelist or an American naïf, it seemed to me, just an original. But I also thought that Conant, who sprinkled references to military battles and monuments and founding fathers throughout his anecdotes, would have been flattered to be considered a noteworthy part of the national fabric. There was a touch of Whitman in his eclectic erudition and his reverence of the natural world, and of course an echo of Emerson in his avowed desire to settle down—"with a woman and a family, like you have," as he told me—while doing the opposite. He'd described five trips in all, including the last one that brought him past my house, with itineraries covering the mountain west, the badlands, the Great Plains, the rust belt, the Bible belt, Indian country, bayou country, Huck and Jim country. "I'm getting to really visit our nation piecemeal, usually on a body of water," he'd said. "And what are my cares? My cares are survival, really."

As for *Into the Wild,* I remembered enjoying the book, as well as the movie, though I recalled that the author, Jon Krakauer, spent a fair amount of time defending McCandless against critics, particularly hard-bitten Alaskans, who thought him a vainglorious dilettante, or worse, and in any event representative of a type of suburban dreamer that the forty-ninth state has long resented itself for attracting. McCandless was twenty-four when he died, evidently after trying and failing—thwarted by a swollen river—to return to civilization. He reminded Krakauer of his own former mountaineering self: foolhardy, idealistic, albeit lucky enough to survive. The story's pathos derived in large part from the future readers were invited to imagine for the bright young man who was deprived of one. The idolatry came after the fact, in the form of so-called McCandless pilgrims, who flocked annually to that iconic husk of a school bus on the Stampede Trail, encountering enough trouble of their own that a helicopter was finally dispatched, in 2020, to remove what had become a literal tourist trap, in the interest of public safety.

To the extent that *Into the Wild* was a useful or pertinent analogy, I thought, Conant seemed to represent a kind of alternative history: not one in which the young seeker dies tragically; nor one in which he survives, wises up, and leads a healthily balanced life; but one where the frustrations of "civilized" life continue to prove inescapable and each survival eventually leads to yet more adventure.

I sort of preferred—or was less discomfited by—the letter I received from a woman in New Jersey, reporting little other than that she had seen Conant "yesterday, Wednesday, around 3:30 in overalls at his red canoe." He glanced her way, she said, but "I didn't bother him." Instead, she hastened to tell her husband, Neil Sloane, the creator of an online database of infinite integers. Curious about what that meant, I looked Sloane up, and found articles in the *Guardian* and *Wired* referring to him as "the most influential mathematician alive" and "the guy who sorts all the world's numbers in his attic." I also found that he was an early proponent, in 1996, of something he called a "perpetual home page," a kind of multimedia tombstone for every American.

"After all, almost everyone wants to be remembered by posterity," he'd written. I wondered about that. I also liked the idea of a whisper network connecting anonymous titans like Conant and Sloane, with only aggregated raindrops serving as a conduit.

. . .

We were seated around a bar table in Nyack, a Hudson River town just north of Piermont. Chris Kelly, the Conants' friend, joined us, as did my neighbor Scott, who accepted a drink, "in honor of Dick," but mentioned that he'd given up alcohol and started exercising more, because meeting their brother had inspired him to reconsider the swift passage of his own middle age. Scott also relayed the best wishes of a few women friends of his, who had met Dick at a Labor Day concert near the Piermont marsh and been charmed by his long-distance devotion to his "sweetheart."

The Conant brothers reacted with looks of restrained skepticism. Dicky was a bit of a "raconteur," Rob said, noting a familial penchant for telling tall tales, beginning with the war stories of their father, whom they seemed to revere. Also, Dicky struggled with what he called "mental barnacles." They tried recalling their first inklings of something amiss, and settled on his college years, when someone "slipped him a mickey," Rob said. The brothers exchanged glances at this mention and seemed to decide not to elaborate. In retrospect, there'd been an earlier warning, from a priest. "Friar Pryor," they said, in smirking unison. This was at a boarding seminary—an Augustinian high school in Connecticut—where Dicky didn't last long. They apologized for being hazy on the specifics. Their attempts to parse recollections were complicated by the breakup of their parents' marriage during the same period. It was a chaotic time, anyway: late sixties, early seventies. I gathered that Dicky wasn't the only family member who had slipped his tether. "He always wanted the white picket fence," Rob said, noting the irony. They spoke about it all with a kind of gallows humor that I recognized from my father's extended Boston-Irish clan. Call it lapsed Catholic fatalism.

Prior to the crack-up, however, they'd been tight—a roving brat pack. And here, as the guys waxed nostalgic about the counterculture, and about what sounded like a prelapsarian boyhood that preceded it, I returned to thinking of McCandless, whom Krakauer had seemed at pains to distinguish from an "outcast" or a "nutcase." The Dicky Conant I was now hearing about—"scary smart," a jock, an artist, a prankster—wasn't an outcast, either, but a star, the linchpin of their gang.

Chris Kelly reached into his wallet and removed a faded blue card with rounded edges. At the top, in gothic script, it said, "Catfish Yacht Club." Below this were a "membership" number (138) and a motto: "First in fun, first in swimming, and first in the heart of holy Bucaroos!" Dicky had had the cards printed, he explained, to ritualize their frequent unsupervised explorations of the Hackensack River, in a banged-up dinghy with a three-horse outboard, in middle school.

"Like Mark Twain!" Rob said.

Kelly assured me that he hadn't just brought the card for my benefit; he'd been carrying it around with him, like a totem, for nearly fifty years. The Hackensack—the *upper* Hackensack, now so thoroughly dammed to form reservoirs that it scarcely registers as a river to the suburbanites who live within its watershed—was their Mississippi.

. . .

Roger, the more taciturn of the two brothers, had brought some documents with him, and eventually slid them over my way, a little sheepish. I discerned that they were two of the "books" that Dick—or Dicky, as I was now starting to call him—had told me about. Roger had received them in the mail over the years.

Both volumes looked to have been printed and bound at Kinko's. One was slender, 131 pages, with a title in the same gothic script used on Chris Kelly's card: "Journal of a Transcontinental Canoe Voyage: Being the adventures of the author upon the Yellowstone, Missouri and Mississippi Rivers at the turn of the Millennium 2000!, by Richard Perry Conant, BA, CST, TD, QM2, etc." CST, the brothers explained, stood for Certified Surgical Technician. "He was a nurse!" Rob said, chuckling at the mental image of Dicky's fat fingers suturing wounds. QM2 was quartermaster, second rank. A naval designation. The brothers vaguely recalled that he might have been dishonorably discharged. None of us could hazard a plausible guess about TD. A card from Montana State University was tucked inside the cover, dated "04 May 04," in the military style, along with a "Remember our Veterans" window sticker. "Dear Roger and Sharon," it began. "I'm sorry I haven't kept in touch for so long. The past decade has been excessively difficult for me; my only respite being that river trip I took five years ago." He went on to mention that he was considering another canoe trip, in spite of a torn rotator cuff ("I expect I'll rent a canoe for a day and see how it goes"), and concluded, "Did you know Alabama has more canoe navigable canals than any other state? Anyway, it was great to see you all at Mom's house 4.5 years ago. I hope all of your delightful family is doing well. Take care and I'll see you when I can. . . . Love, Dicky."

The other manuscript looked more substantial and less self-conscious. He called it "A Canoe Voyage," and it ran to roughly five hundred single-spaced pages, with photographs and captions that he'd laid out by hand, using scissors and glue: "beaver lodge" on the Allegheny; "bovine pals" wading in the Ohio; a forty-two-barge tow on the Mississippi; "foggy morning Rorschach test," in a Louisiana bayou. This was the story of his 2007–2008 trip from western New York to South Texas.

Each volume proceeded chronologically, as travelogue, with occasional digressions into reminiscence, not all of it flattering to the family. While skimming the early pages of the first one and the latter pages of the second, I noticed a couple of things that seemed germane. First, on page 6, was a description of what appeared to be his initial meeting of Tracy: "21 JUL. I met Tracy from Seattle (and her Chesapeake Bay retriever, Haley). She's a very nice lady. I met her while I was packing the boat." It seemed pretty matter-of-fact—not a likely case of raconteur's embellishment.

Second, in the waning Texas pages, I saw an extended description of a swamping, amid waves cresting over his head from abaft, and multiple mentions of sharks, one of whose thrashing beneath the surface produced a spray that resembled "a huge crystal bird's wing." I could see now, in fact, that he had chosen to abort that mission a couple of hundred miles shy of his intended destination, at the Mexican border in Brownsville. "There is a fine line between a man of exceptional courage and a damned fool," he wrote.

This sounded encouraging, I thought. The stormy conditions Conant described on Matagorda Bay, his unplanned terminus, resembled what I understood of those on Albemarle Sound, a similarly large and exposed body of brackish water at a similar time of year. He hadn't saved the canoe in that earlier instance, either. (Instead of abandoning it, he'd apparently sold it, for two hundred bucks.)

The brothers were anxious to know whether I thought the writing was any good. Roger, by his own admission, was not an avid reader, and hadn't ever really engaged with the texts, maybe because of what he perceived as Dicky's loose grip on reality. I found myself unable to come up with a holistic assessment on the spot, and asked if I could borrow them for a closer look, figuring, if nothing else, that they might serve as a vicarious thrill ride for a man stuck at home with a newborn and a toddler and a view of a storied river out the window.

. . .

Not long after, a package arrived for me in the mail, bearing a return address in Peachtree City, Georgia. It was from Joe Conant, the retired Delta pilot, and it included several anno- tated atlases, including the one I'd seen on the west bank of the Hudson. Joe, the second-eldest brother, had driven eight and a half hours to retrieve the still-wet contents of Dicky's canoe, in North Carolina, and then spent days air-drying the written mate- rial on his driveway, in a planned-for-golfing community. It was a painstaking process: gently turning the pages after exposing each to sunlight. Amazingly, most of the ink hadn't bled, and all but a few pages separated without ripping. They were brittle to the touch by the time I received them, and still gritty with sand. More than the phone call from Officer Beardsley, or the face-to- face meeting with Rob and Roger, handling these maps hit me in the gut. It was impossible to run your fingers over them without imagining yourself frightened and alone amid a roiling surf. No one I'd written about before had come close to dying (if that was the case here) in the act of the very thing I'd valorized.

I was relieved, on the other hand, to see that Conant remem- bered me fondly, describing me as a "great guy," not least because he wasn't always so charitable in his notes about the people who startled him en route. "Totally ugly asshole." "He called the cops the dirty rat squealer." "What a profound fuck." There was no mention of the bicycling teenagers I'd worried about, although, not far from that grassy strip beneath the Palisades, he'd written the words "Iceman Kuklinski" and drawn a box around them. Kuklinski was a serial killer, a hit man for the Mob who eventually laid claim to more than one hundred dead bodies. He also led an ostensibly normal suburban existence in nearby Dumont, New Jersey, a few miles inland of the Hudson. Had someone *told* Conant this, or did his casually encyclopedic knowledge of American geography and history extend to the underworld?

I noticed a passing "joke" about using the name Tom Mahoney as an alias. (Why the specificity, if it was just a joke?) More curious, perhaps, were the references to "rent" payments in "Boze" and "Heber"—Heber City, Utah. These were storage lockers, I came to understand. Paid up through Christmas in one case, and mid-January in the other. When I spoke to Joe about this discovery, I learned that Dicky had lived for a time in Salt Lake City, about an hour's drive from Heber. But that was in the mid-nineties, as far as Joe was aware. Dicky was still faithfully paying rent, while on the move, from small towns in the Hudson Valley two decades later. What could be so valuable to a bootstrapping canoeist whose only cares are "survival, really"?

As an ex-pilot, Joe said, he was eligible to fly standby for free, and was planning a short discovery mission out west, to see what the lockers might reveal. Feeling implicated enough already, I asked if he'd mind if I joined him.

4

Pretty Awesome Shit

Joe Conant used a bolt cutter to gain entry to unit #792 at Osterman's Mini Warehouses, a small city of aluminum sheds in the shadow of the Bridger Range, north of the interstate in Bozeman, and found himself staring into an enormous heap of bags and boxes and lumber scraps. Thin and soft-spoken, nearly Dicky's opposite, he looked weary by the time I showed up, an hour later. "Welcome," he said. "It's almost as bad as the one in Utah." The units weren't quite hoarders' lairs—many of the boxes were labeled ("bicycle," "optics," "coffee tea fiber")—but they indicated a disposition toward completism, not necessarily in keeping with one's image of a nomadic spirit. The Heber locker contained antique furniture, correspondence with Ann Landers, a hand-carved wooden fraternity paddle ("Rich Conant '73," with a middle finger extended), and paper currency from Ecuador, Brazil, Uruguay, and Peru. Plus some unmarked bottles containing what Joe, a teetotaler, presumed to be moonshine. This one, meanwhile, reminded me of the closet in my childhood bedroom: full of valuable keepsakes and junk and schoolwork and seldom-worn clothes and private jottings, and organized according to logic discernible only to its creator, who had long since prioritized expedience over organization anyhow.

My eyes drifted first to a pair of homemade crutches in one corner, with repurposed mouse pads for armpit cushioning; and then to a punching bag; and, at the top of the heap, a costume-party giant foam hat.

I could see how for an older sibling it might be a dispiriting sight: less a mystery to begin unpacking than the detritus of a lost brother's barnacled mind. Looking for a bright side, Joe chose to dwell on the setting. "I tell you what, this is just gorgeous country out here," he said. "Holy smokes. On the drive up from Utah, I was looking at some of the valleys. Can you imagine taking a little airplane and just flying around from here to there, if for no other reason than just to bore holes in the sky?" In their capacity for awe and wonder, at least, they were similar. Only the vehicle of preference differed.

Here and there, amid McDonald's breakfast coupons and a "Jon Tester for Senate" button, were various diaries and notebooks, featuring diagrams of molecular compounds on some pages, and, on others, descriptions of sub-zero camping. ("4 layers clothes, jacket, 2 sleeping bags, 2 comforters, lean-to. Very warm and beautiful.") A printed transcript from Montana State lent the diagrams further legitimacy, showing recent graduate-level coursework in microbial genetics (grade: A), medical bacteriology (B), hematology (A), immunology (B), and several other subjects.

The reading material covered a broad spectrum: Dostoevsky, Gore Vidal, *Into Thin Air, The Nation, Paranoia: The Conspiracy Reader, Fox* ("Voted #1 in whores bathed in cum"). A draft of the third canoeing manuscript, as yet untitled, appeared as a dense brick of text inside a pair of plastic Walmart bags, with light pen edits. Plus there were multiple bound copies of the other manuscripts, and what looked like the names of people to whom Conant intended to send them.

We found bags of mail, including credit card solicitations, most of which had been opened at one end, with a knife or letter-opener, rather than using the flap. He always saved the envelope. Joe noticed a stack of birthday and Christmas cards, many of them sent by him and his wife, Lorraine. "It's somewhat gratifying that he got them and kept them," he said, sighing.

Emboldened by the presence of another family member, I opened a slender envelope that remained sealed. "Dear applicant," it began. "We regret to inform you that the University of Nevada School of Medicine is not able to approve your application for admission to the class entering fall of 2007." Presumably Conant had concluded as much, using the thin-or-thick theory. He would have been fifty-six at the time of prospective enrollment.

Inside a manila folder containing photocopied receipts and business cards, meanwhile, was this poem, written in bubbly letters on the back of a Hooters bill, in Newport, Kentucky, by someone named Heather F.:

Your in the hearts
And in the minds
Of the ones you left behind
May your journey be without worry
And your future be filled with happiness!
You are a hero in the upmost respect.

. . .

And then there were the oil paintings, several of them framed and leaning against a wall: Samson wrestling a lion; cowboys and a covered wagon against a backdrop of red-rock spires; impressionistic clouds over a river. Deeper into the locker, other large painted canvases were rolled together like rugs. They were landscapes, for the most part, reflecting the natural world—the American West, in particular—in its epic scale. Big rocks, big skies, little people. "I knew that he had an artistic flair, but I did not know that he was this prolific," Joe said. The Utah locker contained many more pieces, including lithographs, pastels, and charcoal drawings. All told, Conant had saved more than three hundred pieces of original art, spanning four decades.

Not all were dated, but a few distinct phases emerged. The work from the seventies—a period when Joe recalled that Dicky had taken some "bad acid"—was often trippy and occasionally morose. A man's eyes betrayed agony as blood dripped from the stumps where both of his legs had been lopped off above the knees. An etching of a man trapped in an Escher-like maze, with shins and feet that appeared to be sprouting roots, was accompanied by this caption: "Evolution, revolution, they're all the same to me. I live, I die. Even worms get hungry." And there were "some very florid items," as Joe put it—not just nudes, but one, for example, in which a naked woman's lower body devolved into lumpy growths.

Then came a series of bright flowers in the late eighties: individually striking, often set against abstract backgrounds. The later Bozeman works, post 2000, typically portrayed geography from elsewhere. One of my favorites was delightfully absurd, a self-portrait in which a fortyish Conant is standing inside a cracked egg on a snowy mountaintop, dressed only in briefs and holding a glass of milk, alongside deer, raccoons, an owl, and a Dalmatian. He's got the legs of an athlete, but his torso is on its way to acquiring the distinguishing heft of his later years.

A couple of women, one a straight-haired brunette and the other a curly redhead, appeared in more than one painting, suggesting real-life familiarity, but generally the people in Conant's paintings were mood-establishing figures, often young parents with small children or ranchers on horseback or soldiers in a field. Rivers recurred but did not predominate. If anything, the body of work tilted in the direction of saccharine: Western kitsch, reminiscent of dime-novel covers.

Which is not to say that his art, on balance, was lousy. To an untrained eye like mine, the technical mastery across such a range of styles—still lifes and abstractions and animal portraits and religious iconography—seemed noteworthy. I sent a few of the more dynamic images to a friend of mine, an artist in Brooklyn who has worked for Jeff Koons. "They definitely have something," he wrote back. "Those are good paintings."

Back at Osterman's, our focus shifted to the assorted lumber, including a tall bundle of crown molding strips in a far corner. Joe deduced that his brother had been stretching his own canvases and using the molding to build his own frames. What struck me was reconciling all the production, and the effort to preserve it, with the fact that he lacked an apartment.

. . .

He called his residence the Swamp. I found it with the help of Mike Delaney, a big-wheel developer whose card Conant had been carrying with him in the canoe. Delaney was the owner of the property in question, a thirty-acre tract on the eastern edge of town, abutting the tracks of the Burlington Northern and I-90. It had been a dairy farm in the distant past, he explained. A brook trickled through it in the spring, after the start of the snowmelt. Over time, highway drainage brought more standing water, which deterred development, and the acreage became a "forgotten site," as Delaney put it, a kind of buffer between the city proper, which was growing westward, and the freeway.

Not a small man himself, Delaney referred to Conant as a "gentle giant," and brought me to a spot on East Main Street, near a gas station, a liquor store, and a tattoo parlor. In back of the gas station, facing north, he pointed at a steep and partially forested embankment that led down to a marshy meadow: the Swamp. A low green ridge studded with evergreen trees loomed beyond the freeway on the far side of the meadow, roughly a third of a mile across, and rocky peaks jutted above in the background. Standing there, I thought of Conant's initial description of Bozeman to me ("gorgeous town, beautiful mountains") before he delved into the conditions of his unhappiness. You could almost have mistaken the Swamp for a nature preserve—which, in a way, it was, given that it had wetlands protection, which Delaney was trying to overcome. "I didn't realize he was on my property," Delaney continued. "Then one day, he came to get permission to stay there." Delaney was moved, among other things, by Conant's "beautiful speaking voice," and by the fact that he sensed no "brewing hostility" beneath the social pleasantries, as he had grown accustomed to noticing in other homeless people he encountered. "Others are transients—bums," he said. Conant, in Delaney's mind, was more like a nonpaying tenant.

Conant's camp had been on the sloping embankment, under dense cover. "You couldn't see it from above and below," Delaney said. "I'd driven by it a hundred times. He was really quietly stuffed in there." We got in Delaney's truck, and he started driving west, back toward the center of town, and then made a couple of rights, entering a new condominium development of his called the Village Downtown, which he described as "the high end for Bozeman," and part of a grander mixed-use plan, both residential and commercial, that he hoped would eventually incorporate Conant's Swamp. ("Be careful, he'll try to sell you something," another Bozemanite had warned me.) The streets were impeccably landscaped, the structures Disney perfect. Near the terminus of an unfinished cul-de-sac, Delaney steered off-road and soon stopped to unlock a cattle gate between two tall posts. On our left was a berm supporting old railroad tracks from the defunct Chicago–Milwaukee line, which once intersected the Burlington Northern, ahead in the distance. "I told Dick, 'I haven't ever seen you walking through the Village to get to your place,'" Delaney said. "He goes, 'I take different routes all the time.'"

Delaney added, "Circuitous! He was very discreet."

Beyond the gate, we followed tire tracks through high grass, and the leaves of trees and tall shrubs on either side brushed the windows. The effect was of entering a portal. Eventually, the tire tracks veered left, out toward the meadow, and Delaney stopped the truck. There was a narrow footpath now, leading up and in among the trees near the base of the embankment beneath East Main. Low branches formed a defensive web, and continued passage required ducking and occasionally bowing at the waist, as if before a king. Here and there beside the path, amid ferns, lay empty airplane bottles of Bacardi and Jagermeister. I noticed a red-winged blackbird, and swatted at increasingly persistent mosquitos. Finally, we came to a small, slightly charred, clearing, where the underbrush had been flattened in a tidy rectangle. Stashed around the perimeter were a rusty oil drum repurposed as a trash can; a battery-operated drill; plastic bags containing damp, several-years-old newspapers; and a pair of large white socks, draped over a bending branch.

"Nice little spot," Delaney said.

. . .

The proprietress of a gift shop on West Main Street asked what had brought me to town, and I did my best to explain the unusual scenario succinctly: a mountain man canoed past my house back east, then disappeared, and turned out to have been maintaining a storage unit full of treasure here in Bozeman. She asked if

I had a picture of the man, and I showed her one I'd taken with my phone. Her face registered a flicker of recognition. Speaking now with a trace of sadness or hesitation, she said that she recalled seeing him ride his too-small bicycle back and forth in front of her shop window, knees splayed, though not recently. She gave the impression that he was a familiar figure, at least from a distance—a mystery figure who gradually recedes into the tableau.

At the American Legion bar down the street, I showed the same picture, and the manager confirmed that he was looking at an old customer, a man whose name he had never learned. The man used to stop by once or twice a week, in the early afternoon, and sit at a video poker terminal opposite the bar, feeding it a twenty-dollar bill. He kept to himself, never caused any trouble, and seldom stayed for more than two beers. He always had a backpack with him.

"I knew him as Richard," another man, named Mike, said, sitting in a coffee shop nearby. "He was very visible. You couldn't miss him, with those overalls. And he always had a big meal. Like, I'm talking calories, you know what I mean? He did not screw around when it came to eating. Holy crap! We'd have a heart attack with the food he ate." He added, "How do you lose a body that big?"

Mike was small and wiry—he looked as if he could have benefited from eating more—and bald on top, with a reddish-white beard that he had braided into five or six stalactites. These obscured the first few printed words on his T-shirt, such that it appeared to read, "Gynecologist—but I'll take a look." I gathered that he was one of Bozeman's most recognizable street characters, not merely visible, like Conant, but popular. Formerly homeless, he now lived in a trailer on the grounds of an organization called We Do Anything, which put people to work doing odd jobs: painting, roofing, brush clearing. Mike Delaney, the developer, often hired We Do Anything to remove beaver dams in his swamp, and to roust the transient encampments, but the Mike sitting in front of me now said that he always refused those particular assignments, because he believed in leaving people alone. "I keep to myself," he said. "Been that way all my life. I like people—got a lot of homies, you know? But I just need my space."

He sounded a little like Conant, I thought. He said that he'd ridden freight trains around the country for many years, but quit riding in the nineteen-nineties. "The rails were getting crazy," he said. "Lots of murders. It wasn't old-school any more." He sometimes went on bike journeys, as he called them, most recently to Spokane and back. "I'm fifty-three now. My body's just all beat up, so I'm not doing them really long hauls anymore. But I went down to New Mexico and Arizona, like, four times, and I went out to the ocean a couple times—the Pacific. Yep, went to Jimi Hendrix's grave."

He'd settled in Bozeman because he admired the residents' berserker spirit. "Like, I fell out of a tree and snapped my arm in half, just being stupid, climbing this big fucking tree," he explained. "I'd had a few. But everybody in Bozeman is like that! They'll be in a cast—know what I mean?—and they'll be, like, 'When can I go skiing again?' Gluttons for punishment. Bozeman's a lot of fun. There's some very eccentric people here. That's what I love about it—it's just so motley."

While we were talking, a college student walked by, and Mike noticed his "Colorado Springs" sweatshirt. "I was in that town," he said, catching the student's attention. "Hey, you know where Nevada Avenue is? You know where the bridge crosses over the river? I lived under that bridge for a long time."

"Really?" the student asked, struggling to compute the small-world coincidence as it breached familiar class lines. "In Colorado Springs? No way, dude."

"Yeah, there was a used-car lot there, and the salesmen would come over and give me a bottle of whiskey. They'd go, 'It's going to be cold tonight, here you go.' It was awesome."

Mike looked momentarily lost in thought, and then glanced at one of Conant's journals, which I'd placed on the table in front of us. "Everybody told me to write," he said, shaking his head. "There's a lot of shit I wish I would have wrote down, because I forgot so many cool things that happened—pretty awesome shit."

Speaking again of Conant, he said, "I didn't have a *clue* he was that adventurous."

. . .

Mike mentioned that Conant spent "hundreds of hours" at the library, so I went there next and met a couple of reference librarians. The first woman I approached clearly recognized Conant from my photo but was reluctant to speak, out of what seemed to be a combination of professional discretion and the uncomfortable fact that she didn't have anything kind to say. She eventually summoned a supervisor as backup, and they exchanged the kinds of conspiratorial glances that Conant often wrote about observing in his journals. My showing them his manuscripts, as well as images of his paintings, didn't appear to inspire much reconsideration. "You came all the way from New York for this?" one asked. I found myself growing defensive. Conant had managed to visit my town in a cheap plastic canoe. Getting on a plane, as I'd just done, was easy.

Libraries, of course, are bastions of imaginative escapism, and full of books about holy fools and traveling wise men, and I suppose I'd expected a little more enthusiasm about the prospect that a waterborne Don Quixote had been toiling in their midst, undercover. The women looked stunned when I told them that I'd already published a piece about Conant in *The New Yorker,* and I suggested that we call it up on a desktop monitor, lest they doubt Conant's credentials, or mine.

Scanning the article on the screen, the librarians seemed disinclined to view Conant as my German correspondent had, as an avatar for American free-spiritedness. To them, Conant remained a local figure—*that* guy, with the backpack and the overalls—and his apparent canoeing exploits were a peripheral flourish. That these exploits were, on their own terms, highly impressive, both logistically and physically, was beside the point. They could only assume that the character in my prose was, like Forrest Gump, a fiction, composed either out of naiveté or selective dishonesty. It was almost as though we were talking about two different people, one so endearing that he inspires poetry in his waitresses and the other an obese loner and barely functioning charity case. Superman and Clark Kent. (Maybe the canoe was his cape, restoring whatever confidence he had lost throughout his checkered career.)

Was I, in fact, the one clouded by delusions—of my subject's grandeur, as it were? My annoyance at their skepticism abated somewhat the next morning, when I met another local character named Brian and was put more vividly in mind of the challenges public libraries can face, especially in northern climates, where they often serve as de facto warming centers for the indigent. Brian was, on the one hand, another winning example of Bozeman's motley spirit. I'd been told that I could likely find him at Wild Joe's Coffee Spot, at sunup, and that he'd be easy to identify by his safari hat. Sure enough, there he was, quietly reading *The Wild Marsh,* by Rick Bass. He wore a khaki photographer's vest, and his hat was adorned with a red-tailed hawk feather. Dangling from a string around his neck were several bear claws—Wyoming roadkill, he explained. He was an avid birder, and liked to bring his camera down to Delaney's swamp. "Couple years ago, I got a picture of a marsh hawk with babies in its mouth," he said, smiling through jagged teeth.

Originally from San Diego, Brian said that he'd arrived in Bozeman about a decade back, after "there got to be too many people in Colorado." Conant quickly became one of his friendly acquaintances, owing to their shared interest in the outdoors, but then he grew distant for some reason Brian hadn't been able to decipher. "When he was at the library, he just looked all grumpy," Brian said. "He was always writing." Brian added that Conant had had his library privileges revoked on a couple of occasions, as a result of shouting confrontations with other homeless people. In one instance, he'd been suspended for as much as six months. "I got kicked out of the library for a while, too," Brian then said, and explained that in his case the confrontation—with one of Conant's same nemeses—had got physical. "They said I stabbed him in the face. He had a little cut here, and it wasn't even that big. I try not to talk to him anymore."

.   .   .

Further probing produced varied accounts, none of which made it any easier to envision a use for the foam party hat Conant had saved at Osterman's. I called Jon Ford, who was quoted as Conant's boss in the *Daily Chronicle* story about his role as a "weather watcher" at Montana State. Ford confessed that he'd later rearranged his office, fearing a "lone gunman" scenario, from which he wanted to be better positioned for potential escape, after Conant complained about maltreatment at many of his previous jobs—conspiracy theories, Ford surmised. He was relieved when Conant eventually quit. That was in 2003.

A hematology professor who around that same time denied Conant's request to join his lab mentioned that he'd later called the police after receiving an email from Conant that was unsettling if not quite threatening. ("How wonderful it was to see you this morning. Water under the bridge, eh? I didn't think to ask you about your heart problem.") Conant had never *acted* in a menacing manner toward either of these guys, but the archetype of the mountain man who stews too long in his own thoughts—a whiff of Unabomber—was hard to entirely banish.

"Dick is the real thing," another former co-worker at the university told me. His name was Bob Tusken, and I soon gathered that he was the friend Conant had alluded to—"an expert fly-fisherman," he told me—who turned him on to the novels of Thomas McGuane, a local in nearby Livingston. Tusken, an old fishing companion of McGuane's, explained that he'd once accompanied Conant to Osterman's warehouses, and saw enough photographs of remote river scenery to overcome any initial doubt about the paddling resume Conant hinted at. "'Dick!' I said. 'You need to write about this. *National Geographic!*' It was a little hard to believe, wasn't it? And yet the more you talked to him, the clearer it was that he really did it."

The person Conant most reminded Tusken of was Bill Schaadt, a flycaster whom *Sports Illustrated* once credited with catching "more big steelhead and salmon than any man who ever lived." Schaadt was a seasonal sign painter by trade and a word-of-mouth legend on the rivers of Northern California, where through his indefatigable persistence and deep engagement with the local spawning runs he more than made up for "shabby" equipment that "would shock an Abercrombie and Fitch salesman," as the magazine put it. "They were very similar people who just wanted to live the way they were going to live," Tusken said of Schaadt and Conant. "Bill never married. He just loved to fish. He would fix bicycles and give 'em to children."

Tusken thought it especially important that I understand Conant's essential generosity amid hardship, and told me a story about how, a few years back, while enduring some financial and emotional difficulties in his own life, he had run into Conant emerging from a park with his backpack. They hadn't seen one another for several years, since working on a custodial crew together. Conant expressed an interest in touring the town as a passenger in Tusken's car, a rare opportunity to see the sights at high speed. Tusken was hesitant. He lived ninety miles outside of town, and had spent the morning praying that he'd find enough money to make it to Bozeman and back. He didn't mention this to Conant, but Conant seemed to intuit the problem, and suggested that they start by visiting a gas station. Tusken, realizing that his old friend was now homeless, felt guilty. " 'Bob,' he says, 'I've got plenty of money. I'm fine,' " Tusken recalled. Conant filled the gas tank, and insisted on visiting an ATM to give Tusken some extra spending cash as well. "That was the last time I saw Dick Conant," Tusken said. He had taken to believing that Conant was sent by God to answer his prayer: an angel, in overalls. The fact that a stranger from twenty-two hundred miles away was now inquiring about Conant only further strengthened the notion.

.   .   .

Perhaps the fullest picture emerged from speaking to Chuck Hall, a small, soft-spoken man in his sixties who said that he employed Conant for several years, on and off, as a ticket salesman at a Greyhound franchise that he had owned on East Main, at the edge of the Swamp. "I'd seen him riding his bicycle all over town,"

Hall said. "When he first came to me, he was all crumpled up with gout. His fingers were contorted. And his ankles—I almost didn't know how he could walk around. I wanted to help him, but I didn't think he'd be able to use the keyboard. He said he was waiting for a shipment of medicine from the VA, and the next time I saw him it was like a miracle, the transformation."

Hall described Conant as a model employee ("as good as gold"), up to a point. "He had a kind of an ethic—honest like a Catholic, I guess," he said. Conant, for his part, was pleased to have found a job that resonated thematically, writing in a journal, "Opportunities to assist people with travel occur daily. So I get a sense of altruistic satisfaction." They had a special arrangement. Hall let him come and go, when adventure called. "It was kind of a trade-off," Hall explained. "He'd go on a trip, and he'd come back looking red-faced and bearded. Then he'd shave, and tell me about his adventures and show me pictures. I encouraged him to write about them when there was downtime in the office. All the while, he was trying to plan his next trip." He added, "At a certain point, I realized that he was living outside. But he was always on time, and dressed presentably. I have no idea how he did it."

Hall also brought up the med-school application I'd noticed at Osterman's, and said that he helped Conant prepare it and several others. "It was a pipe dream," he said. "I think, more than anything else, he wanted to just be accepted, you know? He wouldn't have had the resources to go, or anything. It was validation he was looking for."

Joe Conant was with us, and at one point Hall turned to him and said, "He often mentioned his mother. Did he have a bad relationship with his mother?"

"It's hard to explain," Joe said.

.   .   .

And what of Tracy? Chuck Hall had heard all about her, as had Mike Delaney, and Bob Tusken, too.

"There was a Tracy," Hall said.

"She was in Livingston," Delaney said.

"He was obviously infatuated," Tusken said.

But none of them had ever met her. The librarians mentioned that Conant once showed up to a public concert on the lawn carrying a bouquet of roses—for his "rich girlfriend," he apparently said in a fit of pique, after one of their colleagues teased him about the flowers. They all watched from the window as he roamed the grounds, seeming to look for a Dulcinea who never arrived.

I felt sure of her existence, because even primary-source material from the locker, a marble composition book reinforced with duct tape, recounted their introduction in the most banal terms, amid descriptions of the weather, and the sprinkler system in Livingston's Sacajawea Park, and the steak that he didn't have the appetite to eat. Whatever role she would later come to play in his life—"Wishful thinking?" Tusken theorized, adding, "I've been that way about women myself, which is why I understand it"—Conant didn't appear to have anticipated it at the time.

The inclusion of the dog's name (Haley) and breed (Chesapeake Bay retriever) gave me hope, until I realized that a decade and a half had passed: a dog's century, or more. Nonetheless, small towns tend to have long memories, and Livingston's year-round population is only seven thousand. I called Yellowstone Veterinary and spoke with a Dr. Murray, who asked me to give him a few days, during which he and his staff would "do some head-scratching here, do some thinkin'." When I spoke with him again, he apologized, and said, "We've had about four Tracys, but I can't place any of them with a Chesapeake."

That left greater Seattle and its nearly four million residents.

At the post office, a sympathetic mailman violated protocol and opened Conant's P.O. box for his brother Joe, handing over an issue of *American Legion* magazine; a letter from the Wilmington, Delaware, VA Medical Center, "extending the opportunity to request free gun locks to the Veterans we serve"; a letter from a pastor in East Millstone, New Jersey ("Dear Richard, It was a real joy to have you as our guest at Calvary Baptist Church"); and a holiday card from Mr. and Mrs. Fred Kelly, in Stony Creek, Virginia. "We are anxious to read your book," it began. "Let us hear from you when you get a chance."

I recognized that name. Among the items Joe had mailed me was another card from Kelly, mentioning his recent marriage, which Conant had been toting along in the canoe. This led me to speculate that they'd been in regular or even recent contact.

Kelly was excited to receive my call. "I was *wondering* if something had happened to him," he said.

But, he explained, "I only had one encounter with Dick. We probably floated next to one another in a channel for maybe thirty minutes." He added, "I wanted to reconnect with him because he was a kindred spirit. My impression was of someone who knew what he wanted to do and by God he was going to do it—not only had a dream but went out of his way to make it happen." He said that Conant had mailed him an excerpt from his travelogue, as it pertained to their visit, and that "it was very accurate."

Scanning the third manuscript, I found that Conant had described Kelly as a "psychologist employed by the Virginia Mental Health Department," a descendant of Pocahontas and John Rolfe, and an excellent mimic of barn owls.

Fred said he took a backpacking trip across Scotland some while ago. One evening he found himself in a remote farming section. It got cold after dusk. He found some large haystacks nearby. Two of the stacks had a neat little cave-like opening between them. He crawled in and used his backpack as a door to block off the opening. It served to keep him out of the wind and to keep in his body warmth. He slept through the night and was immensely comfortable, warm, happy and dry.

Kelly told me that Conant reminded him of an old friend, Harry Heckel, "the oldest man to sail around the world twice." As it happened, Kelly was talking to me from the banks of the James River, near where he had met Conant—and where, more recently, he had scattered Heckel's ashes.

"What a legacy for someone to have," Kelly went on. "I mean, he dropped memories all over the place. We all could be so lucky."

.   .   .

I began to feel like a telemarketer as I refined my cold-calling shtick, looking up the proper names that appeared in Conant's written work and easily confirming Kelly's point. Whether it had been five years or ten or twenty, many of the people I reached claimed to have been discussing our man within weeks or even days ("Yes! Yes! Yes!") of my unexpected status update, and as often as not recalling the very details and episodes I hadn't yet asked about.

Or amplifying them. I understood from my reading, for instance, that an environmentalist named Kirk Forgety had encountered Conant by chance on two different rivers, the Tennessee and the Holston, once in the line of official cleanup duty and then again while celebrating the Fourth of July. I even knew, because it was the kind of detail Conant seemed always to note, that Forgety's wife was pregnant at the time with their first child. What I *didn't* know, until we spoke on the phone, is that it was early enough in her first trimester that they hadn't told anyone else. Forgety confided in Conant precisely because he was a "total stranger." He recalled thinking, "This guy's not going to spill the beans, right?" It came as a relief, unburdening himself of big news without consequence. Like a trial balloon.

But then, a couple of weeks later, there Conant was again, blurting out, in front of the Forgetys' friends, "Hey, Kirk, how's the baby?"

Looking back, the utter implausibility—the Tabasco, the pickled dogs, the overalls—resonated as a sense of possibility. "If there was a river that came through your town, you might see him," Forgety marveled, characterizing Conant as a contemporary folk hero, or the protagonist of a riparian Western, a High Plains drifter gone afloat after the closure of the frontier.

At the same time, as word of Conant's disappearance spread among his childhood contemporaries, I started hearing from people who, like the Bozeman librarians, could only see sadness in what had apparently become of their old schoolmate and neighbor: not unlimited possibility but a foreclosing of it. "You should have met him," one said, seeming to imply that in a sense I hadn't. Another proposed that what Dicky Conant had needed wasn't an article in *The New Yorker* but an intervention. The implication, I couldn't help thinking, was that I bore some culpability for encouraging a potential death march.

Not that there was any kind of consensus about Conant's fate. One sibling, another outdoorsman and romantic, who lived without electricity on a mountaintop in the Catskills, told me that he had taken to sleeping with one eye open as he awaited Dicky's return to settle old scores. An old high school friend told me that he still half-expected Conant to show up at their next reunion, as the embodied punctuation to a practical joke. "This is just like Dicky," he said. "Rip Van Winkle."

In *this* respect, at least, the old acquaintances were in agreement with the riverside admirers. An accountant in Alabama told me that, as far as he was concerned, Conant was peerless: no less rare than Bigfoot. "If you have his journals and you can't make a book, then you're in trouble, dude," he said. "Don't just let him down." He'd met Conant while walking with his daughter outside church one winter Sunday, and the scene he reconstructed, of spying a man-sized creature emerging from the flooded Tombigbee riverbank dressed head to toe in olive mud—"everything except the whites of his eyes!"—was biblical, if not immediately reassuring from a parental perspective. Then, sounding cross, he added, "If he met his end, somebody *did* something to him." He asked me pointed questions about the precise location of the overturned canoe, and said, "I may have to go on a quest."

Still, the accusation of enabling stung a little, because, of course, I *had* felt a significant, almost paternalistic urge, while back on the beach beneath the Palisades, to rescue Conant— but from what, exactly? From loneliness? And I now felt doubly conflicted, because I'd had a few friends who'd drifted away from regular contact for lengthening spans of time, and for reasons that were never easy to isolate, and couldn't decide whether to find solace or greater alarm in Conant's example as I started to fill in the fuzzy picture.

The disparate reactions depending on the context in which people had known him raised interesting questions about what we make of those who reinvent themselves, and why. Our country's common origin story, after all, though glossed to the point of ignoring slavery, is a celebration of the redemption of Europe's castoffs with a lingering shade of I-told-you-so. Much of the Wild West was subsequently settled by desperate characters, men in need of a fresh start. Clearly, for some, Conant had tapped into an unresolved wanderlust, and what Thoreau called "a yearning toward all wildness." The shopping-mall Verizon salesman who taught him how to send text messages with the flip phone that turned up, mud-caked, in the Albemarle, was one such example. He told me that, after college, he had spent weeks at a time living in the woods, until his mother finally persuaded him to come back inside and "be a real human adult." He said, "My idea of life was much different than the way my life actually turned out. Dick was actually what I wanted to be." Was the operative insight that his youthful vision proved a mirage or false (as his mother would have it), or that it was comforting to be reminded that the option remained? And should it matter that Conant himself, as a younger man, had other aspirations? I thought again of that self-portrait of Conant standing inside a cracked egg, which seemed an expression of rebirth in middle age.

· · ·

The old-timers' sense of Conant as a kind of trickster figure sporadically unleashed from his actual past, while understandable at a distance, was belied by the tonnage in the storage lockers. Even setting aside the canoeing manuscripts, which amounted to nearly two thousand pages, you could lose whole weeks, if not months, to the documentation Conant kept, and what I realized, as I continued sorting and parsing the material, was that what others experienced as rare bursts of engagement bracketing fugue-like absences was by all appearances, to Conant, a continuous thread, recorded faithfully without large gaps in the timeline. Just because you didn't see him didn't mean that he was missing. (On the subject of reunions, incidentally, he once wrote, "I figure one should only attend if one is either financially successful or physically thin, or both. I am neither.")

There was something beyond mania to be said, I thought, for his amassing hard evidence of lived experience: receipts by the thousands, and a collection of photographs that would outshine a city block's worth of vacation albums. The benefits as I imagined them weren't only external, in a validating sense, but might have offered reassurance to a habitual self-doubter. He didn't just save old mail; he often made copies or saved drafts of his own responses, as if to preserve a fairer accounting of relationships that had, in many cases, long since gone fallow. ("Dear Mom, Good to hear from you. But you didn't answer my question to you about my art. Those slides I sent you were representative of what I am doing. What do you think of them?") Though not indicative of robust mental health, the behavior struck me as *purposeful* pack-ratting.

By Conant's own reckoning, I gathered, he enjoyed a *Leave It to Beaver* childhood, and growing up in a military family during the baby boom instilled in him an eternal optimism that persisted even long after he retreated to the margins of society. He had a Zelig-like capacity for shape-shifting, as well as a knack, almost uncanny at times, for absorbing the pulse of social currents and trends. ("He could talk about anything, at any time, on any level, and make folks feel at ease," his brother Joe said.) In spite of his Pony Express appearance, he had a Gmail account. Had he been born later, it occurred to me, he'd likely have been blogging, or posting his artwork on Instagram, along with pictures of cantilever bridges and morning mist (#riverlife). There would, at the very least, have been a clearer delineation between the digital stream that he offered for public consumption and the analog deluge that the private storage lockers represented.

Wherever he was, or whatever had happened, the contents of

the lockers now risked lapsing into oblivion, perhaps via a couple of those auctions that had become fodder for reality TV. How would a prospective bidder, self-styled in the art of spotting junk-yard gems, know, as I was coming to understand, that the original owner of the material in question was a ghostly eminence, cel-ebrated by the Freemasons in Rosiclaire, Illinois, who called him Mortimer Smoothbottom ("because of his boat—his canoe—it had a smooth bottom!"), and by the Sioux "Wolfpack," a local protection society, in Mobridge, South Dakota, who named him an honorary member?

Conant was famous, I realized, in an antiquated, pre-internet sort of way that I found alluring, in large part because it seemed likely to vanish from our Wi-Fi-enabled world. No doubt, there remain local celebrities in backwaters, far from major media markets, whose legacies vanish with the memories of their aging neighbors. Conant, on the other hand, was locally renowned in isolated pockets from Arkansas to Iowa to Tennessee to Wiscon-sin. The stray names in his journals provided links to mementos—maps, drawings, letters—saved by fans in Louisiana who gave little consideration to the fact that others were doing the same in Missouri.

He was even a subject of academic inquiry: a case study, for a community journalism course, on the virtues of remaining open to the unexpected. Thousands of students at Central Lakes Col-lege, in Brainerd, Minnesota, have by now heard the story of "Dick," a "gentleman in bib overalls and work boots 'incremen-tally moving forward,'" whom their professor, Kari Frisch, met near a dam one afternoon in the summer of 2009. She was rid-ing her bike. He was engaged in cumbersome portage. At first, she saw only luggage, and an empty canoe. The luggage was so plentiful that she assumed she'd happened upon a group of paddlers, who were probably busy carrying another canoe up from the bank. On a whim, she decided to wait and greet them—or him, as it turned out. She quickly fell under the spell of his "infectious personality." She told him about her recent trip to Egypt, to see the pyramids. He told her about his adherence to the philosophy of Stonewall Jackson: work for fifty minutes and rest ten, to avoid burnout. He offered her a beer and they talked for two hours. But she never got his last name, which explained why I hadn't found the blog (*From Reality Shows to Showing Reality*) on which she'd posted a photo of him proudly holding aloft his jar of pickled sausages.

I shared Conant's account of the same meeting with her. ("Our talk ranged widely and so I much enjoyed her company. She cohabits with her girlfriend and has no children. She is happy in life and is dedicated to her students. . . .") It moved her to tears. "How could a stranger have such an effect on me?" she wondered. My intervention altered the case study, which became an exploration of "the ripple effect," through which chance encounters reverberate ever outward.

.   .   .

A journal in the overturned canoe contained notes for an aborted book project that Conant was thinking of calling *The Anatomy of Failure,* a sort of capstone project begun in the immediate years before I met him, at a time when he believed his canoeing days were finished ("death is near," he wrote). But he wasn't able to bring himself to follow through on it. The same journal shows him keeping tabs on his rent payments for the storage lockers, unwilling to give up hope, growing impatient with his own bitterness and resentments, and starting to dream about rivers again: the Clark Fork, the Columbia, the Cumberland, the Colorado, the Red, the Rainy, the St. Lawrence, and of course the Hudson, on which he floated into *this* book not as a failure but as an unlikely success story.

A sense of eerie obligation crept over me as I contemplated not only the painstaking preservation, rendered almost for naught, but also the dark irony in the fact that I'd been summoned by the first responders in North Carolina because of that fishermen's-forum printout on which, at Conant's request, I'd scrawled my own contact information. It was an artifact meant to highlight his obscurity—a rare digital trace memorialized. I'd never have bothered to print it if there had been many more like it. And now it seemed to have played a crucial role in sparing him from possibly permanent oblivion. Could I at least rescue, if not the man himself, a tale of improbable heroism, by charting a river course through the flood?

5

Keep the Pope off the Moon

Little Dicky, to his parents, was "born among the ashes of war-torn West Germany," in 1951, as he once put it, speaking into a tape recorder for a class presentation. His father, Lieutenant Colonel Perry Conant, was the commanding officer of the 24th Constabulary Squadron, which patrolled the East German border along the Fulda Gap—Freedom's Frontier, the likeliest point of entry in the event of a Soviet tank attack. Perry was an imposing figure, a farmer's kid who had come of age during the Depression—he liked to lecture his children about the virtues of "rock soup"—and then went on to wrestle competitively at Michigan State, on an ROTC scholarship. He was first a cavalryman, with an impish streak, a cigarette dangling from the corner of his mouth, and then he became a tank man, an associate of Patton in the Third Army.

Claire Conant, a Higgins from Queens, was a more recessive figure, sometimes recalled as a shadow by Dicky's friends in later years. She was "blessed with a gentle beauty and a quick smile, her only slight detraction being an oversized nose," Dicky wrote. Within the family, they referred to it as the Higgins Schnoz. (He had one, too.) She and Perry met in the cafeteria of the Supreme Headquarters Allied Expeditionary Force, in Rheims, France, in 1945, while she was working as a censor. She was a member of the inaugural graduating class of Queens College, and was nearly twenty-seven by the time they married the next summer, practically an old maid. "Irish people were raised to feel guilt, whether they did something wrong or not; and to keep their mouths shut," Dicky wrote. "Their guilt was carefully internalized. Outward appearances must be scrupulously scrubbed clean. So nothing must be said. They remained proper to the point of pathological expression. So it was with Mother."

In 1954, the Conants relocated to Fort Knox, Kentucky, where Perry was made colonel; Dicky's earliest lasting memory was of flying over the Atlantic. They moved again in 1958, settling in New York, in the Rockland County exurb of Pearl River. The children numbered eight by then, seven boys and a girl. New friends and neighbors learned to rattle off the names in sequence, like planets of the solar system: Jimmy-Joe-John-Robbie-Dicky-Ray-Roger-and-Mary. (Another boy, George, was born in 1961.) The Colonel, as he became known around Pearl River, went to Saigon that year, and returned a converted Catholic (baptized in the Mekong), with Vietnamese-made bicycles, neon pink and green, as well as the skins and heads of a couple of tigers that he had shot from a helicopter. One tiger skin lay on the floor of the unfinished attic where the four oldest boys slept, in bunk beds.

Borrowing army terminology, the family practiced what it called the muster concept, a strict accountability, with chores charted and posted above the sink, and the threat of a cat-o'-nine-tails for failure to complete them. Outside, however, the kids enjoyed total freedom—in summers, from dawn until dusk. The Conants' new home sat on a ridge, and from the tops of the tall pine trees in the backyard the boys, avid climbers, could observe skyscrapers twenty-odd miles in the distance. Rockland was the state's fastest-growing county, owing to the recent completion of the Tappan Zee Bridge, the New York State Thruway, and the Palisades Interstate Parkway, and yet still remote enough in its inland precincts to seem a world apart.

. . .

Pearl River was just a euphemistic rebranding of what was once Muddy Brook. The boys fished the larger Hackensack, the first running water to spark Conant's imagination, at a swimming hole known as the forty-foot, playing a game they called Poppers. They'd cast their hooks downriver of a short causeway and an old stone railroad bridge, and if anyone got a perch or a sunny on the line, he'd fling it across the street, still wriggling on the hook. Then he'd begin reeling it in slowly, across pavement, while waiting for a car to approach. The goal was to startle the driver with the sight of a dancing fish on the road, and to time the recoil such that—*pop!*—the flopper would become a popper, uncorked beneath the passing tires.

In the dunes, nearby, they played Fire Prevention Week, a year-round pastime that called for setting blazes in order to extinguish them and scavenging for stray bullets and lead slugs to toss into the embers as explosive shrapnel. Another swimming hole lay in a thicket behind a defunct cemetery containing the graves of eighteen Revolutionary War soldiers. Amid cornfields and forest, a hawser rope hung from the branch of a tall, spiked tree that canted out over the bank, precarious; the spikes on the trunk deterred cowardice, providing strong incentive to release the rope over the water. Locals called the spot Neil's, after the name of the family that had owned the neighboring farm, but the Conant boys and their friends conjured an alternate, cautionary, explanation, involving a predecessor (Neil) who had been impaled on the spikes and memorialized. Superstitiously, they renamed it Catfish Yacht Club, and gave one another titles: First

Mate Pete, Deck Swabber Diane, Commodore Kelly. "I don't think anybody ever caught a catfish there," one club member recalls. "A lot of frog torturing went on. We'd cut 'em open and see whose frog had the longest guts." For many of them, the Twainish rusticity amid rapid postwar growth resonated powerfully well into adulthood.

.   .   .

The Conants' marriage, never demonstrably tender, began deteriorating after the Colonel's return from Vietnam. Claire got a job at Rockland State, the local insane asylum, as a teacher of emotionally disturbed children, and later earned a master's in social work, at Fordham. Her increased independence coincided with an escalation in Perry's drinking. The oldest boys' first (unlicensed) driving experiences came while retrieving their father from a barstool. Charismatic when sober, he could be a verbally vicious drunk, with "an acid tongue," as Claire used to lament. Conant wrote, "As I got older and visited more with friends and their families, I noticed that many adults showed affection and warmth not only to us youngsters but to each other as well! How strange."

Amid the domestic discord, Dicky grew precociously spiritual, and, alone among his siblings, was sent away to a seminary, for ninth grade. "His mom was pretty much overwhelmed," one friend recalls. "I was brought up Protestant, but he introduced me to this priest who took us to a beach on Long Island and was trying to convert me to Catholicism. At that point, Dick was discovering his interest in girls was stronger." Was he expelled, as some brothers vaguely recall? If he did something wrong, it wasn't reflected in his report cards. He made first honors in every marking period (his only middling marks were in phys. ed.), and received a certificate of merit for "outstanding accomplishments in scholastic achievement." Yet for some reason, according to memory, Claire was summoned to retrieve him abruptly.

Back home, at Pearl River High School, Dicky thrived, both socially and academically. He was the envy even of those who privately feared his father. "He had a major influence on my life," one self-described "nerdy" friend remembers. "I always looked at Dicky like I wished I could be him—be more spontaneous. Once people got that he was friends with me, I was not bullied anymore." Conant lettered in soccer and track. He was the junior class president (the principal wrote him, expressing thanks for "the nicest Junior Prom that I have ever attended"), and the leader of Senior Prank Day, as well as a member of the National Honor Society. He discovered the city, and brought dates to Carnegie Hall, the Electric Circus, Bill Graham's Fillmore East, and made solo excursions to the Met and the Whitney. Looking back as adults on their high-school years, several classmates claim him as their best friend. "Dicky was the first real love of my life," an ex-girlfriend says. "I took a bottle of aspirin to kill myself when he left me for the next girlfriend. I love that guy so much." For the yearbook, he was voted "Picture Perfect."

·   ·   ·

He won a Regent Scholarship and went to college at SUNY Albany (then called Albany State), arriving in 1969, just a couple of weeks after Woodstock, where he is said to have interacted with Jimi Hendrix. Dicky and friends were among the last to leave the fairgrounds, in a '58 VW bus. Hendrix approached, fixed his eyes on Dicky, and said, "Hey, man, keep the Pope off the moon." Dicky replied, "I promise." To the others, the fact that Hendrix had gravitated to Dicky seemed perfectly normal.

At Albany, Dicky majored in studio art and played varsity soccer, but his primary commitment was to the Edward Eldred

Potter club, a kind of anti-Greek fraternity that prided itself on anarchic improvisation. Gasboy, Hank the Skank, Bullshit Bob, Slimy Bill, Wolfman, The Hat, Locos Carlos: his new friends were given to racing cars (some not their own) around the quad, throwing furniture off of balconies, and squeezing superglue on one another's toothbrushes. Dicky became Crazy Conant, a beloved figure who, stoned or sober, had the gift of heightened presence. He grew his hair long, ditched his shoes for flip-flops, and started wearing overalls, often without a shirt underneath. His artistic talents, meanwhile, came in for special use with the club's love of irreverent public displays. For Parents' Weekend, he built a giant mechanical hand with a retractable middle finger, which they mounted on the back of a pickup truck, and for a Homecoming float he made a sculpture of fornicating pigs. The club was banned from future parades.

Conant's spontaneity also made him a target of sorts—a figure so fun that others came to rely on him for their own amusement. This was especially true of a crew from Pearl River who sometimes visited him in Albany, expecting hijinks. "There was one guy who thought it was hilarious to watch Richard go deep under the influence," an old friend recalls, alluding to the sport of dosing Conant's beer or milkshake with LSD. "They thought it was *so* funny," an ex-girlfriend adds.

How many unexpected trips did he take? People differ in their recollections. One acquaintance put the number at a thousand. But it's not as though he hadn't been known to experiment willingly, and "You can't very well *surprise* someone with drugs a thousand times," another friend says.

The partying eventually got in the way of studying, and the university's provost wrote the Colonel in 1972, informing him that his son's grades were not good enough for continued enrollment. Dicky withdrew and returned to Rockland County for a

couple of years, which were marked both by troubling signs—
"hellacious" drinking, as one friend put it—and by a renewed
focus. Several Conant siblings remember sensing that Dicky
"just seemed different" at that point. The parents had separated.
Dicky often stayed at his father's place, near Catfish Yacht Club,
occasionally sleeping late after overimbibing and blaming others for stealing his alarm clock—early indications of a paranoid
tendency.

Claire asked him to accompany her to a psychiatrist. She said
she'd made the appointment for herself. She was dealing with
the strains of the marital breakup, after all, and her clashes with
Dicky over his rowdy behavior weren't helping matters. In tears,
she pleaded with him to come along, "so that I could help her
overcome her problems and get well," he later wrote. He relented.
The doctor's questions seemed suspiciously focused on Dicky's
behavior, yet Claire answered all of them, without allowing him
to speak for himself. "She was in hysterics," Conant wrote. He
felt duped. "What followed was malpractice"—a recommended
treatment with lithium, which Dicky ignored.

He got a job at the hospital in Nyack, a nearby town on the
Hudson, where he was the only white man on an otherwise Hai-
tian cleaning crew. The Haitians, he felt, were "imbued with the
most jovial dispositions of any group I've ever met." In keeping
with their spirit, and with his own raffish tendencies, he sometimes walked the halls of the hospital on his hands, in the hope
that doctors and patients would be amused by the sight of floating feet outside their windows.

A formidable nurse named Millie, a contemporary of the Colonel's in Patton's Third Army, took him under her wing after six
months and advised him to get serious. He cut his hair and was
moved to the operating room, first cleaning and prepping and
all the while observing surgery from close range, and eventually

helping with suturing and cauterizing wounds. He quickly realized that the gore didn't unsettle him the way it did others, and he began to wonder whether he might yet develop the unflappable bedside manner of the family doctor who had saved his life at age thirteen by diagnosing appendicitis during a house call.

Conant returned to Albany in 1974 and got a job at a hospital there. He resumed his studies, now pursuing a premed curriculum along with his fine arts requirements. Those old friends of his who remained on campus found him to be newly aloof—not so crazy. An old soccer teammate and Potter club member named Steve Lippincott returned for a visit after having graduated. "People said, 'Dicky came back but he won't talk to anybody,'" Lippincott recalls. Lippincott had considered Conant one of his closest friends in the club. "I ran up to him and I said, 'Dick! Dick!' He looked right past me. I said, 'It's me, Steve! I'm your friend.' He said, 'I don't have any friends,' and he kept walking."

.   .   .

Neither parent attended Dicky's college graduation, in 1976. They were recently divorced, and each feared running into the other, or so reasoned the offended son. He applied to medical school but didn't get in, undone by the bad grades of his rowdier years. His brothers John and Ray had gone out west, chasing the energy boom in Wyoming, and Dicky, feeling adrift as his late twenties loomed, decided to follow suit.

He left in the last week of January 1978, flying first to Michigan, to visit the Colonel, who had returned to the farmstead of his youth after his own father, Elmer, hanged himself from the rafters in the barn. The Colonel helped Dicky buy a secondhand GMC pickup, and that first night Dicky took the truck out for a drive around the so-called Thumb Region of the Lower Peninsula. After a few miles, rolling through fields on empty roads as straight as rulers, he killed the headlights so that he could observe rabbits and snowbirds in the pale glow of a full moon. Another truck came speeding up behind him, flashing its brights, and swerved alongside. When Dicky pulled over, he saw two shotguns pointed at his window. The man in the passenger seat accused him of siphoning gas in the dark, and was unimpressed with Dicky's excuse for his stealthy travel ("Why don't you do your bird-watching during the daylight?").

The next day, the Colonel came home drunk and accused his son of being a "goddam thief," so Dicky took off, westward through Saginaw and Flint and Kalamazoo. Midway to Lansing, he got caught in a ferocious blizzard. In a span of fifty miles he counted more than forty vehicles stranded in roadside ditches. His own truck began fishtailing, and in a couple of instances spun fully perpendicular to the flow of traffic, first ninety degrees left, then a hundred and eighty degrees right. He felt that he understood, for the first time in his life, what it meant to say that his heart was in his mouth.

This was the Great Blizzard of 1978, the strongest winter storm to afflict the Upper Midwest since the previous century. Still, he forged on, through Indiana and into Illinois, where, on I-80, he was briefly blinded by the lights of a passing semi. He had never owned an automobile before, and was no longer sure that he wanted to. He slept that first night at a truck stop in Davenport, Iowa, and awoke to discover that the storm was following him west. It had been thirty degrees when he left the farm, and now, as he approached Omaha, he learned from the radio that it was forty below zero. Accounting for wind chill, the temperature had dropped nearly a hundred degrees in twenty-four hours. The cascading barometric pressure had turned his tires floppy, and he had to keep stopping, to re-inflate. Gusting winds nearly blew the driver's-side door off its hinges during a bathroom break; his urine, meanwhile, traveled ten yards before dissipating into sleet.

He continued across Nebraska on Old Route 92, which was lined with mature trees that rebuffed the northerly wind. A day later, having rejoined the interstate, he caught up to another blizzard, in Pine Bluffs, Wyoming. Arriving in Laramie, after dark, he first stopped at a Methodist church to say a prayer of gratitude for having survived the journey, and then, in what was fast becoming a rite of passage for Conant boys heading west, he found the yard of rusting automobiles belonging to Dewey McConnell, an ex–Pittsburgh Steeler and Wyoming's first football All-American. "Uncle" Dewey was a relative, by marriage, of the Colonel's romantic interest, Jean. She was a true western girl, the sister of a rodeo queen. Forty years earlier, Jean had watched from the stands as her sister fell off and then underneath her horse, only to be rescued by a blue-eyed cavalryman named Perry Conant. Lovestruck, she never married while awaiting their fairy-tale reunion, as the story now went. Dewey served Dicky a bowl of moose stew and offered him a bed for the night.

The next morning, Dicky continued on to Rawlins, to the bungalow where his brother John was living with his wife and infant son. John was the older sibling with whom Dicky had the most in common. He was multitalented—almost too casually so—and charismatic, and similarly suspicious of authority, whereas Jim and Joe, the eldest two, were conformists who had gone into the army and the air force, respectively. John shared Dicky's whimsical spirit. As boys, during summer trips to the farm in Michigan, John and Dicky had gravitated to the bog-like troughs and ditches on the property's periphery, and then spent hours removing leeches, as though it were a game. (Dicky used to dream that he'd wake up with legs reduced to toothpicks, beside leg-sized leeches.) John, now a roughneck, was soon to leave for work, and asked Dicky if he wanted to come along and serve as a worm, or lackey. What good fortune!

The rig was a triple, meaning three pipe lengths' tall, or roughly a hundred feet, in the middle of the Red Desert. John Conant, the derrickhand, fed pipe down to the floor from on high. Ray Conant, a year younger than Dicky, was the motorhand, monitoring gauges and maintaining the boiler. Roughnecks by reputation were castoffs and drifters, an untrustworthy lot, but Dicky came quickly to like his brothers' crew, which also included an Okie driller named Floyd and a chainhand named Bo, who came from a Kiwi sheep-ranching dynasty. Their exotic accents only added to the thrill of learning a new vocabulary: mouse hole, bell nipple, worm's corner, monkey board, cow's cock. Dicky, over in worm's corner, was tasked mainly with making the tongs bite, tightening them around the pipe, but at one point, late in the day, Floyd issued an instruction that remained incomprehensible after several repetitions. It sounded like "Latch far on the bluey lahn." Dicky finally consulted John, who translated. They had struck gaseous rock. The blooie line was a tube for diverting the gas away from the rig. Floyd wanted Dicky to ignite the escaping gas, a standard safety precaution.

John escorted Dicky out to the end of the line, about fifty yards downwind of the drilling site, while carrying a pail of sawdust and a rag soaked in diesel. He placed the pail below the end of the tube, stood just upwind of it, and lit the rag, which he then dropped into the pail with a performative, combustive flair. Whoosh! The sun had already descended, making the initial burst of gold and orange all the more glorious. The brothers flashed mischievous grins at one another. They were adolescent pyros again, back in the Pearl River woods playing Fire Prevention Week. Less than a day had passed since the conclusion of

Dicky's cross-country journey, and the West was already beginning to feel like his destiny.

. . .

By the end of the week, he was on his way to the emergency
room, his fingers shattered and wrapped in snow while, with his
good hand, he sucked on a cigarette to settle his nerves. Working
with a new, rougher crew, he had got his hand stuck between an
eighty-pound hydraulic sub and a piston head. On the way to the
hospital, the driver told him not to worry—he was hardly the first
worm to get weevil bit.

The boomtown economy extended to other aspects of energy
production as well, and, after he had healed, he found work in a
coal mine and on the Union Pacific, a gig that better suited his
romantic ideals of the frontier spirit. He believed, as he wrote,
that "the efficient transportation of mail, consumer and capital
goods, bulk commodities, etc., is vital to the health and growth
of our country."

He was a rear brakeman, captain of the caboose, and while he
derived thrills from slinging great masses of metal, and from the
union brotherhood, he also began to suffer from class anxiety,
a sense he couldn't shake that he was shortchanging his talents,
which promised something beyond physical labor. He enrolled
in business courses at the University of Wyoming, thinking that
a job in railroad management might suit him—and make him
marriageable material. Both of his western brothers were married
fathers, and Dicky, in his letters to Claire and the Colonel, wrote
frequently about his intention to raise and support a family. He
said it with an almost martial purpose. He fell in love with a
woman named Mary whom he barely knew, and was devastated
when she didn't reciprocate. ("He just perceived a lot more than
really there ever was," she told me. "He thought people were

trying to run him over with the train, and if I was talking to other men, he would be aggressive with them. I used to think about him sometimes and wonder, Did he ever get run over by the train?") He occasionally sought refuge at Uncle Dewey's, where he blasted Beethoven symphonies if nobody was around, and at the library, listening to LPs of Dylan Thomas and Roger Whittaker. He came to perceive his troubles—social, romantic, professional—as a function of the gap between his ambition and his blue-collar reality. How many other switchers, after all, had requested the graveyard shift so that they could take graduate classes during the daytime? His suspicion of others' resentment set him perpetually on edge.

There were fights, in which he more than held his own. After clocking out at the Laramie rail yards one morning, he stopped in at the Buckhorn, which was renowned for the not-so-ancient bullet hole in the mirror behind the bar, and he was soon clobbered in the ear by a man he didn't recognize. They began wrestling, and Conant pinned his assailant in a Saturday night ride. Determined to elicit an audible concession, Conant then pressed his thumbs into the man's eye sockets. The bartender and another patron intervened, yanking Conant off and twisting his knee in the process. Conant was on crutches for a couple of weeks, and vacillated between pride at having proved himself formidable and discomfort at the thought that everyone was now sizing him up—or, worse, whispering about him.

It could seem as though he took the Western role-playing too seriously at times. While drinking with co-workers at a picnic table on Expedition Island (the launching point, he noted, of John Wesley Powell's exploration of the Green and Colorado Rivers), he got into a scrap with a pit bull that had been playing fetch with a can of beer in the current. The dog bit him in the thigh, the abdomen, and the face before he was able to grapple it to submission. A sliver of his lip dangled loose, and he asked his horrified companions for a knife, with which to sever it. They either didn't have one, or (he suspected) pretended not to. So he smashed a Heineken bottle and performed the surgery with its jagged edge—and then resumed drinking through the side of his mouth.

Not long after, while he was out with his brother John at a saloon called the Silver Spur, drinking the roughneck special of Black Velvet with a beer chaser, another man came at John threatening to bite his nose off. John struck first, with a bite of his own. "Hey, Dicky, you got any dental floss?" he teased. "I got some skin between my teeth." Thereafter, they referred to one another as the Nose Biter and the Dog Fighter.

John was into more than just hard drinking. He'd struggled with drugs, and his marriage was now failing. His only solace was fly-fishing. He wasn't much of a role model for a sensitive dreamer, and his reaction to heartbreak was more volatile than listening to classical music and poetry. In the summer of 1981, after an extended drinking session in which John complained to Dicky about his marital troubles, he went home and shot himself in the head with a Colt .45.

. . .

Dicky was unmoored again. Wyoming as he now saw it had killed his brother, and certain other events acquired greater metaphorical significance as he reflected back on them. Five days before John's suicide, Dicky had been slapped with an animal nuisance charge when his dog Rusty went after another pooch in Laramie. He'd had Rusty neutered, by court order, and this came to seem like a broader form of castration by a town where he'd been unlucky in love. And then there was the case of the eccentric elderly gentleman who planted himself before an oncoming train after enduring years of psychological abuse for his odd habit of conversing with himself while lugging a small ladder around Laramie. The Ladder Man. Subconsciously, perhaps, Dicky had begun to identify with him. Bar patrons still joked about him occasionally, and the lack of sympathy for nonconformists struck Dicky as monstrous.

The economic recession, meanwhile, had caught up to the boomtown, and he lost his railroad job, as cabooses were phased out. His mother wrote him: "I can imagine that the things that have happened have had a depressing effect on you. If you feel bad, don't hesitate to go and talk to someone—a priest, doctor, or professional counsellor." Instead, he headed for Salt Lake City, a saner, soberer, and, he hoped, more compassionate sort of Western locale. Leaving for Utah, he wrote, "I felt like the rejected Frenchman going off to join the Foreign Legion in North Africa." Casting about for a new worldview that might redeem his struggles, he flirted with joining the Mormon church. He volunteered on the reelection campaign of Representative Dan Marriott, and availed himself of the Mormons' extensive genealogical libraries, embarking on a months-long project of compiling a Conant family history, convinced that one ought to know where one comes from in order to realize where one is going. There was to be a Conant family reunion at the farm in Michigan in the summer of 1982, and he set himself a goal of presenting monographs to all who attended.

In the finished document, he described himself, archly, as an "artist and common layabout." But he was proud of the work, and pleased, too, by some of what he discovered about the family's historical significance. He'd even made a pilgrimage back east, to observe firsthand the statue of Roger Conant, the founder of Salem, Massachusetts, an image of which he included at the front. (On the same trip, he visited the Sacred Grove, in Palmyra,

New York, where Joseph Smith had his first vision, but Conant felt only the bite of a mosquito: "no bright lights nor angelic voices nor glorious hallucinations of any kind . . . what a disappointment.") In an appendix, he provided extended descriptions of William Conant, a Revolutionary War colonel who helped conceive the lantern scheme that made Paul Revere famous, and James Bryant Conant, a "distant relation" who served as the president of Harvard and was awarded the Presidential Medal of Freedom.

He also quoted extensively from a nineteenth-century volume published in Portland, Maine, by a Frederick Odell Conant:

> Arthur, in his "Etymological Dictionary of Family and Christian Names," says: "CONANT, (Welsh and Gaelic). Conan, a river, Counant, a cataract in North Wales, from *cau*, a chasm, a deep hollow, shut up, and *nant,* a rivulet."
>
> The radical *con* is not employed in modern Breton, but it is found in many names of ancient places, where it signifies *angle* in the special sense of an angle formed by the meeting of two rivers, in French *confluent.*

His siblings were not noticeably appreciative. Most of them had small kids, and were still mourning the loss of John and adjusting to their father's recent marriage to Jean. After an argument with his sister, Mary, Dicky disappeared for a day and a half. She didn't see him for another twenty-six years.

.   .   .

At thirty-two, in 1983, he took to the sea, enlisting in the navy. Though it seemed an odd, almost unfathomable decision to some of his high school and college friends, who still remembered Dicky as a free spirit prone to discussing *Ulysses* or posing nude for sculpture classes, it was a shrewd move in other respects, among them securing health benefits that would prove invaluable later in life. It was also a good time to be in uniform. These were the waning days of the Cold War, which lent a sense of gravitas to the mission, even as no battles were actually being fought. A world of low-stakes adventure awaited. He graduated first in his class at quartermaster school. He charted Soviet subs—"continent killers"—and chased pirates in the Indian Ocean. He acquired a love of navigation, traversing the Straits of Gibraltar, Hormuz, and Magellan. He was an enthusiastic tourist at South American bordellos. ("Ricardo you are a gentleman," one woman wrote on the back of a calling card.)

Another bonus: becoming a military man endeared him at last to the Colonel, who was in poor health, and who had grown increasingly exasperated by the Mormon interlude and all the heartbreak—the complaints about pitiless treatment by the pioneers in Wyoming. Dicky spent much of his leave time at the farm, drinking with the old man and listening to war stories involving Eisenhower and the pope.

There were problems, however. He was at least a decade older than most of his fellow enlistees, and older, even, than many of his ranking officers, which only exacerbated an instinctual resistance to the navy's rigid hierarchies. Sometimes he couldn't help being insubordinate. His sense of humor wasn't always warmly received. And he suffered from chronic insomnia on board, made all the worse by a nagging belief that his shipmates were slipping amphetamines into his meals as a practical joke—a different sort of acid flashback. It was the kind of cycle from which one couldn't easily escape: grasping to explain his sleeplessness, voicing paranoid thoughts, and becoming further unnerved by the mocking response, as would-be tormentors mimicked the very act of which they'd been accused. He was placed on involuntary leave.

"Our medical corpsman, also known as 'Doc the pecker checker,' conspired to have me ousted from the service through a medical discharge," Conant later wrote. "Some time was wasted ashore as various head shrinkers examined me and tried various exotic psychotropic potions on my delightful yet non-addled brain." He was given Haldol, a stupefying drug often used to treat schizophrenia and mania, and experienced what he called a "sordid quid pro quo," as his insomnia and persecutory delusions subsided in lockstep with his "joie de vivre," as he put it. Under treatment, he had lost his interest in telling stories, and therefore in living.

His lawyer assured him that he was not crazy but "merely eccentric," and contested the service's diagnosis of a paranoid disorder. They appeared before a medical tribunal, where Conant sought to convince the panelists that he would no longer "take on an attitude that someone is tainting my chow." The panelists, in turn, subjected him to an inquisition that reflected bafflement at the general arc of his life.

Q: When you joined the Navy at the age of 32 years . . . like most of us, did you join saying, "I've got to do something and let's get on with it?"

A: You mean a space filler, sir?

Q: A space filler. A chance to promote yourself and your education and your degrees. That's why 99.9% of the people join the Navy or the Army or the Air Force, or General Motors, for that matter—to get along in the world.

A: I felt that the experience would be worthwhile. My primary motivation was patriotic, altruistic.

Q: I'm really interested in knowing—between the age of, say, 20 and 32, twelve years—what spark was lighted within you that got you so patriotic that you joined as a seaman recruit at age 32, when all the other seaman recruits—90+%—were 17 and 18? If we can find what turned you on, we can turn everybody on.

A: All my positions that I held, I always felt the sense of service to the nation, whether it was in manufacturing, medicine, transportation.

Q: And you have a B.A. degree. Why didn't you seek a commission rather than come in with the enlisted troops when you already have a college degree?

A: My thinking was that knowing how an enlisted man feels—that, had I made it into the officers' corps, I may perhaps have had some insight that would have proven valuable in a command position.

Q: I notice in the medical record, the nurses' notes which we have provided point out that at some point you were tearful. Do you recall that?

A: During a group therapy session, I did express myself tearfully, but that was in Jacksonville and I was concerned with how I would tell my family what happened to me. I was concerned about how my father would take it. He has such expectations.

Q: Do you think you got anything out of the psychiatric evaluations and testing and therapy that you went through for those two months?

A: Yes, I sure do. I was made aware of some aspects of my personality that for years I have not even noticed.

Q: What are they?

A: Well, sir, I'm kind of large in build, and I'm very—I

don't know how to say it. Gregarious? Or have been previously. Just the way I walked and the loudness of my voice, certain aspects of how I carried myself, tend to rub people the wrong way.

Q: What, ultimately, do you want to do?
A: Ultimately, I want to get married and settle down, sir.
Q: Career-wise, what do you want to do?
A: I wanted to be—eventually be skipper of a vessel, sir.

Q: Do you know what a personality disorder is?
A: Yes, sir. There are different kinds of personality disorders.
Q: That's true, and there are different degrees of different kinds of personality disorders. And I suppose almost everybody except me has some variety of a personality disorder, but most people, if they can handle it correctly, and understand what's going on, can control some of those traits that you were talking about. Do you think you've gotten your controls pretty well established?
A: Yes, sir.

He beat the rap. ("You have fought well and accomplished much," the Colonel wrote him.) He was back on active duty, in the Caribbean, in 1986, when one of his shipmates was discovered missing in the middle of the night. Presuming that he'd fallen overboard, the crew backtracked forty miles over the course of five increasingly anxious hours. Finally, using binoculars, a boatswain's mate spotted something—someone?—floating half a mile in the distance. He was alive! As the ship drew nearer, Conant was struck by a feeling of cosmic insignificance: his rescued shipmate looked so tiny in the vast and indifferent sea.

Amid rejoicing on deck, Conant received sobering news from the mainland. The Colonel had had a heart attack, and died. He wrote his mother: "I knew his wrath on many occasions. But I knew his love on many more. Most of his anger and frustration toward me was based on love and the determination to see me be proper. I pray the balance of my days will be a worthwhile product of that effort."

.   .   .

Jacksonville, Miami, Gainesville, Albuquerque, Phoenix, Jackson, San Antonio, Sherman, Eagle, Driggs: the postmarks on Conant's letters (to those still receiving them) seldom remained the same for long. He had secured an honorable discharge from the navy and was still studying to become a doctor. He was going to go fight fires in the Northwest, or maybe head out to sea again, on a fishing boat. He'd sold a painting, and was hoping to exhibit in a gallery. He had met a girl. He was still single, and a bit of a rascal. He was also, according to his private writing, at least, experimenting intermittently with living rent-free: "a mouse in my sleeping bag or a spider on my face. There's always something."

At the twentieth reunion of the Pearl River High Class of '69, Conant's old pals compared notes about what might have gone wrong with Mr. Picture Perfect. Some had been disowned, in strange fashion, like Steve Lippincott in Albany. Others had heard only scattered bits of news, from parents and friends of friends. There was a rumor that he had suffered a breakdown and landed in a psych ward after discovering his brother's dead body. One friend who had lost touch would later proffer that Dicky was the casualty of an alcoholic "military bully" for a father, and had probably drunk himself dysfunctional. ("The Colonel was so hard on those boys," another reflected.) And then there was the bad-acid theory. Proponents of this explanation were inclined, to varying degrees, to regard him the victim of a criminal act: personality theft via wanton dosing.

In later years, with an evolving understanding of the biological roots of mental illness, people in and around the Conant family began to speak more openly in terms of a "gene" that had steered Dicky astray. And to the extent that the contaminated beverages may have activated or amplified "trust issues" that were already latent, there was another grim possibility to assess, in the wake of the Catholic Church's sexual abuse scandals. What had *really* been the cause of Dicky's sudden return from the seminary in Connecticut, and why did Claire Conant, on her deathbed, allude to the episode as a source of lingering maternal discomfort?

But the explanation that held perhaps the broadest appeal, in Rockland as well as in Albany circles, was a more cultural one. Dicky Conant was not alone in having drifted, and in having indulged in the vices of the time. But whereas others, spurred by the birth of a child or something similarly grave, had come to a reckoning point, and congratulated themselves on their late-arriving maturity, Dicky stood out as a cautionary tale: the golden boy who refused (or was unable) to grow up.

Sometimes he agreed with that analysis and took it to heart. In the fall of 1992, Conant applied, for the second time, to medical schools, explaining in an essay that he was particularly drawn to the growing field of neurosurgery. "It was a sense of adventure which drove me to work on the railroad," he wrote. "There I worked with heavy, noisy, dangerous equipment in all extremes of weather. In the Navy, I sailed to far corners of the world and met many good people." Neurosurgery, he continued, "is like navigation in the sense that success depends upon truthful information. Facts, good judgment, and deliberate action yield good results." If you squinted, you could see a consistency in his scattered path. He was forty-one, and aware that this made him unusual in his given aspiration, but he encouraged a long view that would grant him three or four more productive decades with which to build a career. His applications were denied.

In a funk, he got busted for drunk driving, near Jackson Hole. To avoid jail, he underwent court-mandated counseling and experimented with AA, but found the program's essential anonymity hard to believe in. Laying himself bare before strangers ("When high on beer, I don't feel so inferior") induced more anxiety than it relieved. Chief among the life goals he listed during his outpatient treatment, higher even than becoming a brain surgeon, was to "see as much geography as possible." The suspension of his driver's license left him with some downtime, while dreaming of vehicular alternatives.

The next summer, 1993, Conant mailed an old Pearl River friend a postcard, from somewhere in the Rockies, saying that he had "fashioned a kayak" and was planning to paddle it to the Pacific Ocean. To another classmate, he described this "highly maneuverable" vessel in more detail. "It looks like a cross between an eskimo kayak and a whitewater dory," he wrote. "It performs beautifully, and is pleasing to the eye." As a postscript, he added that he'd learned from a nurse in Wyoming that his family had been spreading hurtful rumors about him—an allusion to his fear that his mother, upset about his drinking and less than full-throated in her med-school encouragement, had become a character reference gone rogue. With the letter, he included a drawing of rock formations in Utah's Arches National Park, along the Colorado River, where he'd been taking the boat on test runs.

. . .

In the spring of 1994, Dave Call, the former sheriff of Salmon, Idaho, was on the Salmon River, leading a guided tour in rubber rafts. One day, he encountered a "very unusual" man, whom he still recalls vividly. "The boat that he was in resembled a model airplane fuselage," he said. "It had a tendency to tip over and bang into rocks."

Randy Davis, a California firefighter who was on the tour, remembers, "I think some of it was made of papier-mâché. He had truly the explorer's personality. He was very endearing, and sharp in a lot of ways, but he struck me as somebody who wasn't going to be able to settle down."

"He was right out of a storybook," John Litt, of Ozone Park, New York, said.

Conant had left from just downstream of Stanley in a snow-storm on his forty-third birthday, bringing with him three books: a Gideon Bible and biographies of Einstein and Bismarck. Over the next six weeks, occasionally negotiating Class IV rapids, he covered 350 miles. He stopped—far short of the Pacific—only after losing fifteen inches of his bow to a steep plunge off a rock ledge that left him Maytagging, or whirling round and round, as in a washing machine. Speaking of it two decades later, to me, Conant called this a "learning experience," a proof of concept. Among the lessons were that memories should be prized over material possessions (which could easily break or sink), and that traveling light had its downside. Without ballast, you were more likely to be tossed. "The peace of mind I found, largely alone, on that white water mecca convinced me that life was capable of exquisite pleasure and undefined meaning deep in the face of failure," he wrote. "The experience itself is the reward."

6

Psychological Perturbations

Aboat is, of course, a peculiar place to stow away with a
noisy mind. Joshua Slocum, the first man to sail around
the globe alone, became convinced that the captain of
the *Pinta,* from Columbus's fleet, had arrived on board to guide
him through a storm off the Azores, in 1895. ("One may imagine
my astonishment," he wrote later. "The large red cap he wore was
cockbilled over his left ear, and all was set off with shaggy black
whiskers. . . . 'Señor,' said he, doffing his cap, 'I have come to do
you no harm.'") Some seven decades later, in 1968, the *Sunday
Times* of London organized the first round-the-world sailing race
for lone individuals, the Golden Globe. The betting favorite of
the nine entrants was the self-styled French vagabond-philosopher
Bernard Moitessier, who called his boat *Joshua,* in honor of Slocum. Under way, he grew so starved of social interaction that he
summoned his friend Henry's apparition and believed he could
feel his breath. ("I talked to him from time to time," Moitessier
wrote. "I would ask him not to drop the crescent wrench we were
using to tighten the cable clamps. And he helped quietly, without
lecturing me.")

Those were happy hallucinations, at least. Another contestant, a British businessman named Donald Crowhurst, sank tragically into madness. Worried that he couldn't keep up, and that his trimaran wasn't seaworthy enough for the treacherous Southern Ocean, Crowhurst began transmitting false coordinates over his radio, to the point where people following along in the newspaper believed he might win. For months, he maintained meticulously separate realities: a logbook charting his actual course, toward Brazil, and the one for public presentation in which he was speedily rounding the Cape of Good Hope. Then the radio broke, and with it went "the precious link to the world outside the claustrophobic cabin, beyond the empty horizon," as Peter Nichols writes in *A Voyage for Madmen,* his history of the race. Crowhurst "turned away from the world and plunged deep into himself." He imagined a live argument with Einstein, and began scrawling a historical and philosophical tract at the end of which, he felt certain, intelligent readers would recognize that "problems that have beset humanity for thousands of years will have been solved." His tidy handwriting grew messy, the margins cluttered with afterthoughts. Dirty dishes remained unwashed in the galley sink. The tract, which spilled on for twenty-five thousand words, read like this:

That these sentences would at first sight apparently be devoid of physical meaning is hardly surprising, for if we had a complete understanding of their meaning we would indeed have arrived at the stage it is now the object of the exercise to predict.

And yet, and yet—*if* creative abstraction is to act as a vehicle for the new entity, and to leave its hitherto stable state it lies within the power of creative abstraction to produce the phenomenon!!!!!!!!!!!!!!!!!!!

Nine days before his boat was spotted, drifting without a skipper, by a Royal Mail cargo ship in the middle of the Atlantic, Crowhurst seemed to concede defeat in his authentic logbook: "Cannot see any 'purpose' in game . . . No game man can devise is harmless. The truth is that there can only be one chess master."

As for Moitessier, he indeed appeared in contention to win, but in his solitude had grown increasingly disenchanted with materialism and could no longer stomach competing for a monetary prize. Instead of returning to the finish line and reuniting with his children and wife, Françoise, in Europe, he kept on sailing, beginning a second loop and eventually firing a withdrawal note by slingshot onto the deck of another ship off Cape Town. "Please do not think I am trying to break a record," it read. " 'Record' is a very stupid word at sea. I am continuing nonstop because I am happy at sea, and perhaps because I want to save my soul." Alone, he felt, "you can discover who you really are," adding, "You have to choose between your life and a woman." He landed in Tahiti and stayed there, fathering a son with a new partner.

Françoise later reflected of the boating life, "You turn into a kind of small God in your own eyes."

.   .   .

Conant, from what I could tell, kept moving because of his near-constant fear of overstaying his welcome, running not from the law or from a string of broken relationships, but out of preemptive precaution. He often departed towns abruptly, without proper goodbyes, seizing on the weather as an excuse for his urgency. He seemed implicitly to know that if he stayed, he risked becoming *that* guy—the Ladder Man of Laramie—instead of *this* guy, a momentary star attraction. Then his barnacles, inevitably, would get to work, replaying events in such a way that might justify his incivility, or else nurturing guilt that could only be assuaged on the phone or by mail. Being trapped in a small canoe, for all its other virtues, afforded many hours for obsessive reconsideration and little opportunity for escape. "As memories meld into my subconscious they begin to grate on my intellect," he wrote. "I try to make sense of actions whose import I ignored while they were occurring." Uh oh.

When his mind misfired, I began to understand, it was often because he had correctly identified a subtle shift in social dynamics—the faintest hint of a wince, or a half-second's hesitation—and then it was as if time slowed down, enabling him to analyze the possibilities and implications with an inevitably distorting fervor. He couldn't help wondering what he'd done (as opposed to who he was) to trigger suspicion or discomfort. No fleeting moment can bear the scrutiny that a lone voyager is able to give it.

Conant often acknowledged a paradox inherent in boat travel: that the line between bliss and numbing boredom could be virtually imperceptible. A good day on the water—"a day to live for"—might be uneventful and leave him with little to account. To provide "structure" amid endless paddling, and perhaps to stave off cabin fever, Conant counted "cycles," as he called them, or groups of four strokes: one two three *one*, one two three *two*, and so on, up into the thousands, in some cases, without losing track. The numbers gave him a rough sense of distance covered, using a formula that varied depending on the current and the wind: two hundred per mile on slack water, say, versus sixty on the lower Mississippi. He made games of the figures as they amassed in his head, looking forward to palindromes (1881), what he called "repeats" (2525), and "upside down and backwards" (1691). Sometimes, he imagined the cycle counts as dates on a world-historical timeline, which allowed him to view his progress along the country's waterways as part of an epochal continuum. Beginning at 1889, his grandfather's birth year, he'd start interweaving Conant family milestones with the march of time, and from 1951 forward he'd try to summon an event or a pleasing memory from his own life to associate with each advancing cycle.

1957: running in Fort Knox behind the DDT trucks, inhaling the blue clouds.
1965: first stirring of sexual desire, with Susan M.
1972: sleeping on a feather bed in a Bavarian farmhouse.
1985: strolling through the souk in Manama, Bahrain, with a beautiful young woman dressed in a black abaya.
1999: meeting Tracy while packing his boat in Livingston.
2007: being congratulated for his courage at a Kentucky bar by the Cincinnati Reds pitcher Bronson Arroyo.

．　．　．

His marine radio, too, served as a helpful grounding device. Tuning in to Channels 13 and 16, he often eavesdropped on the chatter among tow pilots, admiring the range of accents and ages and absorbing the lingo: "On the two," for instance, meaning starboard, and "kill her out" for reversing to a standstill. Judy to Barbecue. Doc to Dorena Ferry. Bixby to Eva Marie. Roberta Hughes to Robert Posey. There was a music and poetry in the names alone. Here was a well-established gossip network, and a self-contained universe in which he felt justifiably accomplished— less afflicted by a checkered past. As on land, he wasn't wrong to suspect that others might be talking about him. But on the water he had proof! "There is a green canoe out here in the channel. It does not look too sanitary." "Just want to let you know I'm coming up on a canoe and he ain't scared of nothing!" "Boy, I'd never

be out here in a canoe!" "Let's see what the current does to him."
"He'll never make it."

Sometimes he spoke up—"This is Little Green Canoe"—
eliciting surprised reactions. ("Did you hear that? The canoe has
a walkie-talkie!") He coveted the respect of no one more than
the commercial pilots, professional rivermen who, working
three weeks on, followed by three off, lived double existences
not entirely unlike his own. A personal highlight occurred one
December morning on the Yazoo River, in a half-knot current
below the bluffs at Vicksburg, when he was summoned over the
radio by the crew of a Little Rock–bound ship called the *Melody
Golding* and invited to board for coffee and Christmas biscuits.

.   .   .

And then, occasionally, there were the other canoeists and kayakers, on whom Conant sometimes projected his concerns about
the impression he was making. "It's been obvious from all the
evident symptoms you have shown that you are probably slightly
mentally ill," he claimed to have told one such traveler in Greenville, Mississippi. "But it is nothing to worry about or be ashamed
of. Obviously you can exist in society quite well. Hell, you have
successfully paddled many hundreds of miles down the most
powerful river in the country. In fact, you should be proud."

Whether because of the increasing ease of self-documentation,
via Facebook and GoPros, or because of the peer encouragement
that such footage enables, if not because of a deeper dissatisfac-
tion with the effects of these technologies on daily life itself, the
number of thru paddlers has been trending upward. Familiar
faces on a big river become friends by necessity, and the long-
rangers whom Conant got to know on his trips tended to defer to
him instinctually, if warily, as a wiser and more authentic voyager.
One of them even credited him with saving his life, by offering

a tip that later proved crucial about always tying one's canoe to high ground before falling asleep, in case of a flood. This was Neal Moore, a self-described "creative activist" and a former operative for the presidential campaign of Ron Paul, who met Conant in Minnesota, in the summer of 2009, near the start of Moore's own descent of the Mississippi as a "citizen journalist" in search of uplifting human-interest stories. "The man has had a profound impact on my life," Moore wrote me from Africa, where he was traveling, although his home base, he said, was in Taipei. He was in the midst of plotting another canoe expedition, this one spanning the North American continent and connecting many rivers, inspired by Conant. He also acknowledged that a certain primal territoriality was unavoidable on such trips. "It might sound funny, but one becomes possessive of a river," he said, and recounted an episode in which he and Conant had camouflaged their respective canoes in some brush and then scaled a steep bank to find a clearing beneath a tree. During the climb, Conant noticed Moore's Timberland boots, and said, "Those are really nice boots. I'd kill a man for a pair of boots like those."

Moore wrote, "That night in my tent I slept with my Buck knife in hand, just in case."

.   .   .

It was the sight of a similar knife, two years earlier, in Greenville, that had prompted Conant's rumination on mental illness and shame. This was November of 2007. Conant, sitting in a riverside park on the south end of town, eyed a lean young man whittling a pecan shell. The sun caught the knife blade and produced a flash that first mesmerized Conant and then startled him. Eight inches of gleaming stainless steal—an awful lot of knife for a pecan. Conant observed an aimless smile on the man's face, and was further unnerved.

Soon the whittler, whose name was Jason, and his friend Tom departed on foot for Route 82, over the levee and through cotton fields, carrying two sacks full of the fallen pecans they'd gathered to sell by the roadside. The endeavor was Conant's idea. Jason and Tom needed cash, and Conant was sick of giving it to them. ("They had a homing ability for those with the soft touch," he wrote. "Perhaps I was one of their most successful marks.") The previous day, amid persistent gusts, he'd noticed some women stooping to collect nuts, and inquired about the activity, learning that the smaller, oilier variety of pecan could fetch almost a dollar a pound. So he sent the youngsters off, to make their small fortune.

While the guys were gone, Conant sipped his bug juice and reflected skeptically on the events of the preceding weeks.

. . .

He had met them almost four hundred miles upriver, a day's paddle south of Cairo, Illinois, where he exited the Ohio onto the Mississippi. They caught him from behind, each in a green Old Town canoe that featured the logo of a rafting resort in the Ozarks. They often worked there in the summers, and had persuaded their boss to lend them the canoes for an adventure in the spirit of Twain, from St. Louis to New Orleans. Tom had a black beard and wore a wool hat, in spite of the late-afternoon sun. Jason was clean-shaven and had light-colored hair. Both in their twenties, they had set off with a mere $115 between them, using a small road atlas for navigation. They were winging it, relying on youth and charm.

The first thing Conant noticed was that they weren't wearing life jackets. Conant was a hard-liner on the subject. He shared some beer with Jason and Tom, along with his three cardinal rules of Mississippi River travel. First, never take off your life jacket.

Urban portage to the Delaware, Trenton, New Jersey, October 2014

"Yeah, man, what's your whole purpose, though?" a bystander asked.

SALMON RIVER 1994.
ANOTHER VIEW OF ME AND
MY BOAT. THE MANY YEARS
OF MISERABLE BATCHELORHOOD
LONELINESS, HAVE LEFT
THEIR PAINFUL SCARS DEEPLY
ETCHED IN MY COUNTENANCE,
AS YOU CAN PLAINLY SEE.
    I MET THIS OUTFITTING
PARTY ALONG THE WAY.
THEY WERE KIND ENOUGH TO
SEND ME THESE TWO
PICTURES OF ME. VERY
NICE PEOPLE.

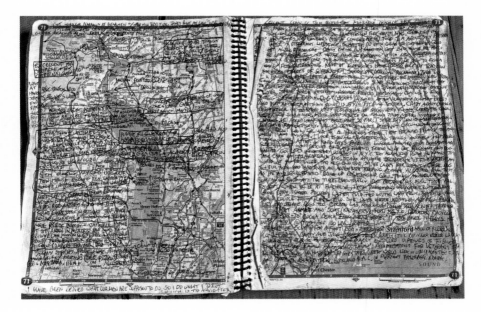

"I started keeping a regular journal, but I found that I was so tired at the end of the day," Conant told me. Instead, he took extensive notes on the road atlases he used to navigate.

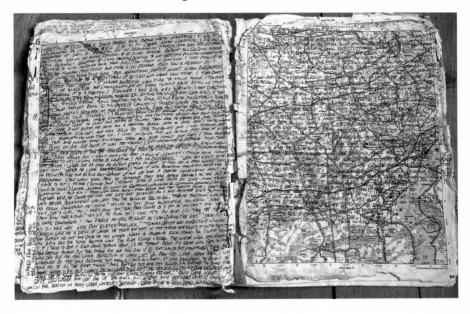

Salmon River, 1994

Missouri River, 1999

Hudson River, 2014

Delaware and Raritan Canal, 2014

As a younger man, Conant produced art that hinted at torment, but his later works reflected a reverence for the natural world: big rocks, big skies, little people. A self-portrait, in cracked egg, hints at a rebirth around the time that he first took to the water.

"I can, and I will!" Conant kept repeating, on an island in upstate New York, of his intention to paddle all the way to Florida.

Second, paddle in the margins of the shipping channel, both for added speed and because the shoreline is rife with subsurface weirs and jetties. Hazards you can see, like barges and tugs, are preferable to those you can't. Third, always tie your boat off to something secure at night, whether a tree branch, protruding rebar, or your own arm, because you never know when the river might rise.

The young men thanked him and pushed on. As they were waving farewell, they were nearly plowed over by an advancing tow, which was so long you could scarcely hear the tug engine's groan at the opposite end. (This caused Conant to shout a fourth bit of wisdom, in jest: Don't forget to look behind you!) They paddled faster than he did, but Conant, often traveling at night, caught up to them in New Madrid, Missouri; again in Memphis; and was hailed from behind once more on the approach to Helena, Arkansas. Gradually they developed a rapport, a nutty uncle and his wayward nephews. They visited museums together. Conant gave them money for booze, and chided them for leaving campfires unattended, or for failing to grease the pan before cooking flapjacks. He marveled at the way they scampered up and down riprap in the dark, like mountain goats. He pressed copies of Custer's *My Life on the Plains* on them, hoping to instill a love of American history. And he was appalled—but also a little jealous—when listening to their stories of reckless gamesmanship on the water itself: "tagging buoys," as if on a slalom course, and "surfing haystacks" (standing waves of seven or eight feet) behind the sterns of passing tugs. What fun, to be young, carefree, and descending a river!

. . .

When they reunited again, in Greenville, the merry magpies, as Conant had taken to calling them, were missing much of their camping gear. Ignoring his advice, they had gone to sleep on a small island without tying off the boats. At 3 a.m., Jason got up to pee and noticed that his canoe was missing. Frantic, they cached the bulk of their effects on higher ground and paddled downriver together, in pursuit. They found it twenty miles later, miraculously still upright, in a maze of mud bars and rivulets near Arkansas City. Rather than try to fight the current back upstream to their cache, they continued on another seven or eight miles, hoping to find someone who might be able to help. The first person they found, naturally, was Conant.

Bad karma seemed to be following them south. That first evening in Greenville, while attempting to hike into town, they were chased by an armadillo and Tom was sprayed by a skunk. Making matters worse, they had angered their boss back in the Ozarks, who received a phone call from the Coast Guard after a towboat captain reported seeing an errant canoe bearing the resort's name. The boss had been generous enough to wire Jason and Tom some additional funds in Memphis, an advance against future earnings, which they'd used impetuously, on hotel rooms and Beale Street carousing. He was now cutting them off.

Conant lent them some tarps, cooked them stew, and even, forgiving the stench, fished a couple of winter jackets out of his luggage to spread over Tom, who lacked a sleeping bag. Their plan, the next morning, was to paddle up Lake Ferguson, an arcing sliver into the downtown, and entice someone with a pickup truck into a ride north and across the river, toward the cache site. That meant leaving one canoe behind for the time being. Conant offered to postpone his departure and watch it for them. He also loaned them some more cash and navigational charts.

So far, so good. He referred to his hapless companions, in writing, as "our modern day Tom Sawyer and his pal Huck Finn."

. . .

The real trouble began, as Conant saw it, when they returned a day later, triumphant. Conant had used the canoe-sitting sabbatical as an opportunity to clean his boat, inside and out, and to do laundry. His belongings were scattered everywhere, clothes drying on the branches of brambles and snags. Jason and Tom were newly standoffish, and cavalier about the fact that they had misplaced his charts.

Here, I'll pause to note that we've come to the sort of dynamic I mentioned above, correctly perceived by Conant as palpably shifting but ultimately misdiagnosed. When I reached Jason, he brought up this same hinge moment unprompted, characterizing it as a spark of revelation. "It was, like, 'Aw man, he's kind of embarrassing to be around right now,'" Jason recalled, explaining that they'd suddenly recognized their benefactor less as a nutty uncle than as a hobo. "So we separated ourselves from him." (Apologetic, he added that he thought they still owed Conant a hundred dollars.)

Sitting in the waterfront park and replaying the events, certain phrases lodged in Conant's mind along with that image of the gleaming knife. For example, "Now it's your turn," said with a weary grin that many might have found playful and routine. Conant wasn't so sure. Losing your boat on a river trip was no joking matter. Were they implying that he might soon lose his as well?

And this: "You're going to need it." The magpies had returned with a gift—or a regift, rather—of a handheld Garmin GPS device. They'd received it up in Friars Point, from a farmer who gave them a tour of his alligator reserve, and then showed them the porch where Muddy Waters pegged Robert Johnson for a dangerous man. Jason presented it to Conant as a gesture of gratitude for all his help. It was true, of course, that Conant could *use* such a tool—but why would he "need" it, as Jason put it, if he had come so far already without it? Jason's tone was sincere but the look in his eyes as he handed the device over was distant and hard to parse. Conant's mind flashed to an image of the raccoon he saw swimming at a horseshoe bend in the Ohio near Henderson, Kentucky. Minutes earlier, on shore, he had caught the same raccoon stealing nuts from his stash, and it had looked briefly bashful, yet its eyes as it later swam beside his boat betrayed cold indifference.

He arrived at the conclusion that these guys suspected him of sabotage—of setting Jason's canoe adrift in the first place, given his penchant for stealthy night travel. What else could explain the furtive glances they'd exchanged while picking up pecans that morning, and the conspiratorial discussions, sotto voce? "I began to think in terms of the infinite variety of turns a human mind can twist to fabricate and mold," he wrote, from experience, while imagining that the fabricating was being done by his potential antagonists. "Given irrefutable facts a determined mind can construct a total delusion out of whole cloth and thereby satisfy a gnawing yet wishful thought process."

Prisoners in striped jumpsuits were brought to the park, as part of a work-release project to remove litter. Conant, meanwhile, found himself preparing a case for his own innocence. The case was foolproof. He had receipts in his wallet. They placed him in Greenville, buying supplies, on the night Jason's canoe floated away north of Arkansas City. Hard facts, not open to interpretation.

He laid out the evidence for Jason and Tom after they returned from hawking nuts on the highway. They didn't seem interested. They were irritable for another reason. Unloading forty-five pounds' worth of pecans had netted them a measly sixteen dollars, far short of Conant's forecast.

The next morning, a retired cop named Norm stopped by the

park with his young son and daughter, and Conant, thinking of Tracy, was pleased to be reminded that it's seldom too late to start a family. In the course of reminiscing about a life spent on or near the river, Norm recalled his own youthful habit of tempting fate behind the wakes of tugboats. He also warned them all about river pirates, not to mention the Louisiana Creoles, in general, who weren't likely to be as friendly as Mississippians. He had a friend whose boat had been robbed at gunpoint on the Atchafalaya. Conant, noting the allusion to haystack surfing, felt that he was on the receiving end of a coded message of sorts: river talk, a riparian currency. "Norm mentioned that the lone traveler was in greater danger," he wrote. "I thought he meant me. I might be in immediate danger from these two whom I had recently befriended. Everything began to add up more clearly. Never mind pirates, I might lose my boat to these morons from Missouri. Or my life. I began to feel afraid."

Before taking his leave of Jason and Tom—he offered handshakes, they gave him hugs—Conant presented them with a regift of his own, in the form of prisoners' MREs. These were leftovers from the cleanup crew, and surprisingly delicious, at least by itinerant standards. ("They swam in a thick, delicious savory gravy," Conant wrote of the dumplings he'd sampled. "Yum yum.") Of the seventeen meals that remained, he kept four for himself, abstemious, and left his would-be tormentors with the other thirteen, "subconsciously hoping," as he put it, that the odd number would prove a source of tension.

.   .   .

The magpies had often spoken of the serendipitous occurrences and surprise discoveries of a river adventure (like the sight of fresh bear tracks) in terms of their "neat factor," on a scale of one to ten, and Conant found occasion to borrow the concept a week and a half later, while paddling on what he believed to be the Atchafalaya River, near Simmesport, Louisiana. This river was much narrower than the Mississippi, and heavily forested, such that the birdsong and other animal noises assaulted him in stereo. "I felt like I was in the middle of a Hollywood jungle movie," he wrote. Then he noticed, on one of the concrete revetments installed by the Army Corps of Engineers, something that he at first took for an olive-colored log—until it moved. A sunbathing gator! Conant was about thirty yards away when it slid back into the water, never to reappear. A neat factor of ten, he thought.

Also a fear factor, which spurred him to reflect more critically on peculiar observations that he'd previously dismissed, like the fact that the sun had seemed to rise that overcast morning in the east, and that the supposed railroad bridge at Simmesport never appeared, no matter how many bends he rounded. He was on the Red River, he now realized, and headed north. After leaving the Mississippi, the evening before last, and locking through on the Lower Old River Canal, he had rested for a few hours and resumed navigating in the middle of the night, evidently choosing a couple of wrong forks amid limited visibility. Ever since, he'd been wondering if the bayou country that he'd now entered weren't some kind of Twilight Zone, with funny currents and miscolored channel markers.

On the bright side, he determined that he'd traveled more than thirty miles upriver in a day and a half's paddling, a sign of vigorous health. And he'd seen—and survived—his first wild gator. But he was concerned about his apparent susceptibility to wishful thinking, or what he termed "psychological perturbations." He'd been so happy to exit the Mississippi, and to ditch the magpies in his shadow, that he hadn't paid enough respect to celestial regularity. After correcting course, and finally reaching Simmesport, he passed a dead beaver—"poor water slapper"—on the bank.

"Ah, mortality," he noted. "Nothing profound here, but I was reminded that I too must croak someday."

·   ·   ·

Another neat factor, this time on the actual Atchafalaya: paddling again at night, now under a waning moon and brilliant stars, and slightly in his cups, he was inspired by the hooting of an owl to begin singing himself. He belted out "The Star Spangled Banner," and "She'll be Coming 'Round the Mountain," and "The Last Farewell," the Roger Whittaker ballad he used to listen to while heartbroken in Laramie. The "personal hit parade," as he thought of it, was joyous enough, but the truly wondrous part came as he raised his volume and other unseen animals piped up, as if answering his calls. For a mile or more, he seemed to be conducting a wildlife orchestra, with contributions from birds, coyotes, dogs, cattle, and even horses. Then the ruckus quieted, and so did he, and a faint train whistle and chirping crickets were the only sounds competing with the rhythmic piercing of his paddle. He was approaching the small town of Melville, population one thousand.

In daylight, now, amid Spanish moss dangling from branches and bushes, he heard much gunfire on either side (black powder, he was pretty sure), and caught a whiff of raw petroleum. "It smells like money, and lots of it," he wrote, and was reminded of his first exposure to the scent, at Muddy Gap, Wyoming, with his brother John, standing beside the blooie line.

Farther south, past Krotz Springs, the river grew more remote, with no buildings in evidence for many miles, and he reclined against his ice chest, to give his back a rest, while still adrift. He also shut his eyes. He started dreaming that his lap was full of water. Wait—his lap *was* full of water! He must have been rolling in his sleep, and inadvertently dunked a gunwale. Fortunately, the bags that he'd tied down were holding the boat semi-afloat, at a forty-five-degree angle, with the bow high and dry and the stern fully submerged, beneath his own weight.

The coldness of the water provided a shot of adrenaline, and he quickly straddled the canoe, using the grip of his thighs and the buoyancy of his life jacket to keep the angle from subtending further. His challenge now was to figure out where the shore was, in the coal-black night. He decided to paddle to his left, urging himself on with a string of expletives and stern admonishment: "Now you are in a world of trouble, Dicky, goddammit. Keep paddling, don't quit." The water was up to his sternum, and, though the river was relatively narrow, it was slow going with a boat so suddenly heavy. Fifteen minutes elapsed before he could make out trees and feel mud underneath his feet. Using the painter line, he pulled the canoe up as far as he could and tied it to a branch, then collapsed on a beach of goopy clay. Taking inventory after he'd recovered, he noted the loss of four gallons of drinking water, a rubber boot, his ice chest, several cans of food, three tarps, and—worst of all—a painting of the Washington Monument that he'd been given by an army veteran in Wellsburg, West Virginia. Irreplaceable.

. . .

Four men in a johnboat approached him the next day, and he was finally grateful for the GPS. He thought again of Norm's warning about river pirates, and decided to hold the instrument to his ear like a cell phone while pretending to talk softly. When the men drew closer, he stuck his other hand into a backpack, as though retrieving a pistol. The johnboat slowed ("It was good manners, actually," he wrote), and one of the men shouted hello, but Conant just stared back, trying to look menacing. The man, smiling, asked if Conant needed anything. Again he remained silent, shaking his head slowly, until the johnboat continued on its way. "My ruse was successful," he wrote. "I continued on still wary of strangers and paddled through the afternoon."

Near dusk, he spotted another johnboat that appeared to be following trotlines on either side of the river. There were two men in this one, and they didn't seem to be paying Conant much mind, but as he prepared to pass them by he repeated the GPS-and-backpack routine, just in case. The older of the two, lanky and white-bearded, craned his neck to look inside the canoe's hull—suspicious of fish theft, Conant presumed. The stout younger man flashed a gap-toothed grin. They were John and Jim, respectively, and they informed Conant that he was only a few miles, down around the next bend, from Morgan City, an industrial port near where Conant planned to pick up the Intra-coastal. John recommended a boat ramp opposite Morgan City, in the town of Berwick, as a safe moorage, and offered compli-cated directions involving numerous wharves and bridges.

Conant was exhausted but also concerned about the loss of so much drinking water. The jungle—"so inviting in the dwindling light"—soon gave way abruptly to dense settlement, and he was amid harbor traffic, with a series of bridges ahead. Contending with shipping wakes as he tried to focus on successive landmarks, per the directions, increased his irritability, as well as his fear that he'd been misled. By the time he reached the third and last bridge, a railroad crossing, he was staring straight into darkness, with only ambient illumination on either side, as he approached the end of the industrial line. Looking to his right, or west, he saw a wharf, with a couple of tugs that "looked like affordable housing for Popeye, Olive Oyl, Pappy, Sweet Pea, Wimpy, and Bluto." Just beyond it was an inlet—"Yippee!" he shouted—leading to a concrete ramp. Welcome to Berwick, just as John had described it. His faith in rivermen was restored.

A car drove up soon after Conant had landed. Hiding in the shadows, he lit a cigarette and watched as a man got out and hurled a box of some sort into the water, while holding on to a long rope. After a few minutes, the man began hauling in the rope. "Hey!" Conant yelled, startling the man, who "looked like he had seen a ghost," Conant wrote. The man introduced himself as Landry. Inside the box—a steel trap—was a drowned raccoon.

. . .

Landry turned out to be a regular at a hardware store, near a bear-crossing sign, that doubles as an informal coffee shop in a town that has none. The proprietor, Gardie Boudreaux, still keeps a copy of Conant's annotated map of Berwick and its surrounding waters amid scattered papers on his desk, and has perused the full manuscript from which I've reconstructed the events described above, which Conant mailed a year or so after leaving town, regretting what he called his bad manners and seizing an outgoing tide. "He must have stayed here about a week," Boudreaux told me. "I don't guess the book was ever hardbacked?"

It was there, at Boudreaux's place, while a Pomeranian named Tika Tequila Maria Rose performed tricks for homemade biscuits, that Conant saw breaking news of a mass shooting at a shopping mall in Omaha. "Another nutcase gone crazy with a gun," he wrote, and reflected on the fact that there were people in Bozeman who might have expected something similar from him. "Instead of shooting people, I bought a canoe and paddled down the river. Perhaps that fellow in Omaha would have been well advised to do the same."

7

Surf and Turf

The American river-trip canon can be understood as a play in three acts. It begins with Lewis and Clark, whose journals of exploring the western frontier on the Missouri, the Snake, and the Columbia Rivers, among others, were literally compelled by the president. The country had just doubled in size, with the Louisiana Purchase. As a *New York Times* columnist once wrote, "More was known about the moon before Neil Armstrong touched down on the Sea of Tranquility in 1969 than was known about the land between the Mississippi and the Pacific in 1803." And thus, the Corps of Discovery. The journals tell a story of economic destiny obscured by scientific observation: wildflower taxonomy, tail-feather analysis. In spite of constant illness ("venerials," dysentery) and the threat of violence from those "vilest miscreants" the Teton Sioux, the overarching tone is of enchantment at the endless-seeming abundance of game and the fertility of the flanking prairies. The authors retain their belief in the binaries of civilization and savagery and that whatever "picteresk" river they traveled on was, as Thoreau would later put it, "an emblem of all progress." Each roasted beaver tail marked the way forward into the future.

Next comes *The Adventures of Huckleberry Finn*, set several decades later in a nation where the river no longer represents a frontier but a world unto its own, offering freedom from an imperfect society ("sivilization," as Huck spelled it, can be plenty savage) and a place for forging unlikely friendships. Just as important was its depiction of the eroding banks on either side of the swift current as a milieu for dreamers and schemers: the Duke and the Dauphin, supposed heir to the French throne by way of the bootheel. Hemingway famously declared that *Huckleberry Finn* was the headwaters, in a sense, of modern American literature, but when it was published, in the eighteen-eighties, Twain was already aware that his story was an anachronism, and that his beloved river's centrality to the national mythology was receding into nostalgia. Arriving by steamboat in Natchez, on a valedictory tour that served as the basis for *Life on the Mississippi,* he observed, "Apparently, nearly all the river towns, big and little, have made up their minds that they must look mainly to railroads for wealth and upbuilding, henceforth."

Last, we get *Deliverance,* James Dickey's novel of city slickers seeking relief from middle-age doldrums and finding trouble afloat. *Deliverance* gives us a river at once threatened by commercial interests, in the form of a proposed dam, and threatening to all who dare go near it. Rather than hastening modernity with the ceaselessness of its current, Dickey's river is primordial—an Appalachian backwater—and the hillbillies the protagonists meet along its banks are essentially stand-ins for the Native Americans Lewis and Clark encountered. Paranoia begets violence begets more paranoia. Or is it the other way around? John McPhee once wrote of embarking on a canoe trip with several other men for whom *Deliverance* had become a standing joke, a coded expression of self-conscious unease in distant seclusion. This was owed largely to the infamous rape scene ("Squeal like a pig!") in the movie treatment, an emasculation nightmare. "Its thought-wave effects seem to have reached to wherever canoes may float," McPhee added.

. . .

Canoeing, for some, is also an athletic pursuit, however ungainly. A columnist for *Sports Illustrated*, thinking recreation rather than exploration, once described it as "the most inadvisable means ever conceived for the transportation of man by his own efforts." Unlike rowing, say, which "drives a boat as straight as a brick-layer heading for a saloon," paddling with a single blade, side to side, leaves a vessel zigzagging like a bricklayer *leaving* one. "That off-center body twisting and straining is man-killing. An AAU official has said that the nearest a man can come to the pangs of childbirth is the twisting and wrenching of competition walking, but he's wrong. The agony of paddling against a headwind is like giving birth to cement blocks."

Yet there are Guinness-certified records regarding the endeavor-as-sport, and a postliterary coda can be found in the example of Verlen Kruger, who is said to have canoed more than a hundred thousand miles in a forty-one-year span that included his early retirement from a plumbing career in Lansing, Michigan. He died of pancreatic cancer in 2004, at the age of eighty-two. When he was seventy-nine, he won a tandem race down the Mississippi, completing the river (with a friend) in just twenty-four days. At eighty, he canoed the length of the Yukon. His pièce de résis-tance was what he called the Ultimate Canoe Challenge, which began in 1980, in Red Rock, Montana, near the primary source—the "utmost" source, completists would call it—of the Missouri River, and concluded, about twenty-eight thousand miles and six hundred portages later, in December of 1983.

He had a partner, an ex–Navy SEAL named Steve Landick, who also happened to be his son-in-law. (He had nine kids.) They used separate canoes, which Kruger designed, and which looked more like sea kayaks, with rudders and zippered spray covers. Sometimes—for instance, while trying to set a speed record for descending the Missouri—they rigged the boats together, like a catamaran, so that one could sleep while the other paddled. "All meals are like filling a tank, and every meal we eat until we fill up," Kruger wrote in his journal.

After the Missouri, they followed the Great Lakes and the St. Lawrence to the Bay of Fundy, and began a long run down the Atlantic Seaboard, to Key West, and on around into the Gulf. Then, in just eighty-three days, they went *up* the entire Mississippi, believing themselves to be ("as far as we've been able to find out") sea-to-source pioneers on the Father of Waters. They continued on up into the Arctic. Along the way, they acquired sponsors: Dow Chemical, DuPont, Johnson Wax, Gore-Tex.

Kruger, then sixty, fell overboard in the Pacific, near Cape Blanco, Oregon, while heading south, and was rescued after an hour and a half by a Coast Guard helicopter. (Unlike Conant, they were traveling with EPIRBs, emergency position-indicating radio beacons.) Medics recorded his body temperature at ninety-one degrees. DuPont offered a two-thousand-dollar reward for Kruger's canoe, which was eventually found by a fisherman, eighty miles south.

Together again, the duo pressed on. It was the summer of 1982 by now, and Landick was a new father. (His wife had visited him on the Yukon the previous fall.) Reaching Long Beach, and a short planned vacation, he flew home to see his baby daughter, Saba. She died in her crib the night he arrived. He took some time off to grieve, and Kruger, Saba's grandfather, went ahead with a new partner whom he had met in Seattle. They got as far as Magdalena Bay, in Baja, before diarrhea rendered Kruger temporarily unable to continue. He hopped a ride on a sailboat into Cabo San Lucas, and thereby forfeited his chance at claiming another record: first to canoe the full length of the North American "west coast," from Skagway, north of Juneau, down to Cabo. That distinction fell to Landick, who resumed paddling three weeks after his daughter's death, and eventually caught up.

Reunited for the second time, Kruger and Landick then went up the Colorado River, through the Grand Canyon: another first. They hiked over the Continental Divide. Landick contracted mononucleosis, though, and had to fly back to Michigan again to recuperate. Then Kruger's canoe was stolen, in Green River, Wyoming, and a high-speed chase was required to retrieve it from the top of a getaway truck.

They were together again at the conclusion, serenaded by a brass band as they floated into Lansing on the Grand River, before a crowd of three hundred, and were given keys to the city. By that point, they were no longer related by marriage. Kruger's own marriage dissolved not long after his return to ground. He married three more times, finally reuniting with his first wife.

. . .

Kruger had a rival claimant to the odometer throne, in Canada. His name was Don Starkell, and, in 2010, when he was seventy-nine, he alerted the *Winnipeg Free Press* to the fact that he was closing in on three circumnavigations' worth of the earth, or 120,226 kilometers (about 75,000 miles). Evidently, he was suspicious of Kruger's imprecise accounting. According to the paper, Starkell "believed he had travelled farther in a more credible time frame—and he had a pair of hand-noted ledgers to back up the claim." Those ledgers (until they burned in a house fire, a couple of years before Starkell died, also of cancer) extended back to 1945, when he was twelve, and already inclined to tabulate his travels. His stats, like Kruger's, were amassed in large part through daily routine and repetition: twenty-two kilometers every morning, weather permitting, on the Red River. (By similar logic, pro bowlers sometimes claim to be performing estimable feats of strength, carrying fifteen-pound balls aloft for miles, in mincing increments.) But he also undertook some maniacal expeditions, including a descent from Winnipeg to the Amazon, with his son (originally two sons, but one dropped out in Mexico, thinking his father meant to kill them all), in which they were threatened with guns and machetes and even briefly jailed, in Honduras, as suspected drug smugglers. He later tried to kayak the Northwest Passage alone, and nearly succeeded, until his boat got trapped in the ice for twenty-five hours, leaving his fingertips and some of his toes to die of frostbite.

An orphan, "Starkell said his drive to paddle was born out of a desire to succeed in one area of his life," the *Free Press* reported. "Retirement and divorce made it possible, he said."

. . .

Just one more example. I mentioned above that Kruger and Landick believed themselves to have been the first to do a reverse Mississippi. But when they were heading north through Manitoba, they saw an entry in a visitors' log, near a riverside monument, that read, "May 22, 1977, Jerry Puschcar, Box 332, Biwabik, Minnesota. Canoe by paddle from New Orleans to Nome, Alaska." Kruger, writing in his book *The Ultimate Canoe Challenge,* added, "I have not seen verification of Pushcar's trip," sounding a little tweaked.

A series of AP wire stories with datelines of New Orleans, Minnesota, and Nome would seem to validate it, however. (I doff my cap to the paddling historian Norman Miller for the finds.) The second of those began:

A bearded young adventurer who is attempting to break the world record for the longest canoe journey has lost his only companion on the trek, a pure white Samoyed puppy named Blizzard.

Jerry Pushcar, 25, a native of Biwabik, Minn., holed up at a farm in the Williams area after completing the first stage of his three-year trip from New Orleans to Alaska.

Pushcar said his dog was also an adventurer, and had learned to avoid wood ticks, bad weather, strange southern food preparations, and ugly weather during the first 2,500 miles of the 8,300-mile trip.

But civilization killed Blizzard.

"I think he was poisoned," Pushcar said over the weekend. "I can't come up with any other explanation for why he died so suddenly."

Pushcar ended up ditching his canoe and walking the final 250 miles, because Norton Sound, an inlet of the Bering Sea, was frozen solid. He married a woman in Nome, and still lives there. When I reached him by phone, mushers were just arriving in town at the finish line of the thousand-mile Iditarod Trail Sled Dog Race. Unlike Conant, he is a man of few words, not given to reminiscing. "I got into gold mining," he said. "Got fifteen claims now, and a couple pieces of equipment." He added, "I'll get in a canoe if the river's running high, and take it across to get to my mining camp." But he had long since lost the urge to travel without a practical purpose. "I figured enough was enough," he said.

· · ·

I've emphasized the family ties—marriage, children—in those preceding accounts because they were important to Conant, who, like the vagabond sailor Bernard Moitessier, was adamant about the fundamental irreconcilability of wild adventure and domesticity. People (men especially) often told him that they envied him, and that they longed to do the things he was doing. He found this only slightly gratifying. What they really wanted, he suspected, was to be able to ignore their social obligations and entanglements for a while and then return to normalcy, guilt-free, as though they'd caused no disruption to the lives of others. You had to be either young or rich to believe in such a fantasy.

Conant, also like Moitessier, was generally dismissive of record seeking ("I have never cared a pfennig for bragging rights"), and of publicity hounds, and the idea of racing was anathema to him. Why, amid such splendor, deny yourself the pleasure of a beer or some barbecue or a long night of sleep? "I'm not a glutton, but I'm sixty-three, and I enjoy eating," he told me. Sponsorship was not his thing, either, despite offers from Chuck Hall, his boss at the bus station, to get him funding. "I ain't trying to sell a damn thing," he wrote. "When I am out on the water in my canoe, I do call the shots. My time is my own, it belongs to me."

Consider this ode to spring:

Life is blooming all around me. I am in my tent warm and dry as rain falls gently upon my tarp and runs quietly down the ponderosa bark. Geese are copulating as my canoe sways along the roots on the nearby bank. I'm reading about Chaucer's England in the fourteenth century. Meanwhile, I am eating peanuts, pretzels, hot sauce and Tabasco sauce, drinking beer and smoking tobacco. I am enjoying good solid peace at eight in the morning.

I've shared that passage with others who can't seem to get past their revulsion at the diet, let alone the time of day. To my (reading) taste, though, it's a welcome relief from the overly earnest strain that runs through the American naturalist tradition. The good things in life are all right there: sex, peace, beer, tobacco, literature, Tabasco. Why *not* at eight in the morning? Here is a narrator who revels in the radical freedom he's achieved, and who is honest enough to remind us that being alone in the wild doesn't make you any less ridiculous. You can run from society, but not from your inner teenager.

By the standards of type A expedition athletes, Conant can't claim even a proper descent of the country's grandest river ("old pal, unpredictable friend," he called it), whose official headwaters are at Lake Itasca, fifty-odd miles upstream of where he put in for his own ostensible full-Mississippi voyage, in 2009. But you can't catch a Greyhound to Lake Itasca, so he settled for Bemidji, where "one of a string of lakes that form the headwaters," as he explained it to me, was within walking distance of a store that sold cheap canoes. Close enough.

.   .   .

Read together, in sequence, Conant's canoeing manuscripts acquire a *Groundhog Day*–like quality: yet another morning waking up alongside a river, avowedly content but nonetheless still compelled to pack up and go—to try again someplace else. There is a revealing progression, however. The first two volumes share a similarly faint narrative arc, beginning with the author in a desperate state, and concluding (or nearly concluding) with his having achieved equanimity, and full of hope—paddling as therapy. ("I can clean the cobwebs out of my noggin.") At the end of each journey, he visits his distant family, as if remembering what really matters and wishing to reconnect. This is the basic quest narrative, loosely plotted, and a continuation, in a sense, of the autobiographical essays that Conant had been writing since young adulthood, likening himself to Casanova and Cellini and using storytelling as a way of making sense of an entropic life. In a prologue to the second volume, he alludes to feedback from Chuck Hall about the first one: "Among some suggestions, he noted that a recurring issue which came up in his mind during his reading was the simple question, 'Why?'" Conant's meandering attempt to answer that question fills twenty pages, but the short answer, again borrowing from familiar archetypes, is women— one (his mother) holding him back, and the other (Tracy) an inspiration. Each recurs as a kind of phantom throughout his writing: the mother, for instance, as a sea monster—"Poseidon's gorilla"—whom he blames for sinking his canoe from below at the confluence of the Missouri and Mississippi Rivers, on her ninetieth birthday. And Tracy not unlike Beatrice for Dante, a beacon in the fog:

> I assumed they thought I was out on the make. I wasn't. I never am. I've been faithful to Tracy ever since we met over 8 years ago.
>
> While I am writing I see two bright stars or planets. They are far apart and remind me of Tracy and me.
>
> Just now a little gray frog jumped across my legs. He too has his purpose! In this rain camp I do not miss Tracy although I often think of her.

The second book also contains an epilogue, in which he describes his writing process: a first draft produced over the course of eight months, two to three pages of prose a day, using his extensive notes, followed by two months of revisions. Enough time has passed for the glow of accomplishment to dim, and he can't help divulging a sense of unease, now that he's back and settled in Bozeman, among landlubbers he distrusts—at the library, say, where nobody seemed to grant that the dyspeptic scribbler could be up to anything significant. The final note is one of resignation. And so a story that begins "I left Bozeman a very bitter fellow" ends with "It seems I am back at square one, right where I was when I started my magnificent journey." The arc circles round: "Unfortunately, some things never change."

The third manuscript is strictly linear, beginning with a shopping trip to Gander Mountain in Minnesota with no elaboration of discontent and continuing for a thousand pages until, in Virginia, thanks to the largesse of a lawyer he'd met in Louisiana, he boards an airplane bound for home. ("No knives or fluids were allowed on board," he wrote. "I was patted down and I did not like it.") There are ups and downs along the way, of course ("due to the many visits and departures, my emotions are on a constant roller coaster ride"), but it doesn't build toward anything other than the abandonment of his canoe. When he gets off the plane and returns to the Swamp, "everything in the cache was just as I left it fourteen months earlier." The hero hasn't changed. His home hasn't changed. And there's no longer any pretense that he expected otherwise.

Each volume is more expansive and livelier than the last, even as the author is gradually losing faith (consciously and unconsciously) in the redemptive potential of his voyages. They all contain comparable helpings of solitary reflection, poignant and trite and aggrieved in roughly equal measure. (Also funny: camped on an island bird sanctuary in Chattanooga, he reveals that he's listening to *Car Talk* on his radio; while drifting downstream after "a paroxysm of retching and bloody coughs," he begins reading *The Plague*.) What changes over time is the amount of attention paid to *other* people, and the choice of paddling routes, perhaps, that put him in more frequent contact with them. Out west, in Laramie and Salt Lake City, and in the navy, even, Conant had arguably been casting about for a sense of purpose, or a calling, whereas now he was shrewdly *using* the questing trope, scripting adventures for himself in order to facilitate the kinds of social experiences he still craved, and on terms—peer to peer, or knight-errant to awestruck bystander—that were unavailable to him as a middle-aged janitor or later as a swamp-dwelling hermit.

Conant refers at one point in the third book to *Deliverance,* while recounting his initial wariness during an exchange he had with "good ole boys" who turned out to be named Jimbo and Bubba, near the sparsely populated border of Alabama and Mississippi. But his experience, both in that particular and as a general rule, turned out to be contrary. Despite a difficult time on solid land, he found ample evidence for believing that the people you meet alongside a river are upright. "In most places I visit I am treated with friendship and generosity and often kindness in the extreme," he wrote. Echoing the lyrics to "Proud Mary," he liked to say, "People on the river are happy to give."

He recognized something essential about moving water, which is not merely a conveyance but an equalizer—an urbanizing force on the prairie and a rural belt in the city, machine in the garden and garden in the machine. A pond (or a swamp) is a microcosm—a retreat, a closed system, which is always at risk of being spoiled by the arrival of an outsider. "Earth's eye," as Thoreau called it, "looking into which the beholder measures the depth of his own nature." But a big river, as T. S. Eliot said, is "the only natural force that can wholly determine the course of human peregrination." Rivers are the basis of civilization itself.

The generosity and kindness—the sense of community, amid a nation that seemed otherwise to be pulling apart at the seams—were a large part of what had so struck me when visiting with Conant beneath the Hudson Palisades and why I was flummoxed by the librarians' cynicism in the face of my presence in Montana. Conant's enthusiastic reception in my town hardly seemed anomalous. Though he spoke memorably about his private observation of birds, it was the social universe he conjured that I came to find most seductive with time, and as I continued immersing myself in his pages, which were teeming not only with colorful nicknames—Captain Catfish, Butterbean, Peg Leg Pete, Tadpole—but with Good Samaritans.

Take the NASA programmer, for example, who delivered Conant and canoe over the mountains in Tennessee, in 2010, shortly after returning from a missionary trip to Alaska. Thanks to the manuscript, I now knew his name: Stanley Lett. ("Stan is a white water kayak enthusiast of two years duration. He is new to the sport but is fairly familiar with a number of southern rivers already.") He still has the paddle Conant sent him, as a gesture of gratitude, as well as a couple of letters that Conant wrote. He felt bad, when I reached him, that he hadn't been a better correspondent. "I sponsor a kid in Africa," he said. "And I have to apologize to the kid sometimes, because I'm not a big letter-writer." During their long drive together, Lett told Conant about the difficulty of his fatherless childhood, and how he viewed his becoming a rocket scientist as proof that the human will is indomitable. (Though Conant told me his escort had worked on a Saturn rocket, Lett clarified that it was actually the J-2X, a successor.) They talked religion and particle physics: Lett, a born-again Baptist, hoped that Conant would be a witness for Christ; Conant, no longer an observing Catholic, articulated an Emersonian view of God in nature, and mused about Heisenberg and Schrödinger's cat and the idea that "history, whether recorded or not, is just a series of events in a magnificent eternal chain reaction"—in essence, a river trip, one thing leading to the next. Lett took a picture of Conant before leaving him on the banks of the James, in Lynchburg. "It was raining and he had a big old smile on his face, because he was back on the river," Lett said.

And there was the lawyer who later bought Conant's plane ticket home from Virginia. They met near a hardware store, in Slidell, Louisiana, where Conant intended to buy the makings of a portage cart, so that he could drag his rig—by hand—eighty miles to Mobile, thereby avoiding the elevated salt concentration in the Gulf. "The heck with that, I'll give you a ride!" the lawyer said. His name was Chuck Hughes. It turned out that he had recently saved the life of a canoeist on Lake Pontchartrain—an ex-Marine, who had gone out fishing, swamped, and clung to a buoy—and felt moved to extend his streak of altruism. "It's a way of making up for the dumb things I did when I was a younger man," he explained. Hughes told me that he couldn't help being drawn to Conant's "expansive vision of life," and confirmed this remarkable fact I'd read: that shortly after he befriended Conant, they ran into a young backpacker from Pittsburgh who happened to be walking from the Pacific to the Atlantic Ocean, after having already trudged the other way. Seekers everywhere. He sent me a picture of himself standing between the two nomads. "I called them Surf and Turf," he said.

A couple of days passed between that chance encounter and the free ride to Mobile, and Conant spent much of the intervening time socializing with a minnow merchant named Bunny. She was a Hurricane Katrina refugee—perhaps the unluckiest of all survivors of that terrible storm. After living in a FEMA trailer and then a hotel, she finally leased an apartment, into which she hadn't finished moving her belongings when her new landlord asked her to follow him to an auto body shop, so that he'd have a ride home after dropping off his car. She did as he asked, but after a few miles he pulled over near a remote, wooded area, got out of his car, and shot her several times—twice in the face. Slumped over the passenger side, with her seatbelt still buckled, she feigned death until her assailant finally drove away. Then she called 911. (They caught him.) She suffered more than fifty bone fractures and underwent multiple reconstructive surgeries. Two of the bullets remained lodged in her body. "She has lost much of the faith and trust she had for strangers," Conant wrote. Nevertheless, she implicitly trusted the enormous "river wanderer," as he called himself, who was camped out in the marsh near her bait shop, awaiting a lift from the lawyer he'd only just met. "She has a wit and voice inflection that brings laughter to all. So Bunny is blessed."

. . .

Carrying a notebook in the bib of his overalls, Conant the inveterate diarist gradually morphed into something more like a journalist, a Studs Terkel of the riverbank, collecting stories and examining them, as alternative ways of navigating life's hardships. "Obviously, there's a little Walter Mitty in everyone," he noted. "I just have a little more in me than other people."

But the people making cameos in his prose had a fair amount!

In Dubuque, while wandering around a Labor Day picnic for the local Democratic Party, Conant met a man, John Harvey, who told of once riding his motorcycle two hundred miles through a California rainstorm without placing his hands on the handlebars. ("It sounded dangerous to me," Conant wrote.) Harvey then drove Conant around town, confiding in him about his struggles with mental illness ("John understands rationally what is the matter with him") and lamenting that many of his fellow Dubuquers never paid the river that slides along their shore any mind. "Hey, man, think of us as ships on the ocean, passing in the dark of night," Harvey said, as they hugged goodbye.

The barista at a coffee shop in Smithfield, Virginia, on the Pagan River, noticed Conant's getup and his journaling and began telling him about her exploits as a railroad tramp. Her name was Abby Street. She had traversed the country north to south and east to west on numerous occasions. He took careful notes as she explained her preference for hopper cars—the "Cadillacs" of the fleet, because of the notched ends that offer roomy protection from rain and wind—and criticized the movie trope of tossing one's backpack ahead before climbing on board a moving train. She had firsthand evidence of the strategy's perils, having seen a man trip and fall after relinquishing his pack, only to watch it glide away. "There goes your house," she said. Conant wrote, "Always wear your pack while running and grabbing onto the car."

People told him stuff, and he jotted it down—sometimes not until much later, even the morning after a long night of drinking, and yet his recall was so extraordinary that a couple of individuals I reached wondered if they'd been the victims of identity theft, given the amount of detail—hourly wage, education, ancestral migration—I was sharing with them. For Conant, relegating his own past to a distant attic of the mind seemed to free up space for absorbing others' multigenerational sagas, in a way that I, as a professional reporter, found humbling. Taken as a body of work, if you adjust the lens and gaze beyond the author's navel, Conant's writing amounts to a scattershot portrait of the people one might meet within a few hundred yards of the country's navigable rivers. The absence of any selection process—culling for relevance or uplift, say—only enhances the cumulative effect: a magnificent chain reaction of human interest.

.   .   .

Why, though, I wondered as my cold calls amassed into the dozens and then triple digits, was I continuing to follow up? At first,

I'd been engaged in basic fact-checking: trying to establish, in light of the Conant brothers' wariness, whether the far-flung stories could be trusted for Walter Mittyish enjoyment. Indeed they could. I'd also been using Conant's mental instability, let's say, as a spur to keep asking around on the pretense that there could still be meaningful *omissions:* behavioral tendencies he didn't dare acknowledge, or clues better observed through the eyes of another. And then there was a gut-check element, pertaining not so much to Conant's recorded observations as to his emotional impact on me. It makes me a little uncomfortable to say it, but I was finding sustenance in other people's concern for him, filling the void of his ongoing absence by working my way through his scattered social network.

Often, I ran into dead ends, however amusing. An Iowan named Marla, the capo of a dockside clique who called themselves the Turtle Mafia, texted me: "Amazing People we meet w/n R Lives! They r Amazing n if u never see them again, Remember how they made ur Day, a Memory! Turtle Girl <3." She also sent me a picture of her recently deceased pet turtle, Muskie ("He had a Tough Shell!"), before she stopped responding to further inquiries.

Occasionally, though, the ripple effect of my curiosity led in wondrous new directions. "Do you have a picture you can send me?" a man named Homer Shrum asked. "Because I tell people this story and they don't halfway believe me that he's real."

Shrum was twenty-nine when he met Conant in September 2009, in Louisiana, Missouri, which is about seventy miles northwest of St. Louis. "A little gem," Conant called the town. He was looking for a place to buy film, and approached Shrum, who was standing outside a bar. They got to talking—Shrum had grown up there, and then moved south to work in a steel mill, but he often visited, especially during deer season—and then to drinking, and, in Conant's case, dancing the jitterbug. The night grew long, and Shrum offered Conant a couch to sleep on at his parents' house.

By the time Shrum woke up, his father had already stumbled on the snoring giant in the living room, and Homer, now sober, was mortified: "I was old enough that I should have known not to bring people home off the river." But the two older men were happily exchanging navy stories over coffee.

Before leaving town, Conant asked, as he often did, for his new friends' addresses, so that he could write with news of his future travels. Homer's was in Columbus, Mississippi. Conant knew Columbus: his brother Joe, the pilot, had been stationed there long ago, while in the Air Force. What was more, Columbus was on the Tombigbee River, one of a string of southern waterways that he planned to ascend after reaching the Gulf Coast. Shrum didn't think much of Conant's suggestion that they might meet again. He nodded gamely, figuring this for the kind of notional optimism that people express all the time without quite meaning it, because it's easier than accepting the finality of goodbyes. Columbus was five hundred miles by car, and probably fifteen hundred by canoe, given that it wasn't even part of the same watershed. It seemed unsporting to call Conant's bluff.

Months passed—nearly half a year—before Shrum, resting at home in Columbus, heard someone shouting his name in the front yard. He opened the door. It was Conant. "He was looking pretty rough," Shrum said. "His feet were swollen. His hands were swollen. He had his toothbrush sticking out the front pocket of his overalls." He had been paddling straight through an unusually frosty Alabama winter, abrading his palms on vines that he used to pull himself forward along flooded banks and admiring icicles dangling from trees. ("They refract sunlight and look like strings of jewels," he wrote.) By dumb luck—wasn't it always this way?—Conant had caught Shrum at the start of four days off from the mill, so Shrum invited him to stay awhile and hang out. Same friend, different couch. Conant soon helped himself to Shrum's tools and fixed a loose board on the front stoop.

"He had a lot of stories about how he'd be on the Mississippi in some random town, and this woman would be sitting there waiting for him," Shrum recalled. "I was like, 'I don't know, man.' But then again, I also didn't believe he'd make it to Columbus."

I had plenty of pictures to offer Shrum, who no longer lives in Columbus, but I was intrigued by the possibility of coming up with a more pertinent memento—a contemporaneous account of their unbelievable rendez-vous, by a third party. Conant had written of giving an interview, while in Columbus, to a weekly newspaper reporter named Roger. He resumed paddling before the next edition of the paper was published, so he wasn't able to read what came of it. I found a Columbus man named Roger Larsen who fit the description and asked if he'd mind exhuming the old article from the archives and sending me a copy. He informed me that there was no article to send. There'd been an interview, all right, but "it just didn't add up."

For a start, Larsen explained, Conant wasn't alone when they met. He had a local resident, a young steelworker, with him: a bug, apparently, not a feature. The two made a motley pair, not natural pals. Larsen caught the younger man's wandering eye a few times and thought it betrayed uneasiness. Larsen couldn't help wondering if he was being had.

After the interview, Larsen accompanied Conant to the river and asked him to paddle a few strokes for a photo op. Conant had so much gear packed in his canoe that when he climbed inside Larsen worried it would sink. "Water up to the gunwales!" Larsen recalled. "That made me highly skeptical. I wouldn't have got in that thing for just a trip across the channel. It was insane."

The "crappiness" of Conant's gear, to borrow from one devotee's description, was like a Rorschach blot: either it made you all the more amazed and impressed; or it was proof alone, almost, that he oughtn't be taken seriously. Larsen, believing the latter, brought up another incident in his own defense. This was two days after the interview, early on a Sunday morning. Listening to the police scanner as he often did, for breaking news, Larsen heard a report of a possible robbery in progress at a convenience mart near the river. He hustled to the scene—and there was Conant, the apparent subject of the complaint, apologizing to the frightened clerk at the counter for helping himself into the beer cooler in back when the display case didn't have what he wanted.

"And then buying the case of beer?" Larsen continued. "The guy weighs three hundred pounds and he's paddling all that distance against the current?"

To me, the moment in question encapsulated so much, both about the limitless ways a solo river voyage could go wrong and about Conant's unique gift for talking his way out of unintended trouble—for creating his own luck. I also saw the episode as another case study, to complement the one at the college in Minnesota—in this instance, on the old journalistic virtues of stick-to-itiveness, resisting first (and second) impressions, suspending disbelief. Inside the store, Conant and Larsen exchanged knowing glances but not greetings. Conant was privately annoyed, thinking quickly of all the mug shots he'd noticed in the local paper, while reading—enjoyably, he had to admit—about "poor saps in trouble." ("What a way to make a living," he wrote of Larsen. "He is worse than an attorney chasing ambulances. At least an ambulance portends recovery and continued health, hopefully.")

Had Larsen only lingered, he would have heard a surprising turn in the conversation between Conant and the responding cops, one of whom noted Conant's Montana ID and mentioned that he'd grown up just across the Montana state line himself, in Buford, North Dakota. Conant knew it immediately as the site of the confluence of the Yellowstone and Missouri Rivers. He recalled seeking shelter from coyotes and lightning at a farmhouse on a bluff outside nearby Williston, in the company of an arthritic bachelor named Charlie Nelson. At this point, Larsen would have seen the officer's eyes widen. "I know Charlie!" Soon, the officer, who had intended to deliver Conant a warning about his perception of the river as a magnet for shifty souls, the site of a recent stick beating, was talking about his interest in kayaking, and about his high-school paddling experiences on the Yellowstone, and his unfulfilled dream of embarking on a long rafting trip as an adult.

"What a great town!" Conant wrote.

"It was better than if he was LaSalle!" Larsen said, reconsidering.

.   .   .

The irony was that Larsen, too, had unrealized big-river dreams. While in high school, in Kansas, in the late sixties, he'd built his own kayak out of wood and canvas, just as Conant did. After graduating from college, Larsen and a fraternity brother known as Crazy Fred planned to float the length of the Missouri, only to get waylaid by some other friends who had commandeered a school bus and a metal detector in order to scour the Rockies for buried treasure. "But there's a lot of square miles out there and not too many clues," he wrote me, in one of a stream of emails that, with the force of a darting current, kept threatening to divert my focus, only to swerve back on course in unpredictable ways.

After abandoning the treasure hunt, Larsen drifted around the country, hitchhiking and "sleeping out," while finding temporary work—loading boxes of cattle ear tags in Mattoon, Illinois;

threading pipe in Mobile. "We all wanted to go somewhere and do something and strike it rich," he said of his and Conant's generation. Columbus, a hospital town during the Civil War and later the site of the nation's first public women's college and an air force base, wasn't a destination but simply where Larsen ran out of money, in 1976. "I washed up here myself."

Larsen said that before getting into the news business he supported himself by working as a handyman carpenter and was sometimes compensated with free lodging in spare bedrooms of the antebellum homes he was renovating. ("They designate the old houses around here with names like 'Something Hall' and 'The Oaks', etc.," Conant wrote.) One mansion had an atticful of sherry bottles and old magazines from the twenties and thirties. There, sleeping in a four-poster bed not his own, amid closets full of flapper gowns, and reading his way through the magazine boxes, Larsen became engrossed in an article that he would recall, with uncanny clarity, many years later, when talking to a writer for *The New Yorker* about a story he couldn't bring himself to publish.

He mentioned it during our first phone call, the way one might summon a headline from last week, as soon as I'd persuaded him that Conant was legit. "The State of Riverbank," it was called. As in: the State of Delaware. The idea was that there remained a cultural jurisdiction independent of any borders drawn on maps, populated by eccentrics and ne'er-do-wells, such as might have entertained Mark Twain's readers fifty years earlier.

How Larsen had come to internalize the old article, and yet remain impervious to Conant's charms, was a story worthy of, well, Conant, but we'll get to that in a bit. I looked it up, and saw that it was published in the March, 1928, issue of *Scribner's*. "Riverbank, U.S.A.—A quasi-anarchistic commonwealth," it began, before providing brief character sketches of a range of rough-hewn types who stalked an indeterminate sliver "between the rail-road tracks and the water's edge on a no-man's-land of willow and cottonwood, of weed-patch, sand-bar, and mud-flat." One of the article's archetypal denizens, Joe Rivey, "has visioned a life of nomadic, romantic adventure, has glimpsed his dream soul-mate; but he can see no hope of possessing either. There is only the river flowing endlessly by at his feet." He sounded like Conant without a canoe. Others had names like Old Fanchers, Waukendaw Chip, the Walrus. Reading it, I found myself thinking again of the parade of colorful names in Conant's own pages and had the realization that not so much had changed in the intervening eight decades, a period that brought nuclear power and space travel and wireless communication to the wider world. It was as if America's rivers, far from delivering the future, had continued vacuuming up ambition as they slid, preserving along the water's edge a snaking time capsule.

8

Chemical Goggles Required

Even locally in my own river town, meeting Conant had altered my perception of the lives of others. There was my neighbor Scott, the zen flooring salesman, for instance; the winter Conant went missing he decided to scale our humble mountain in a straight line, through whichever yards happened to be in his way, using crampons and an ice pick and thinking of John Cheever's "The Swimmer." A wandering Jew, he called himself. And sometime after Conant paddled on toward Florida, I started noticing, near one of the marinas down the street, another time traveler: a man wearing a feathered slouch hat marching around with an antique sword. Conant had found him, too, it turned out: Captain Jack D'Amico, of the 39th New York Infantry, the so-called Garibaldi Guard, a Civil War reenacting outfit. I didn't recognize him as the owner of an Italian cafe in town where I'd once eaten, but Conant saved his business card, on the back of which he jotted down some of D'Amico's cautionary last words: "Be careful in Camden."

Above my desk at home I hung a blank map of the United States, on which I traced Conant's paddling routes—lightning bolts of exploration enlivening a vast white spread, as opposed to the veins and arteries of blue highways and interstates, or the

Mondrianish abstractions of railroad tracks. They showed a slight eastward trajectory over twenty years, a gradual homecoming, beginning in Idaho. In idle moments, between calls, I'd look out the window at the broad Hudson, where barges slid back and forth in the distant channel, and I'd start to think of our village of Piermont less as a satellite of the enormous economic engine downstream than as part of a network of hundreds of small towns in an inside-out riparian nation: the United Riverbanks of Conant. Forget St. Louis and Pittsburgh and Memphis. Bring on Gallipolis and Old Shawneetown and Prairie du Chien and Emlenton and Soddy Daisy and Demopolis and Muscatine, the "Pearl Button Capital of the World!"

My trip to Bozeman had convinced me that, for all practical purposes, the man I and so many other admirers had met didn't really live so much as hibernate there. His proper home was the river town writ large, whichever port he happened to be nearest. Some he just passed through, taking advantage of their grocery stores and post offices. But in others he briefly settled, embedding in civic institutions and attending parades and even birthday parties, like a local. Church, too, no matter the denomination: "It's a good thing to feel sanctified once in a while," he wrote. From what I could tell, he never attended church in Bozeman.

On my map, near the top of a thickened line where three routes overlapped, I drew a star to mark what I thought of as the capital, a place I felt compelled to see for myself. This was Caruthersville, the seat of the Missouri county of Pemiscot, a Native American word for "liquid mud." The British author Jonathan Raban stopped there in 1979, while piloting an aluminum motorboat down the Mississippi, in a kind of Tocquevillean effort to assess the American project. In *Old Glory,* he described Caruthersville as "a muddy un-place," and a "fly-blown town," and joked that it "would have made a perfect, oppressive setting for Emma Bovary." He departed Caruthersville, he wrote, "with a great many questions unanswered and a happy disinclination to pursue them further."

Conant had no such misgivings. "I ended up staying three weeks!" he told me of his most recent visit. "Ha ha, yeah. Because I fell in love with the town—and the people accepted me. They enjoyed my stories. They enjoyed having me around."

. . .

Contra Raban, I found Caruthersville clean, if empty in a familiar way, with vacant storefronts beneath the well-preserved brick facades in the central district, amid vintage lampposts and brushed-steel stop signs. Pharmacies and package stores predominated on the perimeter, along with advertisements for bail bondsmen ("Freedom lost, call Moss") and spiritual solace ("A day outlined in prayer is less likely to unravel"). In a park by the river, I met a pair of heavily made-up women, who were gesticulating and speaking in an agitated staccato—evidence of "a certain diet plan in this area that's not good for your teeth," as one resident later put it. One of the women told me, "I still remember when the presidential yacht stopped at our dock." A cantilever bridge connects Caruthersville with Dyersburg, Tennessee, providing the only river crossing between the confluence with the Ohio, at Cairo, and Memphis. Thanks to frequent flooding, the soil makes for good farming, the primary local industry. The population peaked at around 8,600 in the postwar years and was now inching below 6,000.

Woody's Lounge, a low-slung roadhouse of white-painted cinder blocks, was about half a mile northwest of the park, on the way to Hayti ("Heart of the Heartland," according to the water tower). The bar backed up to an earthen levee, which loomed up like a tidal wave. Beneath a tin awning, a forbidding solid black door seemed to contradict the graffiti scrawled above it, amid cracks in the cement: "Hello all WELCOME here." A couple of yellow signs were bolted to the door. One read "Fallout Shelter" and the other read "Chemical Goggles Required." A painted arrow pointed down to a sticker proclaiming a "Four Tooth Minimum." Inside, dozens of bras, caps, and underpants hung from beams in the low ceiling, or from cardboard that had been fashioned into acoustic tiles which were themselves covered in graffiti. An urn containing the ashes of a regular named Red sat on a shelf behind the bar. Even without goggles, the dust-filtered light was strangely inviting, in the manner of an old photograph.

Tommy Woods, a.k.a. Woody, stood near the door with a customer named Rex Moore, who wore a ball cap, a T-shirt, and track pants. Woods had a white beard, glasses, and a slightly professorial mien. He boasted of having been in the *Guinness Book of Records*. "We had a softball team, Woody's Winos," he said.

"Lost the most consecutive games," Moore said.

"Lost ninety-two in a row!"

If Caruthersville was a fairly generic representation of postindustrial decline, Woody's was its bulwark against anonymity: a triumphant refuge of misfits, whom Conant likened to the protagonists of Steinbeck's *Cannery Row*. Recalling Conant's first appearance, in the fall of 2009, Woods said, "It was raining like hell that day. He was scared he was going to get the place wet. Had a big backpack—he looked like Moses standing there in the door. I thought, Who in the hell is *this* guy?"

"You got to figure how many people we've seen come off that river," Moore said.

"I get so many people, I'm thinking about putting signs on the river north of here, saying, 'Woody's Lounge, 25 miles.'"

A couple of weeks before my arrival, as it happened, a man from Yosemite had passed through town on a bucket-list quest:

smoking legal weed in Colorado, sailing in the Caribbean, and so on. In Caruthersville, he'd been set up with a chance to drive a tractor.

"I wish that was my goal in life: to drive a damn tractor," Moore said. *"Shit."* A faded sticker near the foot of the door, behind him, advertised Moore Flying, Inc., a defunct crop-dusting service owned by his father, who died in a plane crash. Rex worked for a barge manufacturer, and described a favorite pastime of some of his colleagues. It involved an outboard motor, a six-pack, a pump shotgun, and the river's seemingly endless invasion of Asian carp, which have a predilection for leaping out of the water in unison. "Nobody cares how many you kill, because they're destroying the ecosystem," he said.

Conant, typically, had been embraced at Woody's as something other than a tourist. MaryBeth Johnson, Woody's daughter, came in after her son's baseball practice, and joined in the reminiscing. "He was married at one point?" she said. "I can't remember. Or there was a woman. He never said she was his wife. He just said her name."

"Tracy?" I asked.

"That's it," Moore said.

Most nights, Conant camped inside the crumbling remains of an aluminum boat shed between the Bunge grain refinery and the *Lady Luck* casino boat, the town's two most prominent institutions. He spent his days walking through freshly harvested soybean fields or smoking cigarettes atop the levee and watching children roll down the hill. He was an occasional adjunct to the Hole in the Wall Gang, a group of retired men (Bill, Jack, "Joe the Mayor," Curtis) who assembled regularly at a break in the floodwall to bullshit. He befriended a former Green Beret and his pit bull, Thor. And he commuted in the evenings to Woody's, where, as Moore put it, "We would sit here and talk for hours and hours"—about the Asian carp (one of which had struck Conant's forearm while hurtling over his canoe), or the Obama administration (Moore was against, Conant for), or the puzzling (to Conant) endurance of the song "Bohemian Rhapsody," or about Conant's experiences elsewhere. On a couple of foul-weather occasions, Woods encouraged Conant to sleep on the bar's tufted leather banquettes, after closing. It was a level of trust he'd never extended to anyone before, or since. "And when I come to open up in the morning, he'd have the place swept clean," Woods said.

After Conant finally paddled on, one of Moore's friends peeked inside the boat shed and noticed makeshift furniture—a bunk, a chair—assembled from driftwood. "He had the place kitted out," Moore said. "He was like MacGyver!"

Conant left several boxes of his documentation with acquaintances he'd made while in town, to lighten his load, and promised that he'd send for them later. "He said, 'You all can open it up and look if you want,' and I said, 'No, it's not mine,'" Moore recalled. "He said, 'Well, I don't mind.' Though he had it taped up real good."

Conant called the gang at the bar a couple of times from pay phones farther downriver in the weeks that followed, reminiscing about the Halloween party, and sharing delight at the news of MaryBeth's engagement to the man who had been dressed as an Oscar Mayer wiener. But then came months of silence. "I tried to track him down on the internet for a long time," Moore said. "I didn't know if he'd drowned or something. I didn't know what to do. Figured I'll just keep the box and hope he's still alive. Then one day I get a letter."

"He wrote me a letter," Woods added. "One of the nicest letters I ever got from anybody."

Moore mailed the material Conant had left with him back to

the letter's return address, a P.O. box in Bozeman, and Conant responded by asking how much he owed Moore for postage.

The letters he sent had included photocopied pages of his journal, describing his impressions and interactions at Woody's. Moore stowed the journal pages in a locked safe. He had them in hand now, as I stood with him by the bar, drinking a can of Budweiser that the bartender would soon crumple and toss underneath the pool table, to be swept up at the end of the night. He started reading aloud:

> Rex mentioned that I was well liked by everyone and that they were sad to see me go. I said it was hard for me to accept rise of river and my extended stay, but that due to the warm friendship shown me, it was even harder to leave. He repeated that Caruthersville was a small dying river town. Now devoid of a former busy industrial base, the only thing they had to offer was friendship. I told him it was the most important thing in life.

. . .

The existence of people like Woody and Rex, who had feared the worst before hearing from him again, out of the blue, or like Homer Shrum, who was shocked to find Conant in his yard in Columbus, several months after saying goodbye, introduced a tantalizing hint of you-never-know about his current status and whereabouts that offset the poignancy of reckoning with a man who craves friendship but can't seem to maintain it. What's more, the mere mention of Conant's name was like a social lubricant, a fast track to making unlikely new friends of my own. Free plane tickets, moonshine, an apartment in New Orleans, a cabin on the James: these were all offered to me, no strings attached, for the simple reason that I'd inquired about a mysterious man who meant something different to each person he met. In a Louisiana crabbing town, a taxidermist grabbed a large framed photograph—of crawfish and blue-claws—off his wall, and handed it to me, insistent, like it was perfectly natural to share your home décor with out-of-town visitors. When I started to wonder aloud how I'd get it home, intact, on an airplane, his neighbor, another Conant fan, spurred into action, instructing me to follow him to a hardware store, where he enlisted the help of two employees in assembling a padded box, using materials that required a forklift to extract. "Old Dick, he wasn't afraid of nothing!" the friend said.

The residual generosity was intoxicating, a welcome counterbalance to the sometimes tearful calls and letters, and not a little guilt-inducing, in that I was reaping the rewards of someone else's stupendous exertion. My wife, I'm sorry to report, hasn't found a wall in our house worthy of the crustacean photo, so it remains in the padded box, in the basement. (Sorry, Wayne!) In a way, though, that feels appropriate, because the most lasting image from my visit to the taxidermist's place is not of the upturned gator paw ("I made this for a lady to have a party—she can put a plate on it," he said) but of the muscle car stashed in the back of his corrugated, rust-colored garage, unused for years if not decades. It's a '68 Camaro, painted gray, with a white stripe across the front of the hood. From reading Conant, I knew that it had just five thousand miles on the odometer. "California's the only trip I made," the proud owner told me. "I went in 1970. I took my momma and my girlfriend. I showed it at World of Wheels." But for a flat front left tire, it looked impeccable—lovingly cared for as a symbol of possibility, or an embodied memory, rather than a functioning vehicle. A gearhead's canoe. The framed photo and the Camaro both belong to the Walter Mittyverse, accessible only to those in the know.

Where possible, within the bounds of politeness, I declined most gifts, though I couldn't resist the temptation to take Roger Larsen up on his offer of bringing me out on the unsung Tombigbee, knowledge of which had become, in my expanding riparian mind, the mark separating a true river buff from a pretender, someone who knows from Hannibal, Missouri, and guided whitewater bliss, but not the full, gritty sweep. Larsen seemed eager to atone for the missed connection, and provided another, arguably more sympathy-inducing, excuse: overwork. He wasn't just a reporter, I learned, but the founding editor and publisher of the *Columbus Packet*, Mississippi's biggest weekly. And he wasn't just the editor and publisher; he was virtually its sole contributor. Or he *had* been; he told me that he sold the paper a few months after meeting Conant, because the physical strain was getting to be too great. He was nearly sixty by then, and had gone fifteen years without a vacation or a full night of sleep, so intense was his addiction to the police scanner.

He hadn't intended it that way. As a wandering arriviste, Larsen was taken with all of the old families in Columbus whose local roots extended back generations, and he started the paper—printing restaurant advertisements in exchange for free plates of spaghetti—as an outsider's social chronicle, after the established daily ceased printing his letters to the editor. By his own account, at least, he had a soft spot for weddings and animals—" 'Alligator Crosses Highway' or something? People *love* that stuff." But the demands of a weekly publishing schedule necessitated something more reliable than gators. I noticed five mutts inside a heavy-duty cage mounted over the bed of his pickup, down from a dozen in Conant's manuscript. They were strays, he explained, who had served as a security detail, emboldening him to affect the manner of a "cold-blooded reptile" when facing down the relatives of scofflaws who pleaded for leniency in his coverage of crime scenes. He no longer had any need to collect them.

Larsen wore a cap that read "Fuhgetaboutit" and was Conant's physical opposite: reedy, muted. The sale of the *Packet* netted him a quarter of a million dollars, but it wasn't apparent that he'd found much to spend it on. He was living in the old beauty parlor on lawyers' row, which looked like a personal gut-reno that had long since stalled, with several layers of wall exposed. He brought me to his "wood shop," in an abandoned marble factory near the train tracks. Amid scattered cat shit and lumber and a hundred-pound roll of canvas that he'd rescued from the dump, thinking that he might someday build another kayak, were dozens of dusty bins containing back issues of the *Packet* and other files, including the papers of a deceased local character known as Chief, a cape-wearing railroad attorney. Sheets of styrofoam—to thwart rats—framed an eight-by-twelve office inside which, he told me, he'd done much of his writing and editing and upright napping, with the police scanner still crackling. The whole place felt like a sprawling version of Conant's storage lockers.

I asked to see the issue of the paper that Conant would have read. (He called it "a mass-produced vehicle of schadenfreude for popular consumption.") It was the 868th edition. A tagline beneath the banner of the B section boasted of "more than 10,000 copies sold each week." (Columbus has a population of about 23,000.) The masthead named only two other individuals—a woman who helped with advertising and circulation, and a man who helped with "news"—and by my rough count Larsen produced 80 percent of the copy himself, some twenty or more articles, not to mention supplying the majority of the photographs. It was a solo river trip of weekly journalism.

Everyone in Columbus seemed to know Larsen, even the clerk

at a deli where we stopped to buy soda, which made it all the more unusual that after four decades he hadn't told anyone in his adopted town about the formative experience that he began sharing with me. This was in Mobile, the winter before he washed up in Columbus. He was crashing in a flophouse by the waterfront. His upstairs neighbor, a mustachioed middle-aged man who went by Sam Slater, spoke a dozen languages but seemed to have no money, and once, while the two of them were observing a Mardi Gras celebration, Larsen noticed him ducking a camera crew, as if in hiding. They spent dozens of hours together, during which Slater gradually unspooled alluring details about his past: that he had escaped Auschwitz; that his mother had been involved in the establishment of the UN; that he had lived on an island off of Veracruz, and in China, where he was briefly married; that he had taught in college and published several books (in French), including a best seller, *Tanguy*. Slater's room was full of notebooks that he'd kept from his extensive travels, recording basic facts like the cost of bus fare—for verisimilitude in his writing, he said.

"His mind, experience, imagination and good will were so vast," Larsen later wrote me. "Though everything didn't always add up." Larsen likened himself to "Huck Finn listening to the Duke and the Dauphin"—or Dick Conant and Homer Shrum, perhaps. Still, he'd found great solace in the notion that such a learned and warm-spirited man could be hiding out in a backwater, as he felt *he* was. Two lonely citizens in what he would later come to know as the State of Riverbank. "He said once that the most important thing in life is love—and it didn't sound like a cliché," Larsen wrote. "He was not a happy man but had gravitas. Spending time with him helped steady me and gave me a new role model and much to think about."

Larsen's eventual departure from Mobile after a couple of months devastated Slater, who, fighting tears, made reference to "jockstrap Kansas," implying that for Larsen to return home and settle would be tantamount to conceding defeat in a life that still held such promise. The mentor's parting advice to his disciple was, "You have nothing to do, my boy, but read."

In effect, Larsen had gone on to do just that, abandoning his travels at his next stop and thereafter seeking adventure in his woodworking clients' libraries: Casanova, Cellini ("He has more adventures on each page than the rest of us will have in a lifetime"), Waukendaw Chip. He tried writing a letter to Slater, with no response, and twice returned to Mobile, where he could find no trace of his multilingual friend. With time and distance, it all came to seem too implausible, the incongruities outweighing the emotional import, stripped of context. He'd been left feeling a little like the steelworker Homer Shrum, who longed for a picture of Dick Conant, something tangible to show disbelieving friends, lest an indelible experience fade into irrelevance.

·   ·   ·

I sometimes couldn't tell, with Larsen, if *I* was the one being had. "You can look Sam up on the internet," he told me at one point, by which he meant: you can look up Michel del Castillo, the actual author of the best-selling *Tanguy,* and a celebrated man of French letters. Photos of Castillo he'd seen online resembled his memory of Slater, adjusting for age and shorn mustache. By the time Google was invented, making such a comparison feasible for a man living in a midsize Mississippi river town, Larsen had lost the will to reconnect; he was too ensconced in his newspaper life—sleep-addled, deadline-delirious. But, inspired by Conant's example, he seemed now to be inviting me to pursue the lead, at the risk of ruining a fantastical tale.

On the one hand, what difference did it make? But then, taking to heart Conant's advice that the pleasure in a long river trip often comes from digressions up tributaries and sloughs, discovery for its own sake, I found a literary translator in Paris who was said to be friends with Castillo, now in his eighties, and tried to convey the gist of an absurd question: *S'il est possible que Michel del Castillo ait passé quelque temps à Mobile, en Alabama, en 1975, en utilisant le pseudonyme de Sam Slater?* My French wasn't good enough, I feared, to bolster the personal intrusion with the disarming context it deserved: that the man positing this wasn't an obvious fabulist but a successful journalist who hadn't been credulous enough to trust the true stories of a canoeing Santa; that he felt, in a sense, that he owed whatever success he'd achieved to his belief in her friend.

The translator replied at first to say that her friend had had a stroke, and struggled to speak, but she knew that he had traveled a fair amount in the seventies for a French magazine, so it wasn't beyond the realm of consideration. She later followed up to say that she was able to glean from him that he had never been to Mobile—and also that he became aware, in the nineteen-nineties, that another man was impersonating him.

Inconclusive.

My exchanges with Larsen grew to resemble his recounted conversations with Slater, as he gradually revealed more exotic interests and pursuits. For instance: "Three years ago in the ravine behind my shop, south of the railroad tracks, I built a ¾-scale device to raise stones up the face of an Egyptian pyramid." Whoa. He explained that he had long considered the question of how the pyramids were built one of the world's great technological mysteries, and now that he was no longer putting out the paper he had more time to devote to its solution, which he believed lay in Isis knots and slotted levers resembling djed pillars. That note, at least, came with a YouTube link that proved it true: not only was his handmade device, which looked like a giant wooden rowing machine, capable of lifting weighted sleds up the face of a cliff, but there were other perfectly normal-looking people in the frame, evidently indulging Larsen's enthusiasm. "The Egyptology community is heavily invested in other theories, but maybe some professors will give it some thought," he said, and added, "I realize that claiming to have solved such a mystery is like claiming to have created a perpetual-motion machine—it puts me in the kook category."

I shared my growing sense of the similarities between Larsen and Conant, and of the shame it seemed that they had intersected at wrong angles and failed to appreciate one another, in a phone call with the Columbus police officer from North Dakota. "He's even more like him than you know," the officer agreed, and told me that Larsen had recently pedaled his bicycle to Colorado and back.

Larsen confirmed it. He'd added a rack and panniers to his bike, and wore a long-sleeve white cotton shirt, unbuttoned, and affixed a cotton drape to the back of his helmet, as a sun shield for his ears and neck. It was August, and he averaged nearly 150 miles a day, in spite of a heat dome on the Great Plains that sent temperatures soaring intro triple digits (105 in Texarkana, 108 in Coalgate, Oklahoma, 110 in Kiowa, Kansas). He paid a surprise visit to his old college friend with whom he'd once dreamed of floating the Missouri and then prospected in the Rockies. Crazy Fred, to his frat brothers, was now a professional fossil hunter and had since "found the buried treasure," as Larsen put it, in the form of rare dinosaur bones, which he'd managed to sell for millions. "He is pretty well known in T-Rex circles."

·   ·   ·

I'd arguably been on a treasure hunt myself ever since arriving at Osterman's, in Bozeman, and was now amassing nuggets with every vivid detail, each less believable than the last. The Yale-educated polar adventurer Colin O'Brady has spoken of his driving passion "to add one more grain of sand to human achievement," but to my mind the unscripted social elements of Conant's voyages were more meaningful than any strictly solitary endeavor, and more human. In that spirit, I had come to think of Roger Larsen, with his recommendation of "The State of River-bank," as a little like the NASA engineer who delivered Conant over the mountains: an unforeseen collaborator, guiding me back to the water.

Around the corner from the old marble plant–cum–woodshop, Larsen and I wandered into another warehouse, where a man named Glenn Miller stood working on an outboard motor, dressed in a plaid shirt and denim overalls, with a cotter pin in his teeth. He didn't bother looking up for at least a minute or two. (Larsen's presence was so ubiquitous and untiring, I sensed, that few people hastened to acknowledge it.) Then, upon learning that I had come from New York, he mentioned that he'd been mean-ing to visit, because he had a family heirloom that he wanted to get appraised at Sotheby's. It was a playbook of *Marionettes,* written in longhand by William Faulkner when he was still in college. "There's only five of them," Miller said, grinning. He also said that he'd attended a church service the weekend before where the preacher was Tim Tebow. Larsen told me that Miller's father had recently celebrated his eighty-fifth birthday by skiing barefoot on the river.

Just like that, it seemed, I had slid into a riverbank social life as Conant experienced it, full of novelty so matter-of-fact that you had to stop and wonder when and how the rest of us had ceased paying attention to one another's extra-professional interests. Did it require the intrusion of an outsider to draw people out of their workaday shells? We ate dinner at Zachary's, a bar where Conant had sung karaoke with Homer Shrum and friends, who alternated between calling their unusual guest the Commodore and, in less charitable moments, the River Bum. ("It stung when they laughed at this demeaning reference," Conant wrote. "I laughed along.") A decorous white-haired man sauntered in with his wife not long after we'd sat down. Larsen addressed him as Vee, short for Verell Pennington Ferguson IV. Between theatrical doffs of his fedora, Vee confirmed that he was Faulkner's *godson*. His father, V.P., was the original Mississippi beatnik, kicked out of Ole Miss, where he roomed with the jazz pianist Mose Allison, for growing marijuana in the dorm. Vee married into another prominent clan, the Laws family. They owned a large swath of riverfront land that Larsen and I admired the next day from a pontoon boat. Known as Laws Shoals, the family acreage hosted professional water skiing shows in the fifties and sixties, run by an organization called the Tombigbee Stump Jumpers.

The Tombigbee had changed a great deal since then, from a "picturesque if unremarkable river, meandering lazily through the poor cotton fields and depressed rural landscape," as *The New York Times* once described it, to a major shipping conduit—the Tenn-Tom Waterway—connecting the Tennessee River to the port of Mobile. The conversion required an earth-moving project as extensive as the digging of the Panama and Suez canals combined—a hundred million dump trucks' worth of dirt, excavated over a fifteen-year period ending in 1985.

Tombigbee is a Choctaw word, meaning "coffin maker," a reference to a French settler who lived at the headwaters, in the eighteenth century, and floated wooden boxes full of furs downriver, to trade. Those headwaters, in eastern Mississippi, were separated by thirty miles, and a rocky ridge of Appalachian foothills, from the Tennessee as it turned north to meet the Ohio at Paducah. Enter the Army Corps, and a hunger for congressional pork, and you've now got a canal, twelve feet deep and as wide as a football field, connecting the two, as well as a series of eleven locks and dams managing the flow southward into Alabama. The whole town of Holcut, Mississippi, with its shirt factory and several dozen houses, was sacrificed to the cause of ensuring that the river would be traversable at all times, even in summer, by something larger than a rowboat.

The pontoon boat belonged to Stuart Phillips, a third-generation Columbus contractor and barge owner who lives on "the island," as it's called, a harp-shaped piece of swampland created by an oxbow in the original river course, on the east side, and by the dredging of a straight shipping channel, to bypass the oxbow, on the west, as part of the Tenn-Tom project. His next-door neighbor, whom Phillips called "the second-most interesting person in Columbus," is the owner of a boat named *Cirrhosis of the River* and known locally as the Redneck Doctor. "Best doctor in town," Phillips said. "A *doctor's* doctor. He has his own slot machines and a condom dispenser, too."

The first-most interesting person was Roger Larsen.

Phillips stood six feet seven, and possessed what he described as a "muscle gut," or the early stages of a yeasty bloat that hadn't yet gone soft. He told a Conant-like story about picking up Mrs. World 1988, a Mississippi resident who happened to be dating his childhood friend, an hour and a half downriver, and ferrying her back to Columbus in an unrelenting rainstorm, while consuming more than a dozen beers, for courage, as the former beauty queen crouched behind him, sobbing. He considered himself one of only a handful of people capable of navigating the river under such conditions, and second in line, after Vee Ferguson, to the unofficial Tombigbee throne held by a local "river legend" named Buster. "Lakes don't work for me," he said. "You can't *go* anywhere."

The yards of some of the homes on the island revealed mud scars, a reminder of frequent flooding. "When the water's up, it looks like the damn Mississippi," Phillips said. One such yard belonged to a woman named Sadie who used to sit on her porch with a shotgun, to police the "No Wake" signs along the oxbow.

The Corps-straightened river resembled chocolate milk, and was only an eighth of a mile wide, if that, in most places, flanked on either side by dense tree cover. Barges were parked on this or that bank, in clusters, and we passed a couple of active tugs, but the more lasting impression was left by three bald eagles and a swarm of buzzards over an armadillo carcass. Eventually, heading north, we came upon a massive dam, which was releasing enough water to create trails of foam, and the illusion of remoteness was shattered once again. Beside it was a lock with a lift of nearly thirty feet—loose change, when compared with the northernmost lock on the system, which rises eighty-four feet to connect with the Tennessee, but still a daunting and slightly comic sight when trying to picture oneself approaching in an overloaded canoe.

Back on land, and in need of refreshment, I stopped in at the River Hill convenience mart, the site of Conant's near miss with law enforcement. It was across the street from the visitors' center, a handsome Victorian where Tennessee Williams was born, and where, ninety-nine years later, Roger Larsen interviewed Dick Conant, one American original skeptically regarding another. Inside the store, the door to the beer cooler in back, I noticed, was ajar.

9

Off the Edge of the World

T he world on my map only grew more mythical the more
I explored, and I sometimes imagined an accompanying
tourist brochure as I continued populating it with landmarks and Riverbank celebrities. For sports fans, we'd highlight
the clothing-optional volleyball games on Pump-Out Island, a
by-product of sporadic efforts to dredge the Ohio River channel at a horseshoe bend north of Henderson, Kentucky, as well
as TugFest, an annual battle for pride between Le Claire, Iowa,
and Port Byron, Illinois. The Mississippi there is a third of a mile
wide, and ever since 1987, the residents of the respective banks
have been assembling on the second Saturday in August to par-
ticipate in a giant game of tug-of-war, using a river-spanning rope
that weighs seven hundred pounds (when dry). The event can
attract enough spectators to fill Fenway Park, five or six times the
combined population of the competing towns. Dropping Dick
Conant's name, I scored an interview with Dave Roete, a thick-
wristed strategist for the Iowa side, a Belichick of the tug pit,
and asked if it was true, as Conant had written, that "vectors and
Newtonian physics" inspired his famous alteration of the team's
angle of approach. Roete sighed. "That's one of those topics we
could talk about forever," he said.

Not to be missed: the fifteen-foot Superman statue in Metropolis, part of the sparsely populated southern Illinois region known as Little Egypt. (Conant noted a discoloration on the left big toe and remarked, "One may rub this patch of shiny bronze and thereby be assured of good luck, great physical strength, long life, x-ray vision and invincibility.") Then, while still on the folk-hero theme, there's Popeye overlooking the American Nile, in Chester. And speaking of Egypt, let's add Roger Larsen's pyramid-building contraption by the Tombigbee—which also features a modern Stonehenge, in the form of a red phone booth perched unaccountably on a wooded bank. I learned about it not from Conant (did he somehow *miss* it?) but from a sailor named Dave, who, in Pickensville, Alabama, borrowed a van from a woman named Star in order to give Conant a ride to the grocery store. Dave sometimes also goes by Sam, so I'll stick with his last name, Groce. "I think he wanted a couple cigars," Groce recalled. "'Yeah, dude, I can hook you up.' And white bread. He said, 'I'm craving white bread.'"

Groce told me that he was "raised by hillbilly bikers in a freaking junkyard," in Albuquerque, and graduated high school four years early. He did underwater demolition in the navy, and later spent time in a Nevada prison, during which his heroism fighting a wildfire earned him a governor's pardon. ("Dave has an interesting story," Conant wrote.) He supervised construction in the Argentine jungle and dealt in AstroTurf domestically. He was married twice, to the same woman. "I think relationships are sort of fleeting things," he said. "Our youngest son is actually two months younger than our youngest grandson. My oldest daughter is a pediatric surgical nurse."

Conant and Groce shared a fondness for Louis L'Amour. When they met, Groce was notionally on his way to the Dominican Republic, by sailboat, to build an orphanage. "I've got to do something worthwhile with my life," he told Conant. But he never made it to the Caribbean, and I found him still in Alabama, ten or eleven miles from the sleepy marina in Pickensville. A man whose business card identified him as "The Pirate" drew me a map that included no street names, and after half an hour, and some wrong turns, I arrived at a dirt driveway with some trailers parked next to a tin shed and a leaning refrigerator. Riverbank Gothic. Groce exited the nearest trailer, leaving behind a pair of Chihuahuas that he credited with charming some dolphins that had once followed his boat for twenty miles, occasionally tail-walking. (He theorized that they'd been liberated from show business by Hurricane Katrina.) "I had a heart attack, and open-heart surgery," he said, by way of explaining his abandonment of the Dominican mission. "I worry about stuff way too much."

Groce wore a Hawaiian shirt, unbuttoned at the top, and had shoulder-length dark hair that was halfway to gray. He giggled sporadically like a teenager, and lapsed into reminiscence of his life aquatic, which he had since traded for tinkering with motorcycles. "Whatever catfish I caught in the morning, that was breakfast. And if you ain't ever had fresh filleted catfish in the morning for breakfast, on the river? I mean, you pull the thing out clean and cook it right there. Little bit of grits. Just sit back, and, '*Man*, this is pretty. I don't want to leave.' So you jump into the little boat and just go exploring. I got a little Boston Whaler, a thirteen-footer. And the things you'll see, in the middle of what looks like nowhere! I seen a telephone booth on the bank. I actually dropped anchor. There was a guy riding an ATV. He says, 'Go ahead, man, you can make a call.' If it hadn't been nailed down, I probably would have figured out how to get it in my damn boat."

Returning to Conant, Groce recalled the canoeist's arrival at the marina, and the Pirate's dismissive reaction: "Oh, crap, look at this bum."

"I said, 'You don't know his story,'" Groce went on. "'How can you call somebody a bum until you sit back and listen to what they been through?' I've met people, you look at 'em, they're wearing a suit jacket and a pair of khaki pants, but when you get to talking, the dude has lost his entire world, family killed in a train wreck, and has lost the will to continue. I said, 'That right there'"—referring once more to Conant—"'is a man that *knows* what he wants to do with his life.'"

He giggled and added, "For lack of better words, he had pioneer spirit. He was a throwback. He was living in the wrong age."

.   .   .

I sought out the smallest town Conant ever visited, defining town for this purpose as a settlement with at least two of the five institutions (grocery, bar, church, library, post office) Conant relied on for emotional and practical sustenance. New Amsterdam, Indiana, had a small urban grid with a church and a general store, both built in the nineteenth century, and thirteen residents, one of whom rode up to Conant on a quad in 2007 while out looking for her husband, Fuzzy. Her name was Faye Shaffer, and the store, a former Odd Fellows hall with a mason jar collecting dust atop the unlocked ice chest out front, was hers. Its hours seemed to be fungible, determined by the needs of the neighbors.

Both Faye and Fuzzy had died by the time I made it to New Amsterdam, brandishing a copy of Conant's second manuscript, and Shaffer's General Store looked abandoned, along with many other dilapidated structures that gave the place the feel of a ghost town, in early morning light, with only the grinding rumble of a tug pushing pallets upriver to disrupt the eerie stillness. You'll have to take my word for it, given our interest in suspending disbelief, that I showed up without any advance contact or warning, only to learn from a carpenter who insisted on giving me a

T-shirt bearing his surname, McCullum, that the population had ticked upward by one that very week. "We got a traveling artist," McCullum said, greeting me on his sagging front porch. "I don't know his name or nothing. But I visited with him a couple of times down at the landing, and he didn't seem too strange. He's about like your guy." The artist had apparently pitched a tent "in Pat's barn," on the side of which he was now painting a mural.

McCullum was also the "mayor," or the president of the town board. He had impressed Conant with a picture of a record-setting eighty-two-pound catfish, and looked pleased to see that fact committed to print. He summoned his son and asked me to read the brief New Amsterdam entry aloud, as a teachable moment. The son was in elementary school. Conant had referred to McCullum's toddler in passing. "That's you!" McCullum said. The kid blushed and then ran across the street, to the Method-ist church, for an Easter egg hunt. This wasn't the first time I'd noticed the slightly aggrandizing effect Conant's writing could elicit. The fact that the pages in question were in private circula-tion only enhanced their power, however plain their observations. From New Amsterdam to Bozeman to New York, and back. It made anything seem possible.

"Most places don't ever see these people," McCullum said. "Alaska gets a lot of them, I think. And we in the river towns get them, too."

. . .

I'd noticed the mural while driving into town, but hadn't real-ized that it was a work in progress. There were wavy blue and green stripes across the barn's corrugated white siding. Big black block letters above the stripes read "Est. 1815 New Amsterdam." The barn was at the edge of some woods, down a short hill from an unbounded cemetery with enough tombstones to recall more populous days. Sure enough, on my way out, while looking more carefully, I saw a stepladder and a man with a brush, nearly obscured by shadow.

He was thickly built, with a white goatee, and wore a dark argyle sweater, jeans with a wallet chain, and a black beret. "This ain't really large-scale, compared to what I usually do," he said, backing away from some giant sunflowers that he'd begun painting on a side of the barn that faced the tombstones. "I painted a little bit of everywhere, a little bit of everything." He rattled off a list of more cosmopolitan places: San Diego, Birmingham, New Orleans. France, England, Belgium. "Lived in Florida a few times. Man, that's changed. Florida's not the same place no more. Everything's got commercial and plastic—all manufactured. Out here, not so."

His name was Kevin Tipton. He lacked a vehicle, and New Amsterdam, he said, was "just where I ended up," by which he meant that Pat, the owner of the barn, had admired a mural he was painting in Mauckport, a town seven or eight miles upriver, and offered him a ride, some more painting supplies, and some money. "It's like a marriage," Tipton said. "I got to keep my wife happy, and when I'm done with it, then I'm fickle. I have to divorce her and go to another woman—another mural—and do it again."

Tipton was born in Ohio. ("But all my family's in Kentucky, up in the mountains. Big long valley. It's a gorge, got hundreds of arches.") He was married once, to his high school sweetheart, but the relationship didn't survive a four-year stint in the navy. When he got out, he couldn't find steady work. "For about a year there, I went through about twenty jobs," he said. "Kept getting fired. 'What's going on here? I can't do nothing.' Said, 'I'll just start painting.' I was a portrait artist for three years, and then decided to go big-time, and go to L.A. I lived in a van—this is the early eighties—and then all my paintings got ripped off. I got kind of distraught and moved to Phoenix, and was talking to somebody in a coffee shop, and they said, 'Well, you need to just paint a mural. It'd be pretty hard for them to steal a mural.' I said, 'You're right!' And that's how I started painting murals. Been at it ever since."

Murals, like antiques stores, are not uncommon in old towns, of course. The floodwall in Cape Girardeau, where Conant befriended a waitress who made him feel alive again after his grueling bout with dysentery on a flooding towhead, features two dozen colorful panels depicting the history of the bootheel across a span of more than a thousand feet, an Empire State Building's worth of public art. A man named Robert Dafford ("and his assistants," Conant noted) has painted murals commissioned on walls and levees up and down the Ohio: Paducah, Maysville, Portsmouth. I think of him as the muralist equivalent of river-running expedition athletes with their branded websites, compared with Tipton, like Conant a lone wolf leaving his mark by happenstance. Conant took some pictures of Dafford's "impressive" work, "but I couldn't help wondering how long these paintings will survive," he wrote. "They are totally exposed to the elements and a major flood could really do a number on the compositions facing the river."

Here, I thought, Tipton may have had an inadvertent edge. Pat's barn faced away from the water and could only be admired by people who took the time to visit the town, not passersby. Another buried treasure. "They don't last forever, but they last a while," Tipton said of his murals.

Turning his attention back to the barn and the work at hand, he explained that the blue and green stripes were the beginnings of a river scene that would eventually include a couple of Native Americans, a black dog, and a canoe. Depending on the weather, he thought he might be finished by the end of the following week, and then he'd probably "go up in the woods for a month or two, and come back out."

He added, "I'm not real big on big cities anymore. It's like they try to capture you and suck the life out of you. Here, people aren't perfect, but at least you got a little bit of room to breathe." He smiled, and noted that he'd already met half the population. "This place is a bubble. This place is off the edge of the world."

.   .   .

The little Indiana towns along the Ohio seemed a useful distillation of Conant's cultural landscape. Many of them, like New Amsterdam, had names born of optimism: Bethlehem, Rome, Patriot, Rising Sun. (And then, across from Rising Sun: Rabbit Hash, Kentucky, whose mayor, Conant correctly noted, was "a dog," specifically a black Lab named Junior Cochran. "He apparently made postelection public appearances on the Jay Leno show.") They were settled before Indianapolis, and the trees along their shores built wharves in New Orleans. New Amsterdam, the mayor told me, was once a booming port of four hundred, with brandy distilleries, whorehouses, a jail, and a horse-racing track. Then came the flood of 1937, which removed an entire road and many buildings within five hundred feet of where the bank now lies. The flood, occurring in January, weaponized sheets of ice, and rendered a million Americans homeless. It also made permanent a retreat from the river as a primary artery that had been under way since the introduction of the railroad and, later, the automobile.

I'd gone off the edge of the world in part out of a sense that by continuing Conant's work of linking stories I was keeping his spirit alive, and in part because of another missed connection that seemed almost too unfortunate to be accidental. Between

New Amsterdam and Rome, at the junction of two scenic state roads through the Hoosier National Forest, was another little town which had once produced a cockfighting magazine with a national circulation: the *Derby Game Bird*. Derby still had a roofed landing, a general store, a post office, a handsome little bluff (with church tower), and a lively tavern where, over the course of a few days, Conant got to know members of the dynastic Ramsey and Mogan clans, "die hard" families, as he called them, who had stayed and rebuilt after successive floods in '37, '64, and '97. Old memories, new construction: like a chronic river wanderer who never reuses the same canoe. He appreciated the contrast that the residents' deep roots offered with his own experience, and was intrigued to learn from Billy Mogan at the general store that he had a predecessor. ("The local electrician, Ed Gluck, stopped into town some twenty-odd years ago on his way down river," Conant wrote. "Ed never left. He lives there to this day!")

But not so intrigued that he was eager to *meet* the would-be doppelgänger, whose fuller story could only complicate his fantasy of eventually settling. Conant told Mogan, "I better get going before I end up doing the same thing."

· · ·

"I was sorry I missed him," Ed Gluck said of Conant, taking a seat on the porch of a cabin overlooking the mouth of Oil Creek, where river pirates used to stash their stolen wares, and the placid Ohio, which spanned about a third of a mile to unbroken tree cover in Kentucky. "I remember Billy telling me about him." Gluck removed a cigarette from the crumpled pack in his shirt pocket. He wore light shades and a black trilby, and had a trimmed white beard, which showed faint hints of its former red coloring. He mentioned his new set of teeth. By a coincidence that no longer seemed all that remarkable, he said that the cabin, which I'd rented through an online recommendation, had been the first place he stopped when he floated into Derby, in the spring of 1990. It now belonged to a man named Vinnie, who told me that his last customer, who'd left earlier in the week, was in the process of hiking across the country, to raise awareness of the high rate of suicides among military veterans.

Like the peripatetic muralist, Gluck was originally from Ohio. "I really wasn't any kind of adventurer, like Dick," he said. "I'd spent my whole life with my head inside an electrical panel. I was up on a tower one time, and I seen this goddang bug. And that bug sat there on that rail and looked at me, and I says, 'What are you doing up here?' And it just looked at me, like, 'Well, what are *you* doing?' And so I thought about that, and something snapped in my mind. I threw everything I had away, and left."

His voice warbled a little. "I had a wife and kids," he added. "I wasn't smart enough to go to a doctor and get a pill for panic. I didn't know about that stuff. I just up and left."

Then in his early forties, Gluck was a land rover for a while, hitchhiking and hoofing his way up to Newfoundland and down to Arkansas, with a guitar. "Only tried the rails one time and that was a catastrophe," he said. "I was actually in a suicidal mode, so I thought, Well, I'll just eventually die, that's all right. But suicide doesn't *work* when you got something threatening you. All of a sudden, when you get cold, you want to get warm. You get tired, you want to rest. You get hungry, you want to eat, and you gotta *do* something about it."

Gluck was too proud to beg or rummage through trash. "So I learned how to eat wild stuff," he said. "I ate a lot of clover and dandelions and chickweed, stuff that grew along the roadsides and abandoned buildings." From studying books, in libraries, he learned that you could get vitamin C from pine needles and rose hips. "I also had the problem of coming up with water. I was at the mercy of drinking whatever water there was, even if it was out of a mud puddle. Then I finally figured out: the river! There's fish in the river, there's game alongside the river, and plenty of water. All you got to do is purify it."

He launched a canoe in Akron, on the Tuscarawas, which he then took to the Muskingum, and eventually the Ohio. "I was at a complete loss with the world," he said. "I thought I was making my peace with God. I was going to see everything in a natural way."

Unlike Conant, Gluck saw the rivers as a retreat from town life, rather than as a means of dabbling in it, and he isolated himself on islands as much as possible. "Just me, myself, and animals," he said. "I felt like I was a part of 'em. Felt like the river had my blood, sweat, and tears in it, and I owned it. I was kind of oblivious to the fact that anybody else was around in that river. Because, as far as I could see, they were just *using* it. I was sickened by all the pieces of plastic and junk on the bed, by shiny spots on the tops of hills, empty paint cans. Every time it'd flood, there'd be a pile of trash at the heads of my islands."

The Ohio froze at one point, stranding him on an island without food. He'd brought a shotgun, and he used it to kill a muskrat as it skittered across the ice, but he made the mistake of eating the scent glands, which lent a fecal aftertaste. Then he shot two more, and "made some mittens out of those."

He stopped in Derby because he was exhausted from fighting headwinds that had reduced his progress to a single mile in a day. The first man he approached, the former owner of my cabin, "didn't trust me," he said. So he went on down the road, where he ended up helping another man fix the ignition on his truck. That led to a gig dismantling and relocating "Bill Ramsey's cabin," and before he knew it a month had passed. But his story wasn't quite as tidy and simple as Billy Mogan, at the general store, had led Conant to believe. Gluck found that, just as he was unable to let himself die, he couldn't shake his curiosity about what lay beyond the next bend in the river. So he got back in the canoe.

He was nearly two hundred miles farther along when he became frightened by the sight of a huge storm coming upriver toward him. There were sheer limestone cliffs on the Illinois side, and swamp and brush in Kentucky: nowhere to hide from lightning. Then, forging ahead nervously, he spied a cavity in the cliffs, "big enough that you could drive a school bus into it." This was Cave-in-Rock, a shelter once used by Shawnees and a popular tourist attraction ever since. Conant, when passing the cave in 2007, observed an elderly man in a beret taking pictures of a breast-baring woman near the entrance. ("Woo woo," he wrote.) Gluck reached it just as rain was starting to fall, dampening his cigarettes. He tied the canoe to a scraggly tree limb and clambered up to a covered ledge inside, where he drifted off to sleep—until, at dusk, he was nearly assaulted by hundreds of swarming bats. "I'd never seen anything like it," he said.

Several years passed before he returned to Derby, this time aboard an unsteady catamaran he'd made from two canoes and a platform mounted across, with a mast of found aluminum, and a sail sewn by hand. He had a companion then, "an Indian girl," who had a knack for catching minnows, but no appetite for them, and he had aspirations of ascending the Missouri with her. When they passed through West Virginia, he let slip to some dockwallopers that he'd once been a scab, and "all their union buddies got together and tried to sink me." Later, his girlfriend fell sick and could go no farther. Gluck remembered Derby from his previous layover as a place that was "welcoming of a stranger," as he put it. "We came in sailing, and they happened to all be outside, and they had work, and a place to stay." It felt like fate. "I had my guitar with me, and played almost every weekend at Ramsey's campground, and would sing for 'em."

He'd been adrift at that point for ten years, and soon had a reckoning with his conscience. "Had to pay the fiddler for all my sins," he said. "I knew what I did wrong. I just thought I was going to die—and I survived. So I had to live with the consequences." He got in touch with his estranged wife, who then moved down to the area. "So I had to take care of her," he said. "And her mom had Alzheimer's, and I had to take care of *her*. Next thing, I'm working full-time again, mowing grass, building stuff, and doing electrical work."

He pointed at an adjacent property. "I built that stone wall, as a matter of fact," he said. "I helped build all these places around here. Just about every place in town, I've done some work on, whatever was necessary." The ubiquity of his own handiwork wasn't a source of pride for Gluck so much as a reminder of the steep cost of his wayward adventures. He hadn't finished paying off his back taxes and child support until he was seventy. He was seventy-four now. "Got one foot in the grave," he said. His children—"all pretty successful, but not because of me"—hadn't forgiven him. In spite of his contributions to the community, and the fact that he'd been a fixture for more than twenty years, he still seemed like an outsider. "Everyone's related," he said. "I can never keep it straight."

A whirlybird from a maple tree fluttered down onto the porch table. Gluck grabbed it on instinct and started peeling the outer layers using yellow thumbnails so thick they looked petrified. "These things are nutritious and delicious," he said, popping the seeds into his mouth.

I noticed him driving away—in a red sports car—at a speed that I associate with teenagers, and reflected on his adamancy that suicide was not an option for Conant, particularly with the onset of cool and stormy weather. Once you set yourself in motion, he stressed, self-pity is supplanted by greater urgencies.

10

Classified

"Aw, man, you almost trusted me!" In spite of my having spent months trying to get inside the head of a paranoid river wanderer, the question of trust had slipped my mind. Drafting in Conant's wake, as I've indicated, was a generally charmed experience, one that felt like putting on glasses for the first time and seeing the world anew, with brighter resolution. The man who spooked me was no less enthusiastic about our subject ("He had a way of just ferreting out good people!"), but aware that if I could spare the time and expense to visit him, I could probably also afford to buy him some beer and cigarettes and a bottle of something harder. Not offering gifts but extracting them.

He was in his late forties, still wiry, and wearing a small hoop earring and a newsboy cap. He had his dark hair cinched in a ponytail that hung a third of the way down his back. He was sitting, half pickled, in the passenger seat of my rental car, which was idling outside the office of the eastern Tennessee motel that I'd booked online, back in New York. I'd taken a few steps toward the door before doubling back for the key—or the keychain, really, which had the make and license plate information that I figured I might need to give the clerk while checking in. "I was going to be really touched, man, that you trusted me enough to leave the keys in the car," he went on. His gentle voice offset a slightly feral energy. I must have hesitated for a moment, visualizing the laptop and Conant's invaluable journals stowed in my trunk, because he added, "You realize you're just going to have to drive down to the room, so why not leave the bags here?"

. . .

Our day together had begun with entrancing promise, and I imagined myself as rapt at the unfiltered dialogue of Riverbank's worldly dispossessed as Conant had been while eavesdropping on the patter of tow pilots with his marine radio. Picture a couple of men leaning against the bed of a pickup with more than three hundred thousand miles on the odometer, drinking cans of Natural Light and facing a tributary of the Tennessee River. Eleven in the morning, damp and lush. Unrelated, they refer to one another as Big Brother and Little Brother. Big Brother, in his early sixties, is slightly stooped, wearing dirty sweatpants, glasses, and a camouflage cap. He notices a "blue sparrow," or grosbeak, and comments, "You don't see those anymore." He has a gray mustache and a thin soul patch and a scrunched, sensitive face. "I had some specific things I really wanted to say about Dick," he says. "But I'm so tired right now, I really cannot think." He works third shift at a steel plant, and it's past his bedtime. "Dick understood life. He was my friend, a *good* friend, and I didn't even know him but a week. I mean it. I felt like I'd known him all my life. He was smart—he was extremely intelligent, actually—and somebody I could relate to."

"And just strange enough!" Little Brother, with the ponytail and the latent trust issues, says. "I can't believe he came up the Tombigbee waterway. One hundred and twenty miles of *nothing*." (Guess he hasn't seen the phone booth, either.) Little Brother is now modeling a denim beer koozie with a leather patch that reads "Brew Jeans," and Big Brother urges him to be more discreet, because "Daddy," who is eighty-five, could be driving down the dirt road any minute.

Little Brother likes to joke that he grew up in "L.A.," meaning Lower Alabama. "On a pot farm, that's how we got my dad through college," he explains. "By the time I was eight, my job was to go out and clean up all the sucker leaves, and to sex the plants. 'Hey, we got two males coming up on row No. 5, and need to get them out of there.'" He later moved to New York City, and discovered motorcycles and punk rock. He got his welding certification at eighteen. Then he fell off a scaffold rig, quit welding, joined the military, and became a sniper. "I had eight perfect kills," he says. "The best shot I ever made was a thousand and thirty yards—over three thousand feet—and I had nine and a half foot of drop and twelve and a half foot of windage. I caught him right in the bridge of the nose." He turns to Big Brother and asks, "Can I tell him about the last one?"

"No."

"Listen, he wants to know. This is classified. I mean, no-shit classified."

"South America," Big Brother says.

"And I don't know where in South America. They wouldn't tell me. All I got was a grid map. Here's your drop zone, here's your target—"

"Thrown out of a helicopter."

"—here's your pickup zone. You don't know what country you're in. You could be in Ecuador. You could be anywhere. This was during the end of the Reagan administration and the War on Drugs, so we're taking out drug kingpins. Now, what they didn't recognize at the time was that for every head honcho you knock off, there's fourteen other family members ready to take his place. No big loss. Well, I'm on this side of the valley and there's this house out on the other side, and there's a great big terrace. I literally sat in a tree for about two and a half days, waiting for my target to appear. I couldn't shoot him through the glass, because with the deflection and everything, it was too risky. So one day, there's my target, and he's standing right next to the rail, overlooking the glorious valley, and he's king of all he sees. And I'm lining up my shot."

"Shoot him in the fucking head!" Big Brother interjects.

"And it turns out it's his son's birthday, and all these kids come running out of the house. And . . . I nailed him. Took a big divot out of the side of the house. But I covered the kids."

"Blew his head off and blew blood all over the kids. And you think he doesn't feel guilty about that?"

"I had nightmares for twenty years."

"You know what guilt we live with for what we done? You know some of the shit *I've* done?" Big Brother begins recalling his own military service, in Vietnam. "I took out a fourteen-year-old kid one time. Tell him about that."

"He was carrying a grenade."

"Yeah, and maps. And he's running to give our position up, and—seventeen people, after Saigon fell, looking for POWs."

"We were both trained at Parris Island, and we've talked about it on long, cold winter nights. Actually, he fought with some of the people I trained with. When I went to training, they looked at me like some fucking punk kid fresh off the streets. But I made it through basic, and I got respect when we got to the range."

"He could shoot."

"I was hitting pie plates with iron sights at seven hundred and fifty yards. You ever heard of a bio-feedback machine? I can bring my psyche and my mental energy down to almost zero."

"He could drop his blood pressure if he wants to."

"Not so much anymore, because I've been smoking so hard for all these years. But at one point in time, I could slow my blood pressure and breathing to the point that doctors thought I was having a stroke. I could hear my individual heartbeats. I'm not talking about *wump-wump*. I'm talking about: *Wump. Wump.*"

. . .

Little Brother struggled after leaving the military, finding inconsistent work as a mechanic before discovering his true calling, as a builder of docks for rich people. "Took me thirty years turning wrenches to figure out I belong on the water," he said.

They—we—were standing near the site of his old houseboat, which had been lacerated by a falling pine shortly after Conant came and went, in the spring of 2010. It was also the site of one of Conant's favorite stories, which one-upped even his own face-to-face encounter with a great blue heron. A fish tale. This one started with Little Brother testing a brand-new rod and reel and failing to secure it when he got up to retrieve a drink from the galley. It must have hooked something big and fast, because when he returned to the deck it was gone. The next evening, he spied the rod bobbing in the channel, seventy-five yards out, and conceived a plan to lasso it, in effect, using a surfcasting rig with a heavy sinker. He climbed onto the roof of the houseboat. He cocked his wrists, rotated his hips and shoulders, and let fly with a snap, only to watch the cast fall short. After two more failures, he tried an even heavier sinker, which appeared to carry far enough— except on its descending arc it struck a bat in midflight. The bat dropped. And then it, too, vanished, into the jaws of a surfacing bass. ("Nature is funny like that," Conant wrote. "I learned that bats and big fish help to make life amusing.")

Big Brother went home to bed, but Little Brother was just getting started. Conant had left him with a copy of *Undaunted*

Courage, about Meriwether Lewis and the Corps of Discovery, and he was taken with the idea of giving back by contributing to Conant's own adventure story. He described himself impassively as an "incorrigible alcoholic," and he seemed to be maintaining a steady state of sociability, if growing a little more personal in his divulgences, as he directed a tour of the neighborhood of "outrageously large homes," as Conant had written, reminded of castles along the Rhine, where they first met, at the site of a dock-in-progress. (The owners of the dock invited us inside, and began telling me about their friends' son: the first person to travel by stand-up paddleboard from Cuba to Key West.) Little Brother's divulgences included the fact that he had once written a four-hundred-page autobiography and then, on regrettable impulse, tossed it into a bonfire. That he had only recently stopped sleeping with a loaded gun beneath his pillow. (He made a show of placing it in my hands: a .44 magnum, just as Conant had described.) That an old girlfriend pregnant with his would-be child had been rear-ended and killed before her due date. "It destroyed me."

As his chauffeur, not to mention as a writer gathering material, I wasn't in a position to judge him, and it occurred to me that to some fragile souls, Conant—and by extension I—had represented a rare opportunity to make new first impressions in settings where they often felt trapped by diminished expectations. Small towns can be stifling. He showed me the new houseboat he had his eye on, seeking my approval. Its name was *Kid's Play,* which seemed apt given the adolescent pastimes he and Big Brother had recounted on the tributary: plugging electric guitars into an amp late at night, shooting the channel markers with hollow-point slugs, frightening the neighbors' kids with a chainsaw and a ghoulish Halloween mask. "You can get away with almost anything, man," he said, evoking a deranged libertarian paradise. "Go skinny-dipping, fuck in the water." He talked an awful lot about fucking (at one point, he took a call from "the Black woman I'm having an affair with"), and if I'd been savvier, I might have realized that I was approaching the *Deliverance* turn in my story.

. . .

My room was on the second floor of the motel, and I propped the door open, both because Little Brother continued to smoke and because I was beginning to feel that transparency was a safer option than privacy. He handed me a can of beer—"Now you can drink with me"—and suggested that I pour us each a shot of whiskey in the room's pre-stocked paper cups. I sipped, he slugged—and let out a howl that soon brought the manager walking past. Little Brother's girlfriend called—not the Black woman but his "common-law wife," whom I'll call Jane. He invited her to come join the "party," causing me to turn my back quickly so that I could wince without detection.

Then he said that he'd forgotten something in the car, and asked if he could borrow the key to retrieve it. An obvious test. I wasn't worried that he'd abscond with the car, but I *was* concerned that he seemed to be making an explicit game of our short-lived relationship. Affecting nonchalance as well as I could, I handed over the key, and then spent the next minute or two seeking counsel from my reflection in the bathroom mirror. *Wump-wump, wump-wump.*

When he returned, Little Brother seemed to have summoned the courage to address his uneasiness more directly. He reminded me that he had been unusually forthcoming about certain events in his past, and that he'd felt a powerful connection to me through our shared interest in Conant. "So I have to ask you something," he said.

I nodded.

"You can probably imagine where I'm going with this."

I said that I couldn't, though I'd have guessed that it involved money.

"You really don't have any idea what I'm about to say?"

He stepped closer and asked if I wanted a blow job.

· · ·

Suddenly, I was no longer dreading Jane's arrival. I tried reassuring Little Brother that we could remain mere chums. Then, when Jane soon appeared, he proposed marriage to her on the spot. Recognizing his inebriation, she told him to cut it out, and he erupted, shoving her into and nearly over the balcony. She threw her drink at him. I started summoning the courage to call the police, fearing an escalating incident, but the motel manager returned to cast an eye on the peculiar party of three in Room 208 and the tension dissipated.

Jane remained on the balcony, smoking in a swivel chair. She had long, straight dark hair and needle marks on her arms. I understood from Conant's writing that she was diabetic and from Little Brother's monologuing that she sold pills under an arrangement that allowed her to keep one for every three she offloaded.

He followed me back inside the room and placed his rough hands around my neck—feeling my aura, he said—and then on top of my own outstretched palms, as he described the colors that he could see emanating from my skin. I don't remember what the colors were; I was aware that they were meant to be a character judgment, and that the whole exercise was a trial of loyalty and sincerity. Without humiliating the man who might strangle me, I was focused on trying to establish sporadic eye contact with Jane, who was swiveling slowly and looking justifiably skeptical of what my arrival—what the arrival of a well-spoken outsider, with tantalizing hints of adventure and interconnectedness—had done to unsettle their compromised peace. It wasn't clear if she knew we were allies now. We both wanted them to go home without me.

Unlike her boyfriend, Jane was born and raised in Tennessee. Trying to make small talk, I mentioned reading in Conant's journals that the historic Scopes Trial had taken place in the region. "I believe in that trial," she said, nodding and blowing a curl of smoke out the side of her mouth. "We didn't come from no monkeys."

Mentioning my kids, and my desire to call home before they went to bed, proved more effective. She had adult children from a previous relationship and could relate better to homesickness than to wanderlust.

The sky opened shortly after they left, at dusk, still bickering. A great barometric release. I called Leah, who was struggling to get the boys down and impatient with my feverish story. While I was watching TV, under the covers, my phone buzzed with an unfamiliar local number, and I switched it to silent and turned out the light.

. . .

Knock knock.

Jolted awake, I looked at the alarm clock: midnight. I froze, in denial, not wanting to give any indication of alertness. The knocking persisted, and I began to worry about other guests and about the clearly suspicious motel manager. Would he think I was a dealer? A john? Was this going to have repercussions for my Expedia account? (The bourgeois concerns of a river dilettante.)

More knocks—this time knuckles on the windowpane, no more than eight feet from my bed. Though my pulse was already running triple-time (*wump-wump-wump*), I rolled away from the source of the noise and shouted what I hoped was a tired-and-confused-sounding "Hello?"

The window knocks persisted. I got up and crept over to the curtain, which I peeled back just enough to see the dark hair on Little Brother's bare stomach, behind his unzipped leather jacket. He waved with a pleading smile. I closed the curtain again and shouted, "I'm asleep! I'll talk to you tomorrow!"

.   .   .

But I didn't. Like Conant so often would, I departed town at first light, having hardly dozed. I drove through Knoxville and beyond, north and east, continuing on to a mobile-home settlement that Conant had referred to as "hallowed" ground "not noted upon the published maps," though I'd long since flagged it for my own unpublished one. It was in a cove on the north side of Cherokee Lake, a dammed portion of the Holston River: twenty gently sloping acres, with a communal picnic area, and a looping gravel road through well-maintained grass dotted with bird feeders and little garden plots. Wholesome. What made it unique was that it had been settled, two decades earlier, by disabled coal miners—Booger, Doughbelly—from the mountains of western Virginia: Appalachia reconstituted as waterfront Shangri-La. As a former miner who had gravitated to the water for serenity in his later years himself, Conant felt a special kinship.

My hosts, Barbara and Larry Horton, were among the founding settlers. "They're real characters," Barbara's son, Nate Baker, had told Conant, while sharing a campfire at an island two dozen miles downstream, in 2010. Nate was himself a recovering paralytic, owing to Guillain-Barré syndrome, a rare autoimmune disorder, and Conant was impressed to see him wakeboarding capably. But when I wrote Barbara a letter after Conant's disappearance, I learned that Nate had since died, in 2013, of a heart attack. He was thirty-five. She received my letter, she said, after stopping by the cemetery to grieve. "As I sit here writing to you with tears pouring down my face, I can't believe I would ever hear from him or anyone who knew him. . . ."

The Hortons' living room was decorated like a fishing lodge, with fish on the wallpaper and taxidermied fish mounted alongside crisscrossing rods, a display case of lures, and a decorative life preserver. Above the mantel, a plaque read "Life is better at the lake." Larry seemed surprised, though, when I asked him if the fishing was any good. He wore knee braces, a result of his legs having been crushed by a miner's roof bolter ("a double-headed Fletcher, with pins," Conant recorded), and he preferred the steadiness of a golf cart to a boat.

We were joined by a number of Nate Baker's friends, who all had been camping together on the same island when Conant passed through. Pig Island, they called it, although that, too, is not noted on the published maps. It was an annual tradition. They'd arrive by motorboat and anchor off the north side, which has a sandy beach and a sparse-enough tree canopy to re-create a contemporary living room, using generators and electric fans. The south side of the island, by contrast, is rocky, with a beach of shale and limestone gravel, and densely forested and overrun with noisy cranes, which the campers had transmuted into lore as "pterodactyls." More lore: they had also institutionalized a practice of flinging plastic bags full of their own ordure in a southerly direction, treeward, and they imagined that the hundred or so yards of unexplored territory between the two ends had become a jungle of human waste over the years. All the more memorable, then, when a man emerged from the south woods one night, shouting, "Don't shoot!"

"I was like, 'This ain't good,'" one of them recalled. "You just think about movies."

The newcomer had not only survived the pterodactyls and the fecal maze, but he claimed to have just done something even more unthinkable: ascended the Class III rapids spilling down from the nearby dam. And then he reappeared, ever cheerful, the next morning, mentioning that he was in need of new boots and planned to paddle up a mint-green creek to within walking distance of Walmart.

"To me, he was the Dos Equis Guy, the Most Interesting Man in the World," another recalled.

There was something about the timing of that encounter that had amplified the significance of the experience in their minds. Maybe it was the fact that one of them had turned thirty that weekend. Conant detected a nostalgic tinge in the campfire discussions, as the old friends, many now coupled and starting families, reminisced about youthful hijinks, and dangers averted. An unmarried camper named Shane credited Nate Baker with steering him away from drugs, which had already ended the lives of two other acquaintances. ("One of the deceased was called Bruno," Conant wrote. "He was found by his own five year old son.")

In the Hortons' living room, Shane was now standing before me: baby-faced, with a light buzz cut, and wearing a Hulkmania T-shirt. Barbara made him blush when asking the others when Shane was going to settle down with a nice girl. Shane said that after Nate's funeral, the friends began talking about a memorial gathering on Pig Island, amid the pterodactyls. They thought it important that Conant attend, and decided to postpone it until they heard from him; they wrote him a letter, offering to pay his airfare to Knoxville and pick him up at the airport.

They had no way of knowing it, I explained, but Conant wasn't in Montana to receive their invitation, or the awful news it contained. He was dealing with a crisis of his own—"Let's just say a criminal burned my damn tent to the ground," he told me—and was on the move again.

11

There Are No Men Like Me

onant didn't seem to have any idea just how many people were hoping to reestablish contact in a more than
epistolary way. Or, if he did, he may have recognized
that the relationships would likely curdle and memories were better preserved unblemished and full of potential. Those who knew
his cell phone number soon learned or came to accept that he had
stopped answering it. Others tried calling a number they found
on the internet white pages: Conant's old landline. (He'd discon-
nected it long before moving into the Swamp because someone
kept asking for "Dorothy.")

To read about them in the manuscripts, at least, his feelings
about Tracy were unblemished as well. But he found occasion for
unsettling doubt about her role in his life a couple of years before
I met him, which he expressed in a journal that he later brought
with him in the canoe. This doubt was sparked on a fateful day
in the second half of September, in 2012, when Conant returned
from the public library, in Bozeman, to his home in the Swamp,
to find a smoldering ruin. His sleeping bags and tarps, his winter
clothes, and the handwritten edits to a third draft of his latest
opus—in essence, his life, for the foreseeable future—were all
reduced to ash. "The earth was still hot from the holocaust," he

wrote. The apparent use of a chainsaw, to cut thick bushes and trees that obscured his lean-to, suggested that the fire was an intentional act, set by someone intending to displace him. All of Gallatin County was under a red-flag warning, owing to high winds and low humidity, and yet the damage in front of him was curiously isolated and specific.

He visited the office of Mike Delaney, the developer who owned the Swamp. "I come in peace!" Conant announced to the worried-looking receptionist. Delaney was cordial and sympathetic, and said that he knew nothing of the fire, but he mentioned that his insurance policy had changed. He was sorry, but he could no longer permit Conant to camp there. He also, in an arguably misplaced attempt at humor, suggested that maybe Tracy was to blame: a crime of passion. "She'd show up sporadically and they'd make wild love," Delaney told me later, reenacting a casual glibness that Conant struggled to parse. "I think the friction caused the embers to ignite."

Conant dismissed the teasing in the literal sense but couldn't help wondering if there was a larger truth in it, as he reflected back on his time in Bozeman, where he'd stuck it out, often unhappily, because of her. "After the fire, I thought of thirteen years of abuse I had endured for the supposed love of this obscure woman, phantom, wretched occasional apparition," he wrote. "I assumed Tracy merely lived her life keeping an eye on me, testing all the while my constancy and sobriety. I suspect she thought that she was the motive for my behavior. One must ponder, however, how I could accomplish what I did with a sole, albeit true motivation. In fact and in effect she was a viable adjunct, in this wise: I cannot write, nor draw, nor study, nor properly think, nor work, nor plan and execute if I am inebriated and chasing tail."

The Swamp—"the best domicile I've had"—served as Conant's primary residence for longer than any other place since his childhood home in Pearl River. He had moved in during a snowstorm at the start of 2007, amid subzero temperatures, after having a dream—he called it a nightmare—in which he stabbed his landlord and got away with it. And he had come to love its mountain views and the soundtrack of yipping coyotes and rumbling trains. "With this kind of violence, I don't expect to see old age, at least not in Montana," he now wrote.

Later, he passed Chuck Hall, his old boss from the Greyhound station, on the street. Hall attempted a friendly greeting, but Conant brushed past him, in a hurry, then thought better of it, stopped, and waved from a distance. Hall waved back. "His hair is gray now," Conant wrote. "Chances are I will never see him again. Despite his egregious faults, he did help me much through hard times."

He'd bought a bus ticket, and was on his way to Texas.

.   .   .

Four connections: Billings, Denver, Lubbock, San Antonio. At Lubbock, a woman and her young daughter got on, bound for Plano, and slept across the aisle from Conant, who was reminded of the impressionist pastels of Mary Cassatt, which he had seen and admired many years ago at the Clark Art Institute, in Williamstown. "It made me long for hearth and home and a family of my own," he wrote.

It was ninety degrees and muggy when he finally disembarked, in Austin. He lugged his gear onto the Metro, and rode it south, across the Colorado River, to Ben White Boulevard, after which he hiked about a mile to a campsite he had identified online: a wooded drainage basin—another swamp—offering convenient access to a temp agency, a library, fast food, and ATMs with low transaction fees. He suspected that the property belonged to a nearby Methodist church, but the absence of a fence or a "No

Trespassing" sign gave him plausible deniability. "Especially beautiful by moonlight," he wrote.

He bought a used bicycle and quickly found construction work, stripping a concrete slab. The heat exhausted him more than he'd anticipated. He balked at his next potential gig, working as a busboy at the city's new Formula 1 track, after he learned that this would require his buying pants, a belt, and black shoes. He had only his overalls and the size 14 boots that he'd bought at a Walmart in Tennessee, a couple of years earlier, the weekend he met Nate Baker. The heels on the boots were wearing thin and uneven, and a new pair, he figured, would cost $30. His bank account balance—his life savings—stood at $2,735.82. He recalled the time, in Bozeman, in the dark, when he had inadvertently put the boots on the wrong feet and scarcely noticed any discomfort, and he now determined to switch them regularly as a matter of preservation, as if rotating the tires on a car. They looked funny, and he worried about the ligaments in his knees, but he had always enjoyed creative frugality—a poor man's vanity plate.

At a Starbucks, a mile west of his new swamp, he met a pair of beautiful young women from Québec who were new in town, too, and looking to "hibernate" for six months. "We are snowbirds," they told him, and he took to thinking of himself the same way. During their recent migration, they had been harassed by shady strangers at a motel in Memphis, and a trucker had exposed himself on the highway in Dallas. The older of the two, Mélanie, a light brunette with soft brown eyes, had some experience with itinerancy, having previously hitchhiked the length of South America by herself ("That was fucking stupid—I could have died," she said), in addition to traveling around Europe and Africa. He told them that he was "a canoeist who writes books," and offered them a look at one of his manuscripts.

Mélanie recalls:

"This guy has crossed my mind on many, many occasions. These people, they kind of mark you. He didn't treat me like a pervert, or Uncle Creepy, like they all do. He deeply cared. I remember it very vividly. He had this huge bag with him, and he looked like he had a story or two to tell. He wasn't acting homeless, even though he looked homeless. But it was like he had all the knowledge in the world. I wouldn't have been surprised to find out he had five degrees and abandoned everything. I feel like he did what every one of us should do, which is sleep when he was tired and eat when he was hungry—like what Einstein used to do, you know?"

. . .

His first month in Austin coincided, he couldn't help noticing, with a recurring theme in the news of great men fallen: Joe Paterno, David Petraeus, and the local hero Lance Armstrong. It was comforting to think of the equalizing effects of time. In his own way, he, too, was a lion in winter. While he was walking past the American Legion, in his wrong-footed boots, a Latino family drove slowly past him, pointing and laughing. He was now "one of the few anglo men adrift," as he put it, and he found this newfound minority experience more liberating than isolating, affording him a critical distance that he had sometimes lacked in Bozeman, amid "white trash." Conant was aware of having arrived in a place that was culturally vibrant—the Nashville of Texas, he called it—but he couldn't afford luxuries like live music, and he was also struck, in a way he hadn't quite realized before, by the fundamental homogeneity of underclass life on land. He had come fifteen hundred miles, and, though the topography and accents and skin colors had changed, those distinctions seemed almost superficial given the logistics of survival in a highway-dominated environment. "There is too much concrete in my present universe," he wrote.

His chief expenditures were booze, coffee, bus fare, and activating the air pump at the gas station, fifty cents at a time, to keep his bike tires inflated. Most of his food came from dumpsters, or from pecan trees, like the one near his favorite liquor store. At mealtime, he reheated his rescued rations in the microwave of the nearest convenience mart, typically waiting until the cashier was distracted with paying customers and fancying that a man of his size and appearance could go unnoticed. He wasn't especially discerning about his dumpster diving, and believed that the occasional consumption of spoiled food would be good for strengthening his immune system.

It was the city's driest November in more than a century—a swamp no longer. He had a harder time keeping clean, and he became too embarrassed to check in at the temp agency. Around Thanksgiving, some social workers startled him awake and asked if he qualified for veterans' services. They gave him forms to fill out and spoke about the benefits of getting him "into the system." The phrase gave him pause. It wasn't as though he was off the grid, exactly. But what, after all, is a river wanderer if not someone who relishes his own autonomy? He was proud that in all his years of struggling, since leaving the navy, he had never been institutionalized against his will. His time working on the PTSD ward in Boise had hardened his skepticism of government bureaucracies like the VA, which seemed driven to enforce conformity above all else—"acquiescence to the prevailing norm," as he'd once written. He'd regarded some of the vets receiving treatment there as "meek sheep."

On the other hand, he had always been a faithful taxpayer, even with incomes that seldom climbed into five figures, and he was desperately anticipating the rewards of having paid into that system, as a retiree. He had celebrated President Obama's recent reelection by drinking beer with the sunrise, because he had been dreading what Mitt Romney might do to Social Security. And the VA in Montana had been crucially helpful in treating his gout. So, a few days later, he presented himself at the clinic on the interstate, and was promptly set up with a recent college graduate named Kelli who indulged his digressive storytelling.

Then Kelli asked if he'd ever been treated for psychiatric problems or alcohol abuse. "Immediately I suspected she had access to my official med. records from Naval Service," he wrote. "I know to lie while applying for benefits is a crime, so I told the truth. We spoke about benefits available to men like me (there are no men like me)."

. . .

The shaming incident was a jolt, and ultimately persuaded him that he needed to return to the water. Long-range planning enabled happiness by imbuing mere survival with a storyline. He'd need eighteen months of preparation to launch: another half a year until his sixty-second birthday, and then twelve more months of accumulating retirement income, with which to finance his fun. In his last correspondence with the Social Security Administration, he had been promised around $879 a month if he were to file early, as he intended. He considered that figure "a guaranteed source of 'fuck you' money," ammunition against his doubters and detractors.

No longer working, or even looking for work, he felt, he said, like a seventeen-year locust, retreating from civilization and lying in wait until he could emerge again as a river king. He was also in training, of a sort, working purposefully to keep his mind sharp and his expenses low.

He varied his base of morning operations among a handful of fast-food franchises where he charged his electronics: a portable DVD player, an AM/FM radio, and the flip phone he had bought in Chattanooga, which he now used only as a watch. He spent his afternoons in libraries. The branch he came to favor was Spicewood, northwest of downtown, because it had a lockable bathroom (good for washing up), a nice pecan tree, the Sunday *New York Times,* and a robust history and biography section, which abetted his habit of reading accounts of military campaigns as an exercise in tactical thinking. He liked the Battle of Trenton, which was in a sense the story of a river trip: Washington crossing the Delaware. He also liked Spicewood's varied clientele, which made for good people watching. "I think Spicewood Library is a fine example of that diversity which is not only desirable but inevitable nationwide," he wrote. "Whites blacks Mexicans Orientals all in profusion. I've never experienced anything like it."

Back in camp, he looked forward to eye contact with a cardinal friend. He read *The Onion,* increasingly convinced that a daily belly laugh was as essential a component of good mental and physical health as sleep and hydration. After dark, he listened to the radio, an hour of classical music or StarDate, broadcast from the U of T's McDonald Observatory. ("They are always refreshing and allow my humbled being to bask in the greatness of the universe.") If he couldn't sleep, he watched a movie. From a roadside bootlegger, he had bought a set of fifteen pirated classics. His favorite was *Robinson Crusoe.*

. . .

More tactical thinking: on napkins, or on the backs of his receipts, he assessed his finances constantly, calculating his average daily expenditure thus far, and then setting a target date and account balance, weeks or months in the future, and working backwards to see how little he'd need to spend per day to achieve it. To an outside observer, or a storage-locker sifter, his paper trail of ceaseless long division may have looked like madness, but these were, in a way, the gym reps of a man alone in the world, fighting for purpose.

He had been spending $6.85 a day since his arrival, and resolved to be more frugal in 2013. "I could easily accomplish this if I cut out booze," he wrote. "Fat chance, although I have recently consulted with both my esophagus and liver. Both advise restraint."

That spring, he had his more or less annual checkup, and was told that he was on the verge of catastrophic diabetes. Put on new medication both for his blood sugar and for knee pain stemming from the boots, he began sensing a lag between what his eyes saw and what his brain processed, and felt at times "like my muscles were being forcibly torn away from my bones."

He saw Mélanie, from Québec, once more, at a laundromat. She was a snowbird no longer. She had found a restaurant in town that served poutine, and fallen in love with—and then married!—the bartender.

In the fall, he traveled to the Pacific Northwest, where he told an artist couple he met that he was visiting his "sweetie." This was at an Oktoberfest celebration in Deming, a hundred miles north of Seattle. "He said he'd read about Oktoberfest in the newspaper, and wanted to come up," one of the artists recalled. "He was staying on the Nooksack River, which runs behind a decrepit grocery store. He didn't say we *couldn't* visit him, but we could tell he wanted to be alone. He could pretty much live on the river up there completely unmolested. It's the most beautiful place, with expansive views. My husband and I talked about it for days: just this guy doing what he wants to do, and not self-conscious about it."

On sunny days, gazing at the water, Conant had the sensation of someone "turning up the brightness knob on my brain's television panel," and he had several near-blinding episodes where he perceived a glare like a whiteout blizzard that persisted for as long as thirty minutes. The good news was that he was no longer diabetic, but he was still morbidly obese, and he declined a prescription of cholesterol medication in anticipation of the lifestyle benefits a river trip would soon bring.

"I don't get enough exercise back home," he told me. "But on these trips, I get plenty. I don't get younger, but I get fitter. I lose weight. My bones and muscles get much better. My tendons are much more viable. I can start to run and jump again."

12

I Can, and I Will

By June of 2014, Conant had amassed nearly seven thousand dollars, and settled on a homecoming course that would leave him in a climate befitting a retiree: Canada (more or less) to Florida. Lacking an active passport, he bought a bus ticket to Plattsburgh, New York, twenty miles from the border. Another passenger complained about his body odor, and, feeling shame, Conant lied and said that he couldn't help it, he was dying of cancer, and his medications produced a stink.

The bus arrived in Plattsburgh in the middle of the night. The clerk at a 24-hour convenience store, noticing Conant's luggage, recommended the motel next door, instead of some other seedier ones nearby "that cater to the homeless." Conant nodded, walked across the street, and proceeded down a slope into a wooded cove.

He spent the next few days acclimating and fortifying with "many hot dogs," while otherwise maintaining a low profile. "The public was watching me like a hawk, you know?" he told me later. Relying on public transit, he did his preparatory shopping piecemeal, stocking up on peanuts, peroxide, safety pins, salami, and dishwashing soap, among other essentials.

The canoe cost three hundred dollars. He bought it at Dick's Sporting Goods, along with a pair of portage wheels, which he used to drag the boat four miles to his campsite, just north of town. It was a Coleman Scanoe—a skiff canoe, fourteen feet long and with a wider than usual thirty-eight-inch beam and a small transom in the stern. So much for his low profile: a young woman from Saratoga visiting her parents saw Conant exiting the parking lot with a canoe and no truck in which to put it, and phoned home. Her father, a tollbooth operator named Dan Drowne, intercepted Conant beneath the Adirondack Northway and offered a baloney sandwich in exchange for an explanation. The two men sat talking under the shade of a tree for several hours, with the canoe parked on the sidewalk, distracting rubberneckers. Drowne, struck by the journey's unusual beginning, wondered how it might end. What would Conant do with the canoe after he no longer needed it? "He told me if it was damaged, he'd sink it," Drowne recalled. Hearing this, I couldn't help wondering if perhaps that's exactly what Conant had intended to do in North Carolina.

.   .   .

Conant put in on Dead Creek, on the fifth of July, sliding under Route 9 and out into Cumberland Bay, where almost immediately he was overcome with two-foot swells. A few days later, he attracted the attention of a state trooper named Edward Scollon, who wrote me:

> My time with Mr. Conant was brief. He was the subject of a suspicious person complaint. A woman was enjoying a late summer afternoon on her back deck with friends. Her deck overlooks Lake Champlain and Vermont's Green

Mountains from Willsboro Point. Mr. Conant paddled past her home, heading south, in his plastic canoe. Although he waved and offered a 'hello,' his being there unsettled her; especially when she observed him coming ashore behind a neighbor's vacant camp. She called the state police.

I found Mr. Conant in a bed that he had made upon a pebbled shoreline and under a canopy of cedars. He hadn't heard me come around the house and I took a moment to size him up. He looked quite comfortable; he had a book propped up on his midsection and all that was left of his dinner was the can that had once contained it. It was readily apparent to me, from all that he had in and about his canoe, that Mr. Conant was making a long trip. If I hadn't had a job to do, I would have left him alone. He had made this little piece of shoreline his own for the night and even though he was outdoors, I did feel that I was about to disturb his privacy.

As I approached, I called out a greeting to him in an attempt not to startle him. He did start a little, but I offered him my hand to put him at ease. He looked at me a little warily at first. I told him exactly why I had been summoned there and that I could understand why someone may be concerned about him being behind a vacant home. He told me that he had walked up on the lawn, had seen a realty sign posted there, and didn't think he'd be disturbing anyone. I asked him if he had made any attempt to enter the home and he assured me that he hadn't. I took him at his word. He asked me if his being there was unlawful. I told him that as far as I was concerned, it was not; and since it was getting too late to be on the water, I told him that I'd prefer that he stayed put. . . .

It was a short, but very cordial conversation; especially considering the circumstances under which it was initiated. He was an easy man to talk to. I couldn't help but be impressed by his wanderlust and his courage in undertaking such a long journey, all alone. I shook his hand, wished him safe travels and left him to his quiet night on the point.

Scollon continued to think about Conant in the days that followed, and stashed some old two-way radios in his cruiser, anticipating that he might run into Conant a second time, and offer them as a parting gift. "But I wasn't fortunate enough to see him again," he said.

. . .

His progress was slow at first: a few miles a day, seldom more than ten. Lake Champlain, as Officer Scollon warned, could function like a wind tunnel, and eventually a wave machine, and Conant was wary of straining a muscle, which could lay him up for weeks. He mostly stuck to the west shore, although, toward the end of July, at a narrowing south of Ticonderoga, he paddled across to Vermont, just to say that he had, and walked a block or two. Finding only a bald eagle, he crossed right back. The eagles and the ospreys were a revelation to Conant, who hadn't spent much extended time in this part of the country since the nineteen-seventies, when both species were endangered and GE was disgorging PCBs by the ton.

Pelfershire was originally called Pilfershire as local folks were renowned cattle rustlers!
Growl/bark all night close to camp. In AM still noisy. Then chainsaws started felling trees and bulldozer moved

earth. I felt sorry for the critter since they were wrecking his home town. Reminded me of burnt camp in Bozeman.

At visitor center fellow said he was reminded of movie 'The Jerk.' It was a veiled insult directed at me. I said that it was not very charitable but one cannot help what they are reminded of.

Insects are funny. They just land on me like I was a piece of wood or a rock.

The longer he was afloat, the sharper his senses got: hearing, sight, smell. ("Sewage settling ponds. Stinky.") He supplemented his notes with a digital camera, often framing his shots such that his bow, covered in a green tarp and some driftwood, occupied one of the lower corners, creating a visual effect of a primitive explorer in an adventure film. Sometimes he collected lily pads and flowers to decorate the backpack that he stashed in a crate between his legs, along with drinking water and Tabasco. He ate only sparingly, if not always nutritiously, and was losing weight, a pound or more per week. His preferred snack was chocolate-coated peanuts. "The chocolate has—not endorphins, but similar compounds that make you happy," he told me. "And they taste really good!" For a few days at a time, he might not speak to a soul, content with his Western novels and his chores. A circling beaver at dusk. A waning moon over the Green Mountains. Hooded Merganser ducklings at play. And then, feeling a social tug, he would beach in a town and make several of his usual stops: a grocery, a bar, a library, a church.

Navigationally speaking, Lake Champlain and the Hudson were the easy parts: straight, wide shots (for the most part), connected by a canal, with a dozen locks, which reminded him, in places, of the Louisiana bayous, flanked by high, mature trees and swamps. A final lock and dam at Troy marked the beginning of the Hudson as most know it: a river that flows both ways. For the next hundred and forty miles he'd be shedding only five feet in elevation and coordinating his travel schedule with the tides. He bypassed Albany, the site of so many college hijinks, but, at a bar where one of the servers reminded him of Tracy, he soon found himself thinking and talking about Steve Lippincott, his Potter club pal and soccer teammate, unaware that Lippincott still googled him sporadically, hoping without success to make contact.

The days blended together like childhood summers, and he recognized weekends only by the increase in recreational powerboats, which slowed his progress. Seeking respite on an island north of Catskill, he found company: a young man and his dog Mishka, a hybrid Siberian and German shepherd, who had also arrived by canoe. The man, a carpenter named Brad Rappleyea, was soon to become a father and looking to clear his head at what he called "my little zen spot." He had just worked a ninety-hour week. "I was kind of annoyed at first that this guy crashed my afternoon," Rappleyea recalled. "But there was something about him." Rappleyea already had a campfire going, and, as darkness descended, Conant gestured at the groceries in his cooler and offered to cook dinner for two. "He was obviously—I don't want to say a man of good taste, but steak and whole-seed French mustard!" Rappleyea said. "Albeit with gas-station malt liquor from Coxsackie."

"The whole journey he was describing—well, I guess everybody thought Amelia Earhart was insane, too," Rappleyea continued. "I assumed he was on a suicide mission, but he had a matter-of-fact attitude, just smiling. There was this phrase that stuck with me: 'I can, and I will!' He kept repeating that, and with that belly laugh. It surprises me that no one in a position of authority tried to stop him."

Dutchess County was soon on Conant's left, and he thought of himself as entering his mother's "turf," recalling her job as the chief of service at the Wassaic State School for Mental Defectives. "She was proud of it but I don't think I ever gave her due credit, to my shame or indifference or both," he wrote. Up ahead, on his right, meanwhile, were Newburgh, where "Grandpa Higgins" had died, and Cornwall, where he used to babysit his Higgins cousins. His uncle Bob, Claire's brother, was fortunate to spend so many years in such a lovely place, he thought. He was coming up on one of the country's most magnificent stretches, where the Hudson Highlands slash diagonally through the fjord, leaving steep peaks of fifteen hundred feet on either shore that—from the water, at least—register more like the grander mountains out west. ("Not as shocking as a view of the Tetons coming west over Togwotee Pass in Wyoming, but every bit as beautiful.")

He was also due for a medical checkup, and pulled over on the east bank, south of Wappingers Falls, to visit the VA. Feeling the psychic weight of it all, he made a point of speaking only fondly of his mother ("feelings about Mom are of a sensitive nature and hard to express without fear of alienating people"). When the nurse asked him for an emergency contact, he suggested the Red Cross. "They'll get in touch with my kin," he said.

. . .

Soon afterward, floating opposite Storm King and reminded of Jackson Hole, he suffered a gout attack; the flare-up conspired with thirty-mile-an-hour gusts from the north to keep him laid up in Cold Spring ("most picturesque village yet") for a couple of days, popping naproxen pills and discussing the phenomenon of "cityots," or city idiots, with a local dog owner who resented the weekend crowd of heedless kayakers.

Back on the water, as he approached West Point, the home-coming sensation resumed, with a rush of memories of childhood trips with the Colonel, to see the Sherman tank graveyard and the mothballed fleet. Then he reached Nyack, where he had worked in the hospital, and wandered into town for the first time in thirty-seven years, feeling, he said, like Rip Van Winkle, disoriented by the different sameness of everything.

13

Adios, My Friend

Conant made it from his Palisades campsite to Hoboken in what he called "an extraordinary transit": a three-hour pull on an outgoing tide, amid whitecaps and fighting the occasional ferry wake. "Wonderful memories of NYC flood my brain," he wrote on his atlas. "Grant's Tomb, Riverside Church, G.W. Bridge, hurray!" He visited Elysian Fields, the site of the first organized baseball game, in 1846, and asked a lineman from the electric company to take some pictures of him with the city skyline in the background. "Talk about universe and he is drifting," Conant wrote. "I told him to marry his woman. It would help center things." They ended up retiring to Maxwell's Tavern. "Gave me a hug and many heartfelt compliments. Hard to say goodbye. It always is."

The next day, September 5, he rested: "electrolytes, bananas." Police roused him from his beach camp ("blocks from where Frank Sinatra grew up") at 4:30 a.m. on the sixth, and he was under way, into New York Harbor, by 6:15, having promised to write the officers upon arrival in Florida. Through fog, he paddled past Ellis Island and the Statue of Liberty, and was visited by more cops, this time in a motorboat, as he reached the port of Bayonne. Their warnings of heavy commercial traffic ahead were borne out, and steep waves from tugs and container ships chased Conant ashore in the Staten Island neighborhood of New Brighton.

His clothes and sleeping bags were soaked from the harbor crossing. He hung them over some tree branches to dry, and began celebrating by cooking the flank steak my neighbor Scott had given him, as well as a pork roast. A couple of Latino fishermen came by ("totally off the wall, angelic, holy," he wrote), and advised him to go elsewhere—he was too exposed to wakes and crosscurrents, and also too close to the projects. Conant reluctantly packed up and paddled westward for half a mile, along the Kill Van Kull. He felt overcome by lethargy. Exiting a river that he'd spent significant time on always made him sad, like leaving towns that he loved. "These waterways take on a persona," he'd once written, and now the mighty Hudson, "an old uncle who has his moods" and as much a friend as any he'd made that summer, was forever in his rear view.

He had begun noticing tarry stools, and diagnosed himself with anemia, which he blamed on a toxic combination of the naproxen pills, aspirin, and the Hoboken carousing. For several days, he was able to do little more than read stories in the newspaper about the nearby death-by-police-chokehold of Eric Garner, and fret over his advancing age.

· · ·

On September 10, a fifty-seven-year-old harbor pilot named Dougy Walsh went down to the creek on the Kill Van Kull, near his house in West New Brighton, to catch some minnows to use as bait for an annual fluke tournament he liked to fish in, and noticed a red canoe, a tarp, and a bedroll. "You kidding me?" he blurted out. "You're camped in here? What about the rats?"

Smiling, Conant replied, "I'm looking for the Raritan River. You know where that is?"

They ended up talking for four hours, about the tugs, and about Walsh's sick father—also a harbor pilot—and about Conant's plans to game the tides past Newark Bay and on down, in order to ride an ebbing current south of the Rahway River mouth toward Tottenville, at the bottom of the island. "I was blown away by this guy," Walsh recalled. "He didn't have any nautical charts! He was using a road atlas!"

The next day, Conant woke up to the memorial towers of light above Ground Zero. "Unexplained trepidation but determined nonetheless," he wrote. Walsh, after visiting his father in the hospital, returned to the campsite and invited Conant back to his house, a landmarked Gothic Revival dating to the mid-nineteenth century, for crab macaroni and sangria. His wife was away, out on Long Beach Island. Conant was still weak, and struggled to climb the stairs, but he took pleasure in the house's historic significance, as a stop along the Underground Railroad.

"He cut me right to the heart," Walsh said, choking back tears. "He said, 'I thank God there's people like you.'" Walsh added, "My wife said, 'I don't believe you. You meet all these fucking weirdos.'"

. . .

By the time Conant left the north shore of Staten Island, on the morning of the fifteenth, he had been in New York City longer than anywhere else since Plattsburgh, and yet had scarcely ventured more than a few blocks. With a one-and-a-half-knot current behind him, he now slid past the Port Richmond Sludge Docks, under the Bayonne Bridge, past Shooters Island to starboard. Newark Bay, to his north, was an empty slop, largely free of traffic, but when he rounded the corner southward, at Howland Hook, he found himself edging up to a massive container terminal. For the previous week, he'd been observing the comings and goings (and the resultant wave actions) of cargo ships from China, Panama, Norway, the Marshall Islands, and more, and now he was passing the *Kobe Express,* from Hamburg, with boxcars stacked five high and a dozen across, while the cranes of the Port of Elizabeth loomed, like grazing giraffes, on either side of the Goethals Bridge.

In the context of a life spent canoeing the Main Salmon and the Tennessee and the Yellowstone and, more recently, the Hudson, this industrial passage alongside Staten Island, on the Arthur Kill, and then into the heart of New Jersey, on the Raritan, might seem a novelty to be endured, at best—a winking addition to an already unusual CV. But the next few days—dreaming undisturbed in earshot of I-95, waking up to the sight of Rutgers crew practices, no longer anemic—were among Conant's happiest. What this stretch lacked in natural beauty, it made up in rusted ruins and exotic detritus, like the stray gold statue of Ganesha, the Hindu elephant god, in front of some brambles, or esoteric graffiti: "Sic Erat Scriptum Kertwang!" And no longer in a valley, as he'd been for much of the previous two months, he enjoyed a proper view of the western sunset. That was at a sandy beach camp a few miles south of the Fresh Kills Landfill, where he found thick cordgrass, a rarity amid so much invasive phragmites, on which to bed down in luxury. Somebody blasted "The Star-Spangled Banner" from a stereo and he imagined that he was being serenaded as he paddled. Approaching the central New Jersey town of South Bound Brook, he passed a small burial ground for Revolutionary War soldiers, including a Colonel Jerome Rappleyea, a possible ancestor of his carpenter friend from Catskill. Soon after, he admired a towering Ukrainian church ("obvious magnet for new refugees," he wrote) and met a friendly Mexican couple who had just opened a diner, and felt a swell of patriotism. "America still accepts foreigners in need!"

The secret to his inland passage through New Jersey turned out to be a canal that was dug by hand in the eighteen-thirties, to speed the shipping of Pennsylvania coal to New York City. This was the Delaware and Raritan Canal, better known as the D&R: like so many American canals, long defunct, having been outcompeted by rail and road, but with the old towpath reconstituted as greenway. Or runway: Conant chose to regard the pedestrians on the path as participants in his personal fashion show, while he slowly bisected the state. For a change, there were no powerboats to compete with, and only a slight current, flowing southwest to northeast, pushed against his bow. The canal was narrow enough that Conant could smell barbecue through the trees ("I actually salivated like a dog!") while maintaining a comforting sense of seclusion. The inoperative locks necessitated daily portaging, during which he caught up on local gossip—for instance, about a couple of dead bodies that had surfaced on the Raritan in his wake. "Pure coincidence, I promise!" he wrote.

.　.　.

Arriving at Princeton's Carnegie Lake, via canal, Conant put on a button-down and a clean pair of overalls and played Ivy Leaguer for a few days, visiting the Paul Robeson museum, listening to a lecture on justice during the American Revolution, and attending a football game, under the lights (Princeton 56, Davidson 17). He also made himself a regular at the Yankee Doodle Tap Room, in the Nassau Inn, where he marveled at the famous names carved in the wooden tables, including "Doctor Einstein." ("Brooke Shields is said to have carved her name as well but no one can find it.") Another customer, Robert Dix, Class of 1967, and a financial heavy, saved a napkin on which Conant had scribbled his email and P.O.-box addresses, and stored it in his desk, hoping to maintain contact. "He did leave a very favorable impression as an authentic person," Dix said. "Pretty well-dressed in ironed overalls and checkered shirt is what I remember for someone staying in a canoe."

While preparing to leave town, Conant discovered that one of his backpacks, containing months' worth of reserve medication, had been stolen or misplaced. Trying not to panic, he paddled on, toward Trenton. A few of the bridges over the canal were so low that he had to lean back and retract his chin, sliding underneath, as though into an MRI scanner, while cars rolled overhead. Then, eight or nine miles north of the city, he encountered some differences between the canal as it flowed and the map in his mind. He spied a corrugated culvert pipe, off to the left, through which water was leaking down into a creek—the Assunpink Creek, he presumed, recalling his reading, in Austin, about the Second Battle of Trenton—and he decided to have a little fun, paddling into the rusty chute. Down he went, into the dark, gaining speed as he bumped along for thirty feet. He was briefly airborne before splashing out at the bottom and taking on about a gallon of water, a small price for the experience of canoeing "like a ski jumper!" as he put it. The canal runoff provided the creek with some helpful momentum, and for the next several hours he negotiated snags and shoals and descended minor rapids, all while looking for a plausibly private campsite.

He eventually stopped near some woods abutting an abandoned factory, in East Trenton. Squeezing through a gap in a fence, he walked three blocks to a bar, Choppy's Galera, where he joined a man named Carlos, who had just got out of prison, for happy hour, to celebrate a day that had begun in fear and ended in wonderment. Conant paid for the beers and took Carlos across the street, to a bodega, for beans and sauce. "Adios, my friend, *de mi corazón*," Carlos said, as Conant slipped back through the fence and into solitude.

.   .   .

Nearly everyone he'd met on the trip had advised him to bypass Trenton. The objections seemed to be based mainly on the popular conception of New Jersey's capital city as a punch line for despair, and perhaps colored by racial prejudice. But Trenton's real challenge was navigational. Assunpink Creek goes underground as it reaches downtown, buried beneath a highway interchange, some train tracks, and the DMV. Conant spent the morning after his ski-jumping triumph investigating options for portage. His best bet, he concluded, was to disembark beneath the Wall Street bridge, a few hundred yards from the courthouse, amid a partial dam of fallen branches, trash, and tires. For two or three strenuous hours, lugging his gear piecemeal, he scrambled up and down the overgrown bank, at the top of which lay the rotting carcass of a stray dog. Then came the challenge of dragging the canoe itself up the forty-five-degree grade, using a rope. Throughout, a couple of his capped molars were throbbing in pain, which he deemed a "psychosomatic" reaction to his circumstances.

He was sitting at the top, recovering in the shade, in earshot of the scavenging flies, when a slender, middle-aged Black man walked by, dressed in a leather jacket and a leather cap. "What'd you do? Paddle that river?" the man asked, incredulous. His name was Kevin Jolley—"like the Jolly Green Giant, except with an 'e,'" he said—and he was carrying a couple of hot meals home from a nearby soup kitchen. Jolley offered to put Conant up, boat and all, in his open-air garage, for a more proper rest. Conant hesitated at first, and then, an hour and a half later, reconsidered, after having reckoned with the constraints of urban portage: stoplights, crosswalks, potential thieves. At the rate he was advancing, he wasn't likely to see water again before dark. "I rested and read paper as sounds of the not-wealthy neighborhood engulfed my senses," Conant wrote of his stay with Jolley. "It was a very happy sound."

·   ·   ·

Jolley Portage, as Conant took to calling his dry-land slog through downtown Trenton, resumed early the next morning, and became a kind of slow-motion spectacle, as he traversed a couple of city miles in small increments, while parrying questions from strangers about what kind of drugs he was on. He caught the attention of a young civic activist and local booster named Jon Gordon, who, inspired by the poem "In Flanders Fields," had made a habit of planting red poppy seeds in vacant lots as an urban gardener's commentary on the effect of heroin on Trenton and the surrounding region. Gordon handed Conant a Tic Tac container full of seeds, and enlisted him in some future riverbank scattering, but not before shooting commemorative videos, with his iPhone, of "this giant in overalls with a canoe in the middle of the hood," as he put it.

Scene: Conant, sitting on a street corner, leaning back against a green duffel, boots crossed, maps in his lap, hands knotted over his midsection. He has a Camaro Z28 cap on his head, and a toothbrush and a pen poking out of his breast pockets. The canoe is off to his right, parallel to the curb. A white brick building advertising "Plumbing and Heating Materials" squats in the background. Strewn backpacks and bags, a crate, a blue bucket, a Gatorade bottle: a landlubber's boating picnic. A man in a motorized wheelchair cruises west, not on the sidewalk but in the street, against the flow of traffic, and doesn't so much as turn his head to acknowledge the strange voyager.

"Where you headed?" a voice offscreen asks.

"I'm headed down to Florida," Conant says, laughing.

"What made you stop through Trenton?" another voice asks. "Just the map?"

"Well, no," Conant says. "I want to get on the Delaware, so I can head down to—there's a Chesapeake–Delaware Canal that I can take into Chesapeake Bay. Now, Chesapeake Bay's a large body of water, and I'll be exposed. But it's not as large as the Atlantic Ocean!"

The first offscreen voice asks, "Yeah, man, what's your whole purpose, though?"

Before Conant can finish answering, a black SUV pulls up alongside the curb, looming over the canoeist, and the camera turns away. A woman leans out the window. "Excuse me," she says. "I'm looking for Riverview Plaza?"

14

Pirates of the Sun

There were puzzling gaps in the documentary record. Conant's trail began to go cold after the Delaware. A "Waterway Guide to Chesapeake Bay" that he'd been studying in photographs as far north as Catskill, New York, did not turn up underneath the boat in North Carolina. Perhaps, I speculated, it was in the backpack that got filched in Princeton, or maybe it was a casualty of a two-hundred-gallon baptism that occurred near a Sunoco refinery in Marcus Hook, Pennsylvania, when he misjudged the incoming tide while ashore getting groceries. He had lashed the canoe, high and dry, to a crumbling concrete bulkhead, and returned, three hours later, to find it partially sunken from rebounding waves. His luggage was awash in seaweed.

His photographs revealed that he'd visited a Quaker meetinghouse, in Philadelphia, as well as the grave of Ben Franklin, and suggested that he'd enjoyed observing the replica of the tall ship *Kalmar Nyckel,* the *Mayflower* of the Delaware Valley, in Wilmington. But what writing survived of his passage along the Lower Delaware—"its dangerous reputation is well deserved"—made it sound mostly grim, whether because of twenty-knot winds, unsympathetic cops, rocky beaches, sore shoulders and elbows, or varying depths. While contending with shoals alongside an echoing firing range, on the approach to Delaware City, he "had to almost sweep to not drag mud" with his paddle.

It was during that challenging stretch, in the third week of October, that he sent me his gracious note about my article, from the public library in Delaware City, mentioning that his laptop had drowned but that he was of sound body. While at the library, he also responded to a four-month-old email from his brother Jim, who was seeking to confirm his mailing address in Bozeman. Jim replied that same evening, October 20, to say that Dicky's inheritance from their mother's estate (a little less than two thousand dollars) was ready to be disbursed, if only he would communicate "ASAP" with the family attorney, who was assisted by a woman named Carol. Jim wrote, "As you are on another canoe trip (I saw the New Yorker article. Cool!), you have been hard to reach."

Two days later, Dicky wrote again:

Dear Jim and Marie, I survived a terrible storm last night and awoke with a resolve to go to my demise without regret. I want to mend fences with you and not end my days with any (as you term it) angst in my heart. So I am sorry if I wrote or said anything to you that was offensive or unkind or hateful. Of course you have my love as always. Congratulations on successfully disposing Mother's will. . . . With contrite heart, your brother, Dicky. P.S. I have been in touch with Carol.

His photographs in the days immediately following that note show him in the company of several other men. Then they cease abruptly. The last picture, taken at 12:37 p.m. on October 25, more than a month before the ominous phone call that began this book, is of a plush bird hanging inside the cabin of someone else's boat. Conant's memory cards had maxed out.

. . .

Not only was there was no North Carolina atlas like the New York one he'd shown me, but the southernmost maps that were recovered underneath the canoe turned out to be of Maryland. These were part of an inconveniently large Upper Chesapeake Bay "chartkit." And Conant's annotations on them were sparse, mysterious, and at times alarmist. An asterisk in the middle of the shipping channel, south of Annapolis, was accompanied by three exclamation marks and the words "OUCH DISASTER." Elsewhere there were references to "danger," and to swamping waves. A circle around the Hooper Islands was accompanied by the words "BADASS SHITS. BAD PEOPLE. STUCK TIRES." *Tires?*

" 'Moses,' Andrew, and Jim all helped to fix port pontoon, twice!" *Pontoon?* That cryptic note appeared near another asterisk, marking a campsite next to the Selby Bay Marina, in Edgewater, Maryland, during the last days of October. The reference to a pontoon had me wondering if Conant had constructed some type of outrigger system to help absorb the Chesapeake's notorious chop. I called the marina to inquire.

"You mean the guy who came in on a solar-powered boat?" the man who answered the phone asked.

Soon, I was talking to a shipyard hand named Moses Wells. "Dick's a good friend of mine," he said. "He was stranded up in Delaware. He hopped on this other guy's big trimaran. They came in here on a damaged pontoon. Dick feared for his life."

. . .

The trimaran was called *Ra,* in honor of the Egyptian deity. Its skipper, Jim Greer, referred to his rotating crew as the Pirates of the Sun. "You should have found *me* for a story, man!" Greer said, when I got ahold of him next.

Greer's intention was to set a Guinness Record, for completing the Great Loop—a 6,600-mile circuit of inland waterways connecting the Gulf to the Great Lakes—under solar power exclusively. He had been at it, on and off, for three years, when he met Conant, in Delaware City. "He just came paddling up beside the boat," Greer said. "I had heard about him up on the Hudson at some yacht club. Then I got down to Delaware City, and lo and behold, there he is. I said, 'You're the guy coming from up north?'" Greer was seventy-three and roundly built and had an unkempt white beard. A few of his front teeth were missing. "We're similar-type people," he said.

A Google search revealed that they were dissimilar in at least one respect. Greer was a canny publicist and self-promoter. He had been filming much of his travels, and trying to get a TV deal, placing ads on Craigslist for cameramen and crew. ("It's like *Survivor,* on a boat," one fellow-traveler said. Greer added, "Some people last a day, a week, two hours—it's an adventure that's not for everybody.")

According to various newspaper stories, Greer had previously taught at Stanford, photographed wildlife in Africa, fished commercially, and worked in the oil industry as a shipwright. He called himself an "old hippie," and said that he'd tagged along with Ken Kesey's Merry Pranksters for a spell on the Furthur bus, going by the name Fish Monger. He spoke of building his first boat when he was fourteen, and floating south from Wichita until a sheriff in Arkansas presumed him a runaway and pulled him off the river. "I'd like to do the Nile and the Amazon," he told the *Press of Atlantic City.*

Greer built the *Ra* in a frenzied three months, in 2012, using marine plywood and fiberglass. Its cutter-like center hull, painted white, was forty-eight feet long and contained six bunks. Narrow pontoons on either side provided stability, and solar panels spanned the connecting beams. He launched on the Suwannee River, inspired by the song "Old Folks at Home," and piloted the boat forty-four miles out into the Gulf, where he was soon caught in Tropical Storm Debby. (This earned him his first news coverage, in NBC footage of the conditions outside Little Pine Island, Florida.) His commitment to renewable energy was not so much environmental as pragmatic: he couldn't afford the fuel that would enable him to live the life of a Looper, and the solar gimmick was a good way of attracting free help from true believers. The panels powered two battery-operated engines, and on sunny days he could average several knots. But the longer the boat was in the water, the more bottom growth it acquired, and this created drag, such that at times he could scarcely counteract the wind and the tide. In each of his three years on the water he had run into some kind of trouble that caused him to suspend the mission. By the time Conant paddled up to the *Ra* in Delaware City, Greer had cycled through fifty crew members and was all alone, awaiting propane tanks to fire a supplementary—and disqualifying—motor he had acquired to hasten his return.

The two voyagers' first encounter was brief. Greer remained in port while Conant paddled on ahead, sliding into the fourteen-mile-long Chesapeake and Delaware Canal, toward Maryland. Greer caught up to him in Chesapeake City, across the border, where Conant was riding out some foul weather in the boisterous company of Canadian sailors named Serge and Vern. They, too, were headed to Florida, having launched a yellow cabin cruiser, *Gaffeur* (French for "blundering fool"), in Québec, on the Richelieu River.

Conant was now in a bind. He had been hoping to descend the western shore of Chesapeake Bay, which offered greater access to towns and medical services, should the need arise. (He had cited the VA hospital in Baltimore to me as a likely target.) His plan called for crossing the bay at the mouth of the nearby Elk River, where the broad Chesapeake cinches to a relatively narrow two and a half miles: the Hudson at Piermont, a crossing I've managed in both a kayak and atop a sailboard. But he'd learned from the Canadians of a hitch: the far side of his intended crossing was an army base, an ordnance testing area along which camping was forbidden. The restricted area extended southward past the Gunpowder River, to the outskirts of Baltimore. Without any current to count on, it was more than a day's paddle, and left him seemingly without options. The weather of late had been rough, and he had been spooked on the canal by a container ship that was more than a hundred feet tall, leaving steep tumblers in its wake.

Greer needed a first mate, and Conant needed safe passage past the army base. They lashed the canoe to the struts of the *Ra*'s starboard pontoon and joined forces. Conant slept in the V-bunk, in the bow. "He kept talking about this woman he was going to marry," Greer said. "All night, he'd wake up and be talking in his bunk."

· · ·

The *Ra* puttered up the South River, below Annapolis, and into Selby Bay, looking like a bird with an injured wing. It was effectively a catamaran, listing ominously to port, while the starboard pontoon, with a suspended canoe for a counterweight, sailed along in the air. Moses Wells went out to greet the ship on the marina's dock. Around thirty years old, he was of medium build, with short brown hair and green eyes. (His Sioux father was known as B.F.I., for "Big Fucking Indian.") He sported an eyebrow ring and a tattoo on the back of one of his calves that read "Heavy Metal." Conant was the first person he saw, shouting, "Get me off this boat!"

"Jim was a very controlling captain," Wells said. "They were bickering like a married couple."

They had already been turned away from five marinas, Wells soon learned, because Greer didn't have any money that he was willing to part with. His only currency was publicity. In return for a repair job, he said, "We can offer you advertising." Wells wasn't interested, but he admired the voyagers' intrepid spirits. As a teenager, he had hired out on a scalloping rig, and was three hundred miles offshore when Hurricane Isabel struck. Convinced that they were all going to die, he and his crew-mates holed up in the cabin around a table and made a morbid game of the ship's constant tossing, waiting for a bottle of liquor to slide into the hands of the next drinker: a mariner's ouija board. Years later, he lost a sister (to a motorcycle accident) and both parents (to illness) in a span of nine months. When he returned home to collect his old possessions, the basement was flooded. He felt like his entire childhood had washed away, with nothing—not even family photos—left to show for it. He had acquired a fatalist view of life, and vowed never again to take anything or anyone for granted. He was newly married to a woman he characterized as being "like a Gypsy—she doesn't like going down the same road twice."

Wells believed the *Ra* required a dry-docking for a proper renovation, but he didn't think it would hold together in a crane lift, so he welded some supporting brackets and added ratchet straps to fix the sagging pontoon in place, as a makeshift solution. He urged Conant, the heaviest among them, to stand on the bridge and rock back and forth, in a simulation of rough seas. Everything seemed to be holding tight. Fingers crossed, Skipper Greer and First Mate Conant ventured out again, around the bend, and—"DISASTER!" They hit a five-foot wave, which emancipated the straps.

Back at the marina, Greer slept on his boat and Conant pitched a tent in the reeds nearby. "Jim came up to me at one point and whispered, 'You know he's in there talking to somebody, and the phone's dead,'" Wells said. "Then Dick comes out and he's like, 'Yeah, I was just on the phone with my girl. I think she wants me to come back.' Every time he talked about her, he had this glow."

Wells was struck by the fact that Conant seemed never to remove his life jacket. "He didn't go anywhere without it." And he was amazed by Conant's encyclopedic knowledge. When he learned that Conant lived in Montana, he mentioned his only experience with the state, visiting a friend in the small town of Shelby, up near the Canadian border. "Dick was like, 'Yeah, there's a split canyon there, and it runs down to a gully—got a lot of super-clean mirror water there,'" Wells recalled. "It blew me away."

Greer eventually borrowed money to buy a train ticket down south, where he planned to fetch some new equipment. Conant offered to stay behind with the boat, like a responsible first mate. While they awaited the captain's return, Wells, a part-time commercial fisherman, took Conant with him up the South River, looking for white perch. "I enjoyed his company," Wells said. "And he enjoyed being on a boat that had a motor." Conant seemed not to know that his camera had run out of memory, and continued taking pictures, in many cases of campsites that he thought looked promising. He also took copious notes, in a small yellow notepad that didn't turn up beneath the canoe in North Carolina. Wells admired Conant's attention to detail—for instance, pointing out the four great blue herons that were standing in a circle, hunting minnows together. "My whole entire life on the water, I'd never seen blue herons work together before," Wells said. "Course, Dick was writing that down."

Greer phoned from Florida to say that he was comfortably settled and no longer planning to return until the weather warmed up again in the spring. He intended to spend the winter building another solar boat, which he was calling his "Ferrari," because it would be faster and less bulky than its predecessor. He talked about sailing it to Cuba. "Nobody's ever done that!"

Conant, Wells said, became distressed at the thought of how much time he had squandered on a dead-end solar adventure. It was November now, and he knew that he needed to be making more reliable southward progress if he hoped to stay warm. What was more, he was in need of medication, and the *Ra* had bypassed Baltimore, with its vaguely boatable VA.

Wells tried to console him by arguing that he wouldn't likely be faring much better in his canoe. The west side of the bay was fraught with peril in general: there were sheer cliffs down at Chesapeake Beach, and there was another restricted area by a natural gas plant, which would have chased him off shore. And then there was the mouth of the Potomac, which Wells considered the most treacherous spot of all, because of the convergence of the Atlantic Ocean, the bay, and the ebbing river. "On a good day, it's two-foot waves there," he said. "On a day with fifteen-mile-per-hour winds, you have six- or seven-foot seas, and eight and a half miles of water to cross. And you can't go all the way up the Potomac, either, because it ebbs out at like nine or ten knots, so you can't paddle against it."

Conant apparently talked about enlisting a friend in Virginia for help with automotive "portage." I wondered if this was Fred Kelly, the man whose holiday card he had been carrying with him among the many papers in the canoe. But Wells, hearing this, decided to take a day off and drive Conant himself. They first raided the galley of the *Ra* for canned goods to add to Conant's supplies, then loaded the canoe and everything else into the bed of Wells's white Ford pickup, and took the scenic route, avoiding I-95 and instead detouring past Chincoteague Island, where Wells's mother had grown up. "He wanted to see where my family was from," Wells said.

At a rest stop, they overheard a couple of men in the parking lot making disparaging references to the spectacle of the two of them, with their truck bed full of junk. "They called us Sanford and Son," Wells said. "It kind of hurt Dick's feelings. I was like, 'Dick, don't worry about it. Those guys are stuck in Hampton, Virginia, picking up trash. Their whole lives, they could try, and they won't see the things you've seen, and meet the people you've met.' "

Wells dropped Conant off near the visitor center in Portsmouth, a short walk from the naval hospital where Conant had concluded his previous trip, in 2010. Conant knew the area well enough to give Wells directions from memory. He tried to slip him a couple hundred dollars for the taxi service, but Wells refused. "The way I looked at it, his stories were a payment," he said.

. . .

What about the Hooper Islands, and those notes on the map about bad people and slashed tires? "I lived a short period of time on Hoopers Island," Wells explained. "I told Dick the majority there don't like outsiders. I had my tires ice-picked as I cut my neighbor's grass one time."

As I spoke with Wells, the *Ra* was still there at the marina: an eyesore or a tourist attraction depending on whom you asked. He had already heard about the missing boater on Albemarle Sound through the Intracoastal grapevine, and had tried reaching out to law enforcement down in North Carolina, to share his theory—that Conant was alive and living somewhere warm, under an assumed name—without gaining traction. Wells said that he and Conant had gone shopping together at Walmart, and bought a new tent ("because he had an old green one that had holes in it") and a portable propane heater, items that he hadn't seen mentioned in the news accounts he'd read. "This wouldn't be the first time he's done this," Wells said. "When he left here, he was already talking about just giving up. You can't put a fourteen-foot canoe on a Greyhound bus."

Wells then mentioned that he had recently returned from a vacation to Florida—Fort Lauderdale, not Naples—and had struck up a conversation there with some canoeists who claimed to know his friend, though he went by something other than Dick. "He wore overalls, had a big beard, and camped out," Wells said, characterizing their description in hopeful, if generic, terms. As a commercial fisherman, he emphasized, he was accustomed to finding bodies and stray life jackets floating in the surf. "It's just weird, you know what I mean? That nothing turned up."

"I still think about him all the time," Wells went on. "I'll do, like, random Google searches in the middle of the night: 'strange man canoe,' 'big guy in overalls,' 'river man.'"

He had also told his wife, "If we ever get divorced, you know what I'm doing. I'll start from up north, and I will canoe every-where."

15

Budgets, Man

As it happened, I was on my way to the airport, headed for North Carolina, when Moses Wells informed me of the Chesapeake misadventures and of his belief that Conant had bailed on the voyage purposely. Nearly six months had passed since the discovery of the canoe, and John Beardsley, the wildlife ranger who had first called me with the news, was finally ready to talk about his investigation. He picked me up at my hotel in Elizabeth City in a 4x4 pickup with a laptop mounted above the gearshift. He had a buzz cut and wore a khaki uniform with a badge, belying a romantic streak. On the laptop he opened Google Earth and loaded a satellite view of our surroundings. Not too far north of our current location was a dark green rectangle. "That's what this entire area should look like if it wasn't for humans," he said. "If we didn't come here and destroy it all, it'd be covered in trees."

The rectangle, he explained, was the Great Dismal Swamp, a hundred-thousand-acre National Wildlife Refuge preserving what was once a million or more acres of forested wetlands straddling the borders of what are now Virginia and North Carolina. It had been Conant's portal to Elizabeth City. At the end of the first week of the previous November, a lockmaster named Robert Peek escorted an overloaded canoeist into what he liked to call "the oldest continuously operated manmade canal and locking system in all of the Americas," while privately noting the oddity. The canal marked the hard eastern edge of the rectangle on Beardsley's screen, and was used primarily by snowbirds sailing boats that are too large for trailers. "People dug it by hand," Beardsley said. "That just blows my mind. That's a huge feat in itself." The digging took twelve and a half years and finished in 1805.

The Great Dismal was in a number of ways a fitting conclusion, or near conclusion, to a pilgrimage like Conant's. "Nowhere in North America will you find wildlife in greater abundance than right here in the Great Dismal," Peek says. "We actually have the highest bear population in North America, 1.5 bears per square mile. And you can find up to two hundred species of bird in one season. This has been described as nature's paradise." The water, purplish and foamy, is so high in tannic acids that bacteria can't breed; drink freely, in other words, without boiling. "We learned that from the Indians: this water won't go bad," Peek says. The poet Robert Frost, after a devastating breakup in 1894, skulked into the swamp hoping to commit suicide by wilderness exposure. (A biography of Frost describes it as "a place where those who have lost hope run away from the world.") Peek gave Conant a map of the refuge and recommended some places to camp, including the perimeter of a lake in the middle, a natural depression that connects to the canal via a feeder ditch. The depression has its own unique "Lady of the Lake" mythology, involving a ghost canoe spotlit by fireflies that sometimes appears at night, and a lovesick suitor who ventured into the swamp, never to return.

But Conant did emerge, six days later, and I soon interrupted Beardsley, excited to mention what I'd learned from Wells about the trimaran and the truck ride and the tent and the propane and

Conant's apparent misgivings. "Well, that all sounds great, but here's the problem," Beardsley said. "We found a tent. It was still in the bag." He conceded that they hadn't found any propane, but argued that if Conant had intended to hop a bus down to warmer weather, as Wells suggested, then he would have been better off abandoning his canoe in town, where there was public transportation within walking distance—whereas, through the tip line printed in the *Daily Advance,* Beardsley had learned of a sighting that placed Conant paddling happily south beyond the city limits. He offered to take me out on the water to show me.

.   .   .

We met Beardsley's colleague Chase Vaughan at the Coast Guard base, several miles southeast of downtown, and launched a twenty-foot boat, with a center console, into the Pasquotank, an Algonquian word meaning "where the current forks." The river seemed about as wide as the Hudson at its broadest but without the steep slopes on either side that lend a feeling of containment. After ten minutes, with the two-hundred-horse Evinrude on full throttle, we passed a blimp factory on our right; it looked like an elongated planetarium, stretching the length of a football field. "He paddled right by here, so there was no missing that," Beardsley noted. Before long, there was nothing to see but trees. Thirty minutes in, with the sound starting to loom on the horizon, the forest on the west bank yielded once more to settlement: a small neighborhood known as Glen Cove, with about two dozen houses fronting the water. An adult male Glen Cove resident reported the Conant sighting. He and his daughter were fishing out of kayaks on the sixteenth of November when they noticed a man piloting a canoe with a tarped mound in the bow slip past them, hugging the shore. The canoeist looked capable and untroubled, but the father worried about what might happen when he reached the sound.

Gesturing to his left, meanwhile, Beardsley indicated an area where three dead bodies had recently been recovered. These were crabbers from a Vietnamese community on the east bank. Their boat still hadn't been found and Beardsley didn't expect that it ever would be.

We rounded the point into the sound. The wind was blowing five to ten from the northeast, producing conditions similar to those on the afternoon they'd begun searching for Conant. It was a pounding, hold-on-tight chop. After heading west for another ten minutes, Beardsley slowed down and raised some binoculars. "Hey, is that another tarp in there, right near the green bush?" he asked, pointing toward the cypress knees, and the scrub growth behind them. I saw only an errant crab pot, and an osprey perched on a branch. Vaughan thought he saw plastic wrap from a case of bottled water. We were a couple of hundred yards from shore. Vaughan took a long boat hook, stuck it in the water until he hit muck, and then pulled it out again; the pole was wet only up to his navel. If we got much closer, we'd be bumping.

From Glen Cove to our current location was four miles, give or take. It wasn't very far to travel in thirteen days, the time elapsed between that last sighting and the canoe's recovery—or even ten days, between the sighting and the big northeaster. A photograph taken on the evening of November 15 placed Conant at a bookstore downtown. From there to Glen Cove was more than a dozen miles, and Conant had evidently covered the distance in a single day. "Now, if he wanted to ditch the boat and live like a native in the brush there, I mean, it could be done," Beardsley said, speaking of the swamp woods. "And avoid detection? Yeah, there's a chunk of land here, pretty dense forest and swamp. If you *really* really really wanted to, you could do it. Now, anybody who was going to do that would, in my mind, keep their sleeping system to sleep in, and bring their food with 'em. Especially the dried beans, because they're not going to go bad. That's my only issue with the whole survivalist thing. Is it feasible? Absolutely. Could happen. There's just certain things that I think he probably would have took."

. . .

There was another detail that didn't augur well for Moses Wells's scenario. They'd recovered Conant's wallet—something else he might have wanted—and run a trace on the bank account associated with the credit cards in it. The only transactions since November were automated monthly deposits from Social Security.

Back on land, Beardsley brought me to a locked yard full of trailers in front of a large aluminum boat shed. Resting on the dirt underneath the shed roof was a familiar-looking red canoe. "She's in great shape still," he said, with a trace of pride. "I mean, there's scratches all around it, but being that it was used to travel a pretty good ways down the Atlantic Seaboard, it's going to have some rubs here and there." I rocked the boat and could hear the sloshing of water that remained trapped inside its molded plastic benches, a mixed broth of New York Harbor and Delaware River and Albemarle Sound. Inside the hull were several objects that Joe Conant hadn't bothered to bring back to Georgia with him: a fifty-quart cooler, the tent, a brown tarp, a black milk crate, more than a few fathoms of rope, the portage wheels that had delivered the boat through downtown Trenton. I opened the cooler and found a magnet from the post office in Florence, New Jersey, stuck to an interior wall, as well as a stray receipt for a sixteen-ounce coffee in Plattsburgh, on June 19, 2014, at 8:13 a.m. "Yeah, I don't think he threw much away," Beardsley said.

The paddle, with yellow blade, was still tethered to the stern. "There was only that one paddle, but it was tied up," Beardsley said. "Maybe he had an extra paddle?"

He didn't. Of that much I was certain. It was the same paddle I'd seen him using on the Hudson, and the one that recurred in countless among the several thousand photos on his camera's memory cards. Moses Wells, after helping to load Conant's gear into his truck less than a month before Conant went missing, was adamant that there was only the one paddle. To me, this meant that the prevailing theory among locals—that Conant was caught unprepared for the violent wave action of the sound, and tossed overboard—was, at best, incomplete. Even if he had swamped, which seemed plenty possible, he clearly didn't lose the boat in the act of paddling. In a sense, the incredulity of awed Conant acquaintances like the accountant in Alabama who insisted that Conant was "too good" of an explorer to be defeated by mere water seemed vindicated. In order to secure the paddle, Conant had to have been standing on solid (or at least mucky) ground. Yet he hadn't set up camp, either. Could he have been sleeping in the boat, as he often bragged about, and then rolled overboard? Or was he towing it by the painter, only to slip and lose his grip?

Beardsley had spent a lot of time puzzling over the vagaries of decomposition and flotation, wondering if the reason they hadn't found Conant's body was because it was submerged. Human bodies sink when the lungs fill up with water, and then float again when their cavities fill with gas, a process that varies in speed depending on the temperature of the water and the makeup of the body itself: the relative fat content, the nature of the gut bacteria. The Vietnamese crabbers had been missing for six days before their bodies surfaced—or were noticed, at any rate, by the fleet of some fourteen boats that went looking for them. But that was in late April. Colder water delays decomposition. Two years earlier, in nearby Coinjock Bay, a young man had disappeared while baiting duck blinds from a canoe, a couple of days before Christmas. A Coast Guard search in the first twelve hours after he was reported missing turned up the canoe, a bucket of corn, and a pair of waders, with a cell phone inside. But the man's body wasn't seen floating until three weeks later.

Maybe the Coast Guard and the Wildlife Resources Commission had called off their Conant searches too soon—for a recovery, if not a rescue, at least. ("Budgets, man," Beardsley sighed.) Or maybe, given the nearly two-week period that remained unaccounted for, they were already too late. "Unfortunately, a lot of times what happens, especially in the cooler water, is the gases in your body don't expand as much, because it takes heat to help expand them gases," Beardsley said. "The body may float, but then it'll go right back down before long." He added, "We don't even know where our accident scene's at. If them guys never found that canoe, we *still* wouldn't know he's missing."

I found myself modeling various scenarios in my head, accounting for Conant's girth-enabled buoyancy and speculating about the postmortem digestive properties of pickled hot dogs and Tabasco. But ultimately, returning to the stowed paddle, and to the wading depth, I was inclined to suspect that the reason no one found a body, let alone a life jacket, was because it wasn't in the water in the first place. Heart attack? Conant's doctors wouldn't have been surprised. Maybe he went inland, in search of help. But then what? Mistaken for a bear, or a burglar? Lost in the woods, hypothermic, with a bum knee or a twisted ankle? Reunited with Tracy in a fever dream?

In his writing, Conant often contemplated his own mortality. He believed, not without reason, that his adventures had extended rather than shortened his life span, but he also faced down more near-death experiences than most, and found occasion to speculate about how his incredible story might end. Near the conclusion of his trip to Texas, in the winter of 2008, for instance, he wrote:

> The waters along the shore of Matagorda Peninsula are too shallow to allow the passage of a rescue boat should I encounter trouble. The peninsula appears on my charts to be not only remote but largely uninhabited. I can not be certain that I will have enough fresh drinking water, especially in the event of a broken limb or some other injury.

Noticing purple lesions on his toes a couple of years later, amid a storm alongside a flooded Tombigbee River, he feared the sudden onset of diabetes.

> Well, I have to die of something. Frankly, I wouldn't mind croaking out on a trip like this. It's better than getting smashed in a car wreck or wasting away on a cancer ward while doctors use experimental drugs on me. Then again, I don't want to end up like that doe this morning, lying around with her guts all eaten away by wandering carnivores and buzzards. I guess once I'm dead, it won't matter. That is something the nuns from my youth had correct; namely, from dust to dust we merrily go.

Buzzards, incidentally, were what Grover Sanders, the duck-hunting farmer, told me he had in mind—"This don't sound good"—when he returned to the cypress stumps in his skiff during a brief warm spell around Christmastime, three and a half weeks after hauling the canoe ashore. The failure to recover a life jacket especially had nagged at him. "I mean, the boys down there are fishing all the time, with nets, up around that whole shoreline, and you know if he had fell over and was in the water, they would have found him," Sanders explained. The unseasonal weather, with temperatures soaring toward seventy, seemed likely to hasten decay, he reasoned, or at least to inspire vultures to stake an anticipatory claim. As a hunter, he was familiar with the sight of birds circling for days above deer carcasses too deep into the swampland to be retrieved by men or dogs, supervising rot.

But he saw a lonely sky.

He put on waders and treaded carefully around the muck, for a hundred or more yards in either direction, half expecting to see a lifeless body slumped against a tree. "I felt confident," he said. "But never found *nuthin'.*"

.   .   .

The Conant case, technically, was still open, but the officers were chagrinned to admit that they had lost the file associated with it. It had been stored on a laptop that slid out the back of Chase Vaughan's pickup truck on the highway. This meant that any notes from interviews with the last people known to see or speak with Conant were gone. It seemed to me a fitting indignity, which was compounded by my realization, after visiting the *Daily Advance* offices, that the paper had misspelled his surname throughout their coverage of the search (thereby preserving his slender Google profile). For two days, "Richard Conan" was front-page news in Elizabeth City. Then he slipped to the B section on December 2 ("Missing canoeist hoped to reach Fla., get married"), and, in the absence of further local angles, fell out of the paper altogether. "Yeah, he kind of disappeared on us," a reporter said. "We ain't heard from him since. And we lost these

Vietnamese fishermen. We get all *kinds* of things happen here. We've had missing canoeists, we have drownings, we have murders. For a small town, we got a lot of news."

I took it as a journalistic paraphrasing of Heraclitus: the news, like the river, stops for no one. Let it flow. But Beardsley was bothered by what he perceived as tabloid glibness. In eight years on the job, since leaving the army, he had never before failed to locate a missing person, whether dead or alive. "I've had plenty of boating accidents in my career, and some of them are more personal, where kids are hurt or killed, or a mother or father is dead now, and leaving all their kids behind," he said. "That kind of gets you. But do you take as much *interest* in that?" As with countless other people whose paths crossed briefly with Conant's, Beardsley couldn't help seeing aspects of himself in the traveler. "Do you ever think about doing something like that yourself— just going on a crazy adventure?" he asked me. "We, as wildlife officers, are by ourselves a majority of the time. There's a reason I like to be out here, in the field. I don't like to be cooped up in an office." Yet, like Conant, he also prided himself on his ability to talk to strangers—to defuse tense situations involving people with weapons.

The reporter from the *Daily Advance* had said that I was lucky to be arriving "at the time of the biggest festival in town— celebrates the area's potato-growing heritage." Noticing the street closures by the riverbank and the arrival of a giant Ferris wheel, I realized that Conant would have agreed. It brought more potential conversationalists down to the riverfront, including a group of retirees sitting on lawn chairs, one of whom wore a live mammal on his head.

"No . . . shit!" Beardsley exclaimed. "That man has a freaking monkey."

We approached for a closer look. Beardsley recalled encountering a similar-looking monkey—light brown with raccoon eyes and a long, thick, dark tail—in Afghanistan, and mentioned that it had developed a fondness verging on addiction for the Skittles in soldiers' MREs. He called out, "Now, that is a pet you don't see very often."

"Capuchin," the man said, a little wary.

"Are you from around here?"

"Yeah, I'm local."

"Where do you get such a pet?"

"Not around here."

Beardsley's badge seemed to put everyone on edge, no matter his laid-back manner. I, doing my best Conant impersonation, can give you only this: the capuchin drank purple Gatorade and wore a cloth diaper, which his owner said he changed "about six times a day, sometimes eight." He traveled in a modified birdcage adorned with baby toys. His name was Ozzie.

.   .   .

On Water Street, we stopped by Page After Page, the bookstore where the last known photograph of Conant was taken. In the image, he is wearing at least five layers (a plaid jacket over a cardigan over denim overalls over a plaid button-down over what appears to be a dark thermal undershirt), and carrying a Gatorade bottle in his right hand and a green cloth shopping bag in his left. His beard is whiter than I remember. A silver pen clip shines over one of the chest pockets of the overalls. His face is ruddy, of course, and his countenance sweetly plaintive.

"And I got to say, when he first walked in I was like, 'Oohhhhh,'" the owner, Susan Hinkle, said, mimicking fright. It was a Saturday, just before closing, she recalled, and she was working alone. "But he was super nice."

Conant stayed nearly an hour at Page After Page, telling Hinkle all about his various travels, and about his recent appearance in *The New Yorker,* and about his sweetheart, whom he intended to wed. "He was showing me how he has to paddle along the edge, because the canoe was so loaded down, you know, that he couldn't take any waves," she said. He showed her a piece of paper that he kept in the bib of his overalls, on which he was recording the names and addresses of future pen pals, adding her to the list, one spot below his new friend, "a fisherman, I want to say, from Assateague or Chincoteague, one of those islands." That would have been Moses Wells. She gave him a discount on the Intracoastal boating guide he bought.

The next day was stormy, and Hinkle found herself unable to get Conant out of her mind. "Nice to see that there's still people like that, you know what I mean?" she said. "I was like, 'God, I hope he didn't go today,' because it was so windy, and pouring rain." In the afternoon, she went out for an errand, and she kept an eye out the window, looking at the water, but, like so many of Conant's friends, she wasn't fortunate enough to see him again.

Epilogue

I n January 2018, I heard from a Conant family member that "human remains" had been discovered along the northern shore of Albemarle Sound. An internet search led me to the following headline, accompanied by a photo of ominous storm clouds over water: "A human skull washed ashore in North Carolina. So far it's a mystery."

The skull was missing its bottom jaw, and only three teeth, all molars, remained attached to the maxilla—two on one side, and one on the other. One had a gold crown. Splotches of moss appeared to be growing on the frontal bone, or forehead, and in cracks around the nasal bone, suggesting that it had been exposed to the elements for some time. No dirt or mud clung to the exterior, as you might expect if it had been unearthed from a previous burial. It was amid fallen leaves near the edge of a six-foot bank, behind which lay dense forest, extending inland for a third of a mile before yielding to farmed plots in an unincorporated community called New Hope.

A head with no trace of a body. The sheriff speculated at first that it might belong to an escaped criminal: a young man, who, after phoning his mother one Easter Sunday, had fled an Edenton jail wielding a sharpened toothbrush. He had alarmed her by insisting that he planned to visit his five-year-old daughter, no matter the incarceration. But he never showed up, and, ten days later, a hunter found a naked, decapitated, and partly decomposed body in a field, thirteen miles from the jail. Investigators identified the headless body by its fingerprints, but had been stymied ever since, lacking any leads into suspects or motive or—until now, perhaps—the whereabouts of the head.

TV news crews descended on New Hope. One report showed footage of the sound looking deceptively placid—no trouble for boaters—and included an interview with a resident who allowed only his legs to be filmed, lending an air of further intrigue.

But the jailbreaker was an African American, and the medical examiner believed that the Albemarle skull likely was a Caucasian male's. John Beardsley called Joe Conant, in Peachtree City, and alerted him to the development, explaining that they hoped to make an identification using dental records, if the Conants could provide any.

Here, in a roundabout way, they seemed to be in luck. In his third manuscript, Dicky had written at length about a toothache that drove him off the Tennessee River, beneath a highway interchange, and up Roseberry Creek, into Scottsboro, Alabama, where he found a dentist.

I looked to my right and saw a computer screen with a blown up image of the affected tooth. It was an intricately detailed, black and white, x-ray-like picture of my jagged tooth and root with adjoining structures. I could not discern the soft tissue. I exclaimed, "Holy cow! Look at the resolution!"

Naturally, he also recorded the name and address of the dental office—which still had his X-ray on file, nearly eight years later, when the Conant family suddenly found itself looking for records to share with the medical examiner in Perquimans County, North Carolina.

. . .

By this time, I had written another story about Conant—and his overturned canoe—for *The New Yorker*. A doctor in Chesapeake, Virginia, wrote the magazine to say that he had spoken with Conant nine months after his ostensible disappearance and had the pictures to prove it. Canoe, tarp in bow, ruddy complexion, patchy beard: check, check, check, check. The resolution of the photos wasn't great. The canoe was dark green. The paddler didn't really look like Conant—he was thinner, for one thing— but it wasn't inconceivable; the note mentioned that the would-be Conant had diabetes. "He was controlling his blood sugar by not eating and he was losing weight." There were other intriguing, if vague, similarities: complicated feelings about a deceased mother, a fire in which the canoeist had "lost all his belongings." Could there really be an unknown army of such men wandering the country's waterways?

I called the doctor. "It has to be the same man," he said, although he admitted that they hadn't exchanged names, or not that he could remember, anyway. He had been out on his morning row, on the Gilmerton Canal, an extension of the Dismal Swamp, he explained, when he saw the canoeist, and, feeling moved, invited him back to his house for tea. An offer to use the laundry room was declined. "All he wanted was to fill his plastic water bottles," the doctor said. "He talked about paddling down the James against the wind, and taking a wrong turn into the western branch of the Elizabeth River." Crabbers towed him back to the southern branch, which he had used to reach the canal. He was headed next for the Albemarle. It was as if Conant were returning to unfinished business. The doctor sent him off with some nav charts.

Setting aside the logistical questions—where, lacking a wallet, had Conant got the money to buy a new canoe?—I was skeptical, because of one essential detail: the doctor reported that his man was "not very sociable." Nonetheless, I passed the images on to Joe Conant, in Georgia. He shared them with some other relatives and sent back the family verdict: not Dicky.

.　.　.

The site of the skull's discovery, eight miles due west of the cypress stumps where Conant's canoe was recovered, had interested me for some time. Looking at Google satellite images, as Conant often did, and at the weather archives, I'd tried reconstructing what I supposed to be his final two weeks, which came to seem like the only significant period of his life that *hadn't* been preserved with abundant documentation. They can't have been fun. The wind almost never let up: fifteen knots one day, twenty the next, with only narrow windows of relative calm. He passed Glen Cove, leaving the creature comforts of Elizabeth City behind, on a waning crescent moon, meaning that night passage, with its more typically placid seas, would have posed challenges as well.

There were whole days, I imagined, when he would have chosen to stay put—and not happily, given the nature of the stump-ridden, occasionally swampy terrain. He might have felt claustrophobic, unable to roam freely and staring into a vast expanse of violent water. (I thought of what he'd once said about his impatience on Jones Towhead, in the Mississippi, amid flood levels and dysentery, likening himself to Odysseus when he was enticed by the Sirens: "The water is calling me but I should not go.") He preferred not to spend more than eight hours at a clip in his sleeping bag, fearing "cabin fever," as he put it. In late

November, he'd have been working with only ten or eleven hours of daylight.

He had plenty of food, but, given the sound's brackish composition, potable water would have been a concern—and an inducement to keep moving, before long, in pursuit of the next available town: Edenton, as he'd mentioned to the Bible College administrator, or Hertford, a short digression up the nearer Perquimans River, as he'd suggested to Susan Hinkle at the bookstore.

I thought of the fact that, the day before the canoe's discovery, Grover Sanders had been out on the sound in the same vicinity and saw nothing unusual. It didn't seem likely to me that after all that time, Conant was only *just* approaching Big Flatty Creek from the east, or that the boat, long lacking a pilot, had been bobbing around for days near the mouth of the Pasquotank, where traffic is fairly regular. It seemed more plausible that the boat had drifted back to the stumps from the west—from farther up the sound. The wind in the couple of days after the storm was primarily northwesterly.

The big navigational challenges, aside from weather and its effects on the surf, were the open-water crossings: first Big Flatty, a mile broad at the mouth; then the Little River, a mile and a half, or slightly more; and next the Perquimans, three or four miles, depending on your line of attack. That would have rivaled the longest crossings in his career. The peninsula between the Little and the Perquimans seemed to me a likely regrouping point, and a particular wooded patch struck me as an inevitable campground, sandwiched as it was between a mile or more of private waterfront residences on either side. Playing detective, I looked up the property records of those surrounding neighborhoods, and sent an email to one of the owners of the house nearest the woods, apologizing for the random intrusion but wondering if, by any chance, she recalled seeing an unusual man during the second half of November 2014. It was a shot in the dark, not unlike John Beardsley's initial decision to call the name—*my* name—on the back of that soggy fishermen's-forum printout, just in case.

She replied, politely, to say that she hadn't been at the house during the time frame I described. It was a weekend house, not a primary residence. But imagine my surprise when, less than a year later, I began reading the news accounts of the unclaimed skull—and saw my correspondent's husband quoted as one of the people who had discovered it. They had been gathering driftwood on the beach in front of the woods, just west of their house, when one of their friends hopped up the steep bank and saw something glinting in the winter sunlight.

The husband doubted the prevailing theory suggested by all the headlines: that the skull had washed ashore in the waves. The bank, he told me, was too steep, and perpetually eroding. He thought it more likely that the sound, in its continual assault on the shoreline, had claimed the rest of the skeleton. He thought, in other words, that someone had perished there in the woods, overlooking but not *in* the water.

.   .   .

Resting in those woods and studying the maps in the boating guide he'd bought from Susan Hinkle, or the ones that he photo-copied in the Elizabeth City library, Conant would have noticed a potential problem. Across the broad Perquimans River mouth was a large "restricted area" extending well into deep water, like the one that had confounded his plans on Chesapeake Bay and led to his teaming up, unhappily, with the Merry Prankster. He may not have known why. There were undetonated bombs beneath the surface over there. Harvey Point, the spit of land on the far side, is home to a mysterious military operation that originated before the Bay of Pigs invasion. Former code name: Isolation

Tropic. SEAL Team 6 rehearsed the assassination of Osama bin Laden by constructing a scale model of his Abbottabad compound at Harvey Point. "That's a local big secret," one Elizabeth City resident told me. "They chase my sailboat off if I come close to their markers."

Reading about Harvey Point, I came upon stories of black helicopters at dusk, window-rattling explosions, and a jet-skier who was startled by the surfacing of a black-clad scuba diver. "My stepdad, he's heard of people going down there too close in boats, and looking in there with binoculars, and they get shot," a fifteen-year-old boy once said. "The law around here is, if you get a hundred feet from the fence they can shoot you." Apocryphal, perhaps, but now imagine a paranoid navy vet approaching in an apocalyptic canoe.

Surely, I thought, such a place would have security cameras trained on the water 24/7. These would offer definitive proof of whether Conant made it as far west as I suspected. Then again, as the *New York Times* reported, Harvey Point "has a spokesman who prefers that his name not appear in print." (It added, "Blackbeard's booty is supposed to be buried somewhere nearby, beneath the waters of the sound.") Another article—"In Nearby Hertford, the Echo of Bombs Is Business As Usual—and Nobody's Business"—detailed the runaround its author got from the navy to the CIA to the Pentagon, ending in a "highly classified" stonewalling.

Blackbeard, bombs, bin Laden. Who would believe it? I was still working over all the permutations in my mind, picturing Conant shivering on a bank, with dark storm clouds approaching from the east, capped molars rattling to unexplained ballistic thunder due west, when I received a text message from John Beardsley. "We have been able to confirm that the remains do not belong to Mr Conant," it said, and I smiled, just a little, realizing that I didn't have to give up dreaming of a more mysterious ending to my bedtime story.

.   .   .

Missing persons in North Carolina are not typically considered dead before seven years have elapsed, but the occasion for an informal eulogy presented itself a few springs ago, when I heard from a Catholic priest who had met Conant while walking his dog along the Hudson, a little north of me. "I haven't stopped thinking about it," he said. "It was like in the gospel when Jesus meets Nathanael: here is a man without guile. And remember, what does Nathanael say about Jesus? 'But what good can come from Nazareth?' I said this to my spiritual advisor last night. I told him the story of Dick, and I said—I hate that it sounds like a cliché—'We've got to think differently.'" Pentecost Sunday was approaching, and he wanted me to know that he was planning to devote his sermon to Conant's memory. I got his permission to invite Conant's siblings.

The priest's name was Rees Doughty, and his parish, in Cornwall-on-Hudson, turned out to be of familial significance. Uncle Bob Higgins, Claire Conant's brother, belonged for years. Speaking to a congregation of several hundred, including Jim, Rob, and Roger Conant, Father Doughty described his riverside encounter ("I suppose I might have thought he was crazy, and just said, 'Well, good luck to you,' but there was something about this man") and then read a couple of excerpts from Conant's journals that had appeared in the *New Yorker* story. "He was convinced, quote, that 'Life was capable of exquisite pleasure and undefined meaning deep in the face of failure,'" Doughty said. "He apparently had many, many challenges that he had to deal with, and disappointments, I guess, yet all throughout there was a sense of courage and of hope."

It had been a long while since I'd been in a church, and I caught my mind drifting into reverie, cycling through a slide show of Conant's photographs, records of what he would have called the reward of his experiences in natural settings of almost unimaginable beauty. My favorites among them hinted at untold stories, like the shot of sand castles adorned with flowers on a beach in radio range of Saskatchewan, amid no other evidence of human presence.

I have tried here to make Conant the hero of his own epic, while not giving anyone the illusion that it was an enviable life. Was he a tragic figure? I believe he went to extraordinary lengths to repudiate the notion. ("Overall I think that despite great hardships I have managed to survive and progress in my own humble way. . . . Despite my poverty and low status, I remain undisgraced, healthy, still striving, still planning and happy. If no one else respects me, too bad. I still respect me, and I am the one that counts.")

The problem with hope, of course, for a self-chronicler or any writer, really, is that you have to abandon it if you want to maintain control of your ending. By continuing to pay rent on your precious storage lockers, you are accepting on some level that you will never get around to organizing their contents.

Sitting in a pew toward the back, I thought, not for the first time, of something Conant had written near the end of his penultimate trip, feeling the usual melancholy that dogged him when his paddling time was almost up.

When I was about to nod off I felt like I was floating in the night air. I felt extraordinary peace and contentment. I felt like I was doing what I was supposed to do and where I was designed to do it. I felt that my existence had purpose in the universe, as humble as it may be. It was not elation. It was merely a recognition of my place and a resigned, unemotional acceptance. I heard no dogs this night and few insects were about, except for ants. It was peaceful. I thought of Tracy from Seattle.

Had I tried hard enough to find her? As I said earlier, I can think of no reason to doubt that she is indeed a real person, as well as a disembodied idea: something to live for, the thing with feathers. I thought at times about launching a social-media campaign to locate her, but never followed through, fearing that it would convey the wrong message: that her input, however curious I might be, is crucial to what we ultimately make of Conant. All I can say with confidence is that they met once, in Livingston, on the heels of a day that left Conant brimming with an expanded sense of possibility about the future. My own meeting of Conant fifteen years later had much the same effect on me, and though I never met Tracy, I did meet Ginny, a college librarian who lives down the block from Nyack Hospital, where Conant used to work in the nineteen-seventies. She wrote me a letter, recalling that she used to love to watch him dance—always smiling, eyes alight, seemingly more present in the enjoyment of the moment than anyone else, a centripetal force. They never dated, but he told her that she reminded him of a bird on a wire, and handed her a painting he'd made, of a snowy night scene, under a dim crescent moon, with a man carrying what looks like an axe or a bindle toward a well-lit country cottage. She brought it with her when we met for coffee, explaining that she'd continued displaying it in her home across the decades, through several moves and a divorce, in spite of the fact that it lacks a frame and seems to be on the reverse side of a scrap of faux-wood paneling ripped from a basement wall. It reminded her of the last time she saw him, in the back of a crowded bar in his trademark overalls, and of her regret that she never made it over to say hello.

Outside the church on Pentecost Sunday, the three Conant brothers waited in a receiving line to introduce themselves to Father Doughty, and to tell him that, as luck would have it, his church was just two blocks from the house where Dicky used to babysit his cousins, back in the nineteen-sixties.

"Did you know that he was a seminarian?" Jim said, astonishing Doughty further. "Yeah, he was a seminarian for a year, and then he wasn't asked back. I don't know why. He was a character."

"He always wanted to be a doctor," Rob said.

Roger turned to Rob and said, "Dicky accused you of being a raconteur, but he was the real one. Except his stories were true."

Acknowledgments

Three people never wavered in their belief in this story, or at least they betrayed no doubts to the author. Given the extent to which writing is a confidence game, this book wouldn't exist without them. They are John Bennet, David McCormick, and Andrew Miller.

But a project like this is, as Dick Conant might say, the result of a series of events in a magnificent chain reaction: an unscripted river trip of journalism. Absent my neighbor, friend, and guiding river spirit Scott Rosenberg, I would never have known about the man canoeing to Florida. But for the enthusiasm of Susan Morrison and David Remnick, I wouldn't have chased him down beneath the Palisades. Had the Conant siblings not trusted me with the stewardship of their missing brother's papers, I'd have been at a loss for whom to call or write to begin corroborating the fantastical tales therein. By the end, I'd connected with more than two hundred people whose paths crossed, at some point or another, with our protagonist. Some are named in the preceding pages, but my gratitude extends to them all.

About the Conants: I've yet to meet one whom I haven't liked. They are a remarkable family, and I hope this book can serve as a source of pride. I know Dicky wasn't always the easiest to get along with. Special thanks to his nephews Rob and Cornelius: Rob for archiving all the artwork, among other things; and Corn for poring over receipts and journals with a keen eye and an open heart.

I am blessed, meanwhile, to have a family of my own full of professional readers: Sarah and Edward, Mom and Dad, Leah. I'm especially grateful to my parents for instilling an awareness of the imaginative possibilities of rivers through our annual trips to Westport, and to Digs and the boys for their enthusiastic embrace of the Hudson.

At *The New Yorker,* Katia Bachko, Peter Licursi, and Nimal Eames-Scott were cheerful and tireless checkers of facts, and Betsy Morais was a wise reader and confidante.

Friends who read portions of the manuscript without any professional obligation to do so include Will Cohen, Lauren Collins, Willing Davidson, Matt Dellinger, Raffi Khatchadourian, Jesse Lichtenstein, Field Maloney, Nick Paumgarten, and Elihu Rubin. Call in your favors.

John McPhee, at Princeton, and Austin Kelley, at N.Y.U., invited me to discuss the project with their students, whose questions and suggestions were invaluable. The Wilderness Paddlers Gathering provided a crucial early audience, and a gift that keeps on giving in the form of an introduction to Vermont's Lake Morey.

Thanks ongoing, also, to Bridget McCarthy and Susan Hobson at McCormick Literary, and to Maris Dyer, Dan Novack, Patricia Clark, Jenny Carrow, Reagan Arthur, Erinn Hartman, Demetris Papadimitropoulos, Laura Keefe, Sara Eagle, and others at Knopf.

Marc Ruby, another Piermont neighbor, was adamant that we keep recreating on the river, no matter deadlines. Now that it's done, I guess he was right?

A Note About the Author

Ben McGrath is a longtime staff writer for *The New Yorker*. He lives outside New York City in a small town on the Hudson, with his wife and two children. This is his first book.

A Note on the Type

This book was set in Adobe Garamond. Designed for the Adobe Corporation by Robert Slimbach, the fonts are based on types first cut by Claude Garamond (ca. 1480–1561).

Typeset by North Market Street Graphics,
Lancaster, Pennsylvania

Printed and bound by Berryville Graphics,
Berryville, Virginia

Designed by Michael Collica